Legal Research Simulations

Second Edition

Warren Rees
Librarian Emeritus
University of Notre Dame Law School

BRIDGE TO PRACTICE SERIES®

WEST ACADEMIC

860 Blue Gentian Road, Suite 350
Eagan, MN 55121
1-877-888-1330

Published in the United States of America

ISBN: 979-8-31770-447-6

I would like to express my gratitude to the students in my classes who, by asking questions, helped clarify the material and to my research assistant, Kira-Khanh McCarthy, who read through it all and greatly improved the final result.
A special thanks to my wife, Anita, whose support made it possible.

PREFACE

As we begin examining the process of legal research, I would like to offer a few introductory comments. As the name suggests, the goal is to teach the process of basic legal research. While it is an introductory work, it aims to teach more than just the bare bones of basic legal research. We will cover the origin of different forms of legal authority (cases, statutes, and agency regulations) and their relationship to each other. For each form of legal authority, we will then look at the tools available to locate them and how each tool works. Next, we will look at the tools needed to locate the current version of each type of law. Finally, we will look specifically at locating cases that discuss each form of law; it is imperative that you know how the courts have interpreted and applied the various forms of laws in actual litigation. Our discussion of the different research tools will also include details about the information provided by each. This will help you understand what you know when you finish using it and what you must still do to complete a legal research project.

This book presents an outline of the steps involved in conducting legal research. The material is organized according to the steps needed to conduct research using many different resources or tools. Some resources serve multiple functions; in these situations, the same resource will be discussed in different parts of the book according to its use and function.

This book also provides information about the content and use of specific sources and the steps to follow when conducting research that requires beginning with the information you know and locating additional information to reach the desired goal. The latter situation is what you will be required to perform when writing papers in law school and in the practice of law. This is part of the process of thinking like a lawyer. This book is organized to assist in understanding the process of legal research and how to proceed based upon already known information. Assignments that accompany this book will give you practice in this discipline.

Will you be an expert legal researcher after working through this material? No! But then, neither will you be an expert in any subject after completing an introductory class in law school. This is only an introduction.

Once a basic understanding of legal research is acquired, law students and newer attorneys still struggle with two major issues: becoming familiar with the terminology in an area of law that is new to them and knowing whether they have found all the relevant sources and aren't missing a critical piece of information. Regarding the former, becoming familiar with new terminology is specific to the exact problem you are researching and really can't be taught in a book on legal research. We will look at a few examples as we investigate the process of legal research. Books and articles written by experts on a specific subject will obviously provide help. We will cover how to locate books and other helpful materials. Artificial intelligence (AI) can also provide assistance at this early point in legal research and we will discuss the use of AI in helping to learn the legal concepts involved in an unfamiliar subject area.

Regarding the second issue, becoming familiar with the tools discussed in this book will help you understand the necessary steps to assure that all relevant authorities are found. Also, books and articles will be helpful in this scenario. Additionally, new tools using artificial intelligence are increasingly available and will no doubt continue to evolve and improve. For example, Westlaw has "Quick Search" which can take an existing article or brief and locate relevant authority and help update the law. The algorithm performing this task uses the tools discussed in this book to perform legal research. This use of AI is important and will definitely save valuable time when you are engaged in the practice of law. AI has become a useful method for beginning research even when you do not know much about the subject. Queries that only reference facts of the cases, without using any legal terminology, can be a good way to begin research on an unfamiliar subject. However, the tools upon which the algorithms depend have limits and may still miss important points and laws. For this reason, it is important that you understand the tools and their limits so you can take steps on your own to assure that your research is complete.

In addition to research, this book will also cover the basics of how to cite various legal resources according to the rules in the latest version of *The Bluebook: A Uniform System of Citation.* I will refer to this source as *The Bluebook* throughout. This text will emphasize how to cite to legal resources when writing memos and briefs, which is what you will do during your first year of law school. Citing the same materials when writing law review articles and books are similar but varies slightly from what is discussed here. In your practice of law, you may need to adapt to variations of these rules as required by local courts; however, learning the basics of *The Bluebook* will provide the basis for citation of legal sources throughout your career.

Working through this book will require access to two of the major legal databases, Westlaw and Lexis. You will have free access to these databases during your years in law school. You need to use and become as familiar as possible with both databases while you have free access. At this point in time, you do not know which database the firm you work for will use, so become familiar with both. You may also have access during law school to similar electronic resources, such as Bloomberg Law. I have not included information about Bloomberg Law but the basics of using Lexis and Westlaw will transfer to any other online legal database that may be available. The look and feel of other legal databases will obviously differ but the process will be the same. Additionally, this book covers several free resources available through the internet, primarily government websites.

The layout of screens on Lexis and Westlaw changes from year to year. The location of links to various functions described in this book may change but the functions remain. When using Lexis and Westlaw, take a few moments to locate the link discussed if it does not appear exactly where this text indicates.

Throughout this book you will encounter references to various exhibits. Some exhibits are located near the relevant discussion while others are in the Appendix, which is located at the end of the book. If you don't see the exhibit near the relevant text, check the Appendix.

Like most things in life, learning a skill requires knowledge and application of that knowledge in specific contexts. Hopefully this book will aid in beginning the process of learning and mastering the skill of conducting legal research.

WARREN REES

April 2026

TABLE OF CONTENTS

LEGAL RESEARCH SIMULATIONS

Second Edition

CHAPTER 1

INTRODUCTION TO LEGAL RESEARCH

I. INTRODUCTION TO THE BASICS OF THE AMERICAN LEGAL SYSTEM: LAWS

Legal research involves locating information about a specific subject in materials that constitute the law in the legal systems of the United States of America and other materials that explain the laws. Laws, in our legal system, take various forms. The major types of laws are:

- Constitutions
- Statutes
- Administrative Regulations (a.k.a. Administrative Rules) issued by government agencies
- Written opinions issued by courts (a.k.a. cases or common law)

II. FOUNDATIONAL CONCEPTS YOU MUST UNDERSTAND TO PERFORM LEGAL RESEARCH

To perform legal research and work effectively with the laws of the nation, you must understand the following foundational concepts.

A. You must understand the following information about each type or form of law.

- Who creates each type.

  Laws are created by those (individuals or groups) who are granted the power to issue them when acting in their official role. For example, statutes are created by members of legislatures when acting in their official capacity as legislators. Judges make law when they write opinions. In both cases, they make law when they are acting in their official capacity. A law review article written by a judge or member of a legislature does not have the force of law since the individual is not acting in her/his official capacity when writing the article.

- The difference between laws and other sources you can use to understand the law.

  Laws are referred to as "primary sources." All the types of laws listed above are primary sources. All other materials, such as books, articles, etc. are called "secondary sources." If something isn't a primary source, it is by default a secondary source.

- The process of creating each type of primary source and how it is organized when published.
- Different options for locating relevant laws of all types.
- The relationship between the various types of laws.

B. Jurisdiction (whose law applies in a specific situation).

The types of laws listed above exist at the federal as well as the state level. At the federal level we have a federal constitution, statutes, agency regulations, and decisions issued by federal courts. Each state also has the same types of laws.

In some situations, federal law alone will apply; in others, state law only. Federal and state law may both apply; in this case, federal law may preempt state law while in other instances they may apply concurrently. Determining the exact relationship between federal and state law involves many different factors which we cannot cover thoroughly here but we will look at a few instances to get an idea of the general rules.

C. Hierarchy of laws within a jurisdiction and between jurisdictions.

Some laws carry more weight than others; when two laws of different forms (e.g., statute vs. common law) are applicable, there is a hierarchy that determines which one controls if they are found to conflict with each other. We will examine the hierarchy of legal authority within a jurisdiction and how this hierarchy applies when both state and federal laws apply.

D. Some laws are mandatory while others are persuasive.

In any given situation, not all laws that are relevant will have to be followed; some will be mandatory while others will be persuasive only. Federal law in all forms apply (is mandatory) to anyone within the United States and a state law applies (is mandatory) to anyone within the state. Case law from California courts is not mandatory (persuasive) for courts and individuals living in Illinois. On the other hand, a lower New York state court is obligated to follow (mandatory) a common law rule created by a higher-ranking court in the New York judicial system. You must understand the steps required to identify which primary authorities are mandatory and which are persuasive.

The question about what is mandatory and what is persuasive is important when an issue is litigated in court. What is mandatory and what is persuasive depends upon whose law (federal or state) is applicable and which court is deciding the issue. Your job as an attorney, when performing legal research, is to identify all laws a court might apply to a given set of facts and determine whether they are mandatory in your client's case. There are tools designed to help identify relevant laws based upon the subject matter of your legal issue.

We will discuss and examine all these aspects of legal research.

III. STEPS OF LEGAL RESEARCH

With this foundational knowledge, you will have sufficient background information to perform legal research. You must next understand the procedure of conducting legal research. Legal research involves the following steps.

A. Identify the relevant legal issues in a problem:

1. Identify the legally significant facts.
2. Identify the legally significant relationships between parties involved.

B. If you are unfamiliar with the subject matter, locate secondary sources that explain the law and assist in identifying relevant primary law.

C. Use the appropriate tools to identify relevant primary sources within the jurisdiction involved:

1. Federal.
2. State (which state?).
3. Both (those issues to which both federal and state law applies).

D. For each primary source identified in B and C above, which are mandatory?

1. Is federal or state law involved?

2. Which court will hear the case?

E. If both federal and state law apply, does federal preempt the state law where the two conflict or do they co-exist?

F. Identify the exact language of the law at the time the events happened. This may involve identifying how the law read at some time in the past or determining how it reads today.

G. Read court decisions that interpret and apply the language of the law.

We will cover steps B through F in as much detail as possible in an introductory resource. Step A, identifying the relevant legal issues posed by a set of facts, is highly context specific. We will look at some examples, but we obviously can't cover all possible subjects. That is what your other classes in law school are designed to cover. Step G is also a skill you will learn throughout your years in law school.

IV. COURT CASES

In your law school classes, you have already (or will soon) read opinions (or excerpts from opinions) written by judges that apply a rule of law to the facts involved in order to resolve a dispute between the parties. The common law is derived from these opinions. The statement in a case which applies the rule of law to the facts is known as the "holding" in a case. The holding is what carries weight in future court decisions; in other words, the holding carries precedential authority.

Locating relevant court opinions and determining the law derived from them is more complicated than working with statutes or regulations, so we will spend over half of this book learning about them. Specifically, we will discuss how they are created, what authority they carry, how they relate to the other forms of law, how you can locate relevant cases on a subject, and how to be sure that the rule of law applied in a case is still valid today (or at some time in the past).

The term "case" is ambiguous. It may be used to reference the entire litigation between two or more parties from start to finish. Other times, it is used to refer to just a written explanation (an opinion) by a judge that discusses the court's application of the law to the facts. These written opinions are only one small part of the complete case, but they can carry a great deal of weight. Let's look at a full court case in more detail and see how opinions fit into the larger picture.

A. CASE LITIGATION

Court cases, or litigation, usually are of two types: civil and criminal. Civil cases begin when the plaintiff files the complaint with the court. Criminal cases normally begin with the state (either federal or an individual state) filing an indictment charging the defendant with violating a criminal statute. For our purposes, we will concentrate mostly on civil cases.

The filing of the complaint initiates the case. The next major event is usually the filing of an answer by the defendant. Several pretrial motions may be filed followed by discovery, which consists of depositions, interrogatories, etc. Eventually a trial will be held, which may either be a bench trial (where the judge decides the facts of the case) or a jury trial (where the jury decides the facts). The judge will decide the rule(s), or law(s), applicable to the facts; this application of law to the facts results in a judgment.

The progress of ligation, from the filing of the complaint to the final judgment, can be followed in what is known as a docket. An abridged version of a sample docket is included in Exhibits IV-A through F, which is located in the Appendix.

Starting with Exhibit IV-A, the court where the case was filed is shown at the top-center of the first page of the docket. This case was filed in the U.S. District Court for the District of Columbia. (We will talk about the different courts a little later.) Just below that is the docket number; in this case, the docket number is 93-cv-01791. The docket number is a unique number assigned by that court to this specific case. (The docket number is unique within a specific court, so you must know in which court the case was filed to locate it using the docket number.) The number before the dash identifies the year in which the litigation began; the following letters indicate whether it is a civil (cv) or criminal case (cr). The number following the second dash is a unique number generated by this court for this specific case.[1] Docket numbers assigned to cases in federal courts will follow the same pattern used in this example. Each state, however, has its own system. As a result, docket numbers assigned to state cases may look slightly different. Regardless of their exact form, they serve the same function.

Below the docket number are the names of the parties involved in the litigation along with the attorneys who represent them. The dated entries, following the names, is the list of documents filed and actions taken by the court. For our purposes, you don't need to know the meaning of everything listed on the docket, so we will move through this docket quickly. Notice that each document filed with the court, such as the complaint, is numbered; Exhibit IV-B shows the complaint is 1 and the defendant's answer is 5.

As I mentioned before, after the litigation is started by filing the complaint, you will see entries in the docket related to pretrial discovery; here you see references to depositions and interrogatories (numbers 7 and 8 in Exhibit IV-C). On the 21st of November 1995, a trial was held and a verdict for the plaintiff was given by the jury. (Exhibit IV-D) In most cases, the judgment by the court will be issued (it is number 31 on the docket) and that usually ends the case.

Occasionally a trial court judge will write an opinion about a legal issue that arose during the litigation. Most opinions are written by judges that sit on an appellate court. In those rare instances where a trial judge writes an opinion, the attorneys representing the parties to the litigation will receive copies but very few are ever distributed to the public. Copies of these opinions are usually only available by accessing the docket of the case. However, in the case before us, the court faced some type of legal issue and the judge wrote an opinion to resolve it. The opinion is number 46 on this docket (Exhibit IV-E) and was issued on Sept. 6, 1996. This opinion was released for publication in a reporter; the beginning of this opinion is found in Exhibit IV-G.

A judge writes an opinion when some dispute arises between the parties about the interpretation or application of the law to the facts involved in the case. In this case the plaintiff was a "whistleblower" (one who discloses events that are illegal) and was ultimately fired from his job. The plaintiff in this case claimed that he was fired because he reported illegal actions by his employer, which is a violation of the False Claims Act (FCA), a federal statute. The court here, in its written opinion, held that the ". . . employee did not establish [a] claim of retaliatory discharge in violation of whistleblower provision of the FCA."

The judge addresses a second issue; the plaintiff also claimed that his employer breached the contract agreed to by the employer and employee when he started the job. On this issue, the court held that ". . . under District of Columbia law, employee reasonably relied on provisions of employee

---

1 For the curious, the three letters following the number, in this case HHK, represents the initials of the judge to whom the case was assigned. Here, the case was assigned to Judge Henry H. Kennedy. The initials are not a part of the docket number. Sometimes, as shown in Exhibit IV-A, a number appears at the beginning before the year; this is used to designate a division of the court when the court has more than one location.

handbook to his detriment in that he followed handbook grievance procedures at the expense of much time and money and thus, university was liable as a matter of law on employee's breach of contract claim under theory of promissory estoppel." In other words, the employee handbook, given to him when he began working for the employer, extended a promise to the employee on which he relied to his detriment. The employer should have realized that employees would rely and act upon this promise and is responsible to employees for harm caused by the employer's failure to comply with provisions in the handbook.

Now direct your attention to the first docket entry for October 7, 1996, and the following entries in Exhibit IV-F; one of the parties appealed a part of the decision by the District Court judge to the higher court of appeals, the U.S. Court of Appeals, District of Columbia Circuit. When this case goes to the court of appeals, it gets a new docket number because this is a new case at the court of appeals; the docket number for this case at the court of appeals level is 96-7225, which is listed in the docket entry for October 18, 1996.

The docket for the court of appeals is shown in Exhibits IV-H through J. At the appeals court level, a new trial is not held. Instead, specific issues are appealed and only those issues are considered on appeal. The appeals court accepts written briefs from the parties in support of their position and holds oral argument where the attorneys will appear before the court to present their arguments and answer questions posed by the judges hearing the appeal. Finally, the appeals court will issue an opinion that contains the decision on the issues that were appealed and the reasons for the decision. Opinions written by appeals courts are often made available but not always. The beginning of the appeals court decision in this case is shown in Exhibit IV-K.

Where can one locate and view dockets? The sample screen shots shown here are from an online service called PACER, which is the official docket system for federal courts. You will not have access to this as a student. However, you do have access to dockets through other online databases you will use during law school. Westlaw, Lexis, and Bloomberg Law all contain docket information. The best option for accessing dockets that you have during law school is on Bloomberg Law (www.bloomberglaw.com/). (Information about registering for access to Bloomberg Law, along with Westlaw and Lexis, will be provided by your law school.)

Enough discussion about dockets. Hopefully the information covered so far is sufficient to convey the general idea of what a docket is and the information it provides.

I now want to focus on opinions written by judges. These opinions constitute the "common law" or court made law. When there are no written laws, like statutes, regulations, or constitutions, on a subject, courts can make common law by creating rules of law in court opinions. The holding in these opinions become the law and are usually enforced by courts in future cases. The "holding" of the case is the part of the opinion that states the rule of law being applied and the application of the rule to the specific facts involved in the case. In some opinions, a court will interpret and apply a statute or administrative regulation to specific facts in a case. We will discuss this situation later, but for now we will concentrate on cases in which a judge applies a common law rule to the specific facts involved.

We will discuss the authority case opinions carry in greater detail later. For now, let's look at an opinion issued by a court and see what information it contains.

B. CASE OPINIONS

Opinions written by judges, or sometimes called justices, are collected and published together in reporters; all other materials, like complaints, answers, etc. are only available through a docket service. By far the largest publisher of American court opinions, or cases as we will often refer to them, is a company called West Publishing. This publisher is now owned by a parent company,

Thomson Reuters. West was one of the earliest publishers of legal court opinions in this country and continues to dominate the print market today. West also operates an online database, known as Westlaw[2], that contains court cases along with many other materials related to the law. You will use Westlaw extensively during law school and possibly throughout your legal career. We will look in greater detail at the various reporters published by West a little later, but for now, let's concentrate on case opinions and the information they contain.

Exhibits IV-L and M, found in the Appendix of this book, display the full text of a case decided by the Washington Court of Appeals which is a state court of appeals; Exhibits IV-N through T highlight selected parts of the same case with each part enlarged and labeled. In the following discussion, follow along in both the full text and the highlighted portions.

At the top of the first page of this case is a reference to the West reporter that contains this case. The reference here is to 748 *Pacific Reporter,* 2d Series. This tells you where West has published this case and you will use this information to cite this case. 748 is the volume number and the name of the reporter is *Pacific Reporter,* 2nd Series. At the top left of the same page you will see the number 276. This is the page number on which this case begins. (We will examine the specifics of citing cases a little later.) We will discuss the various reporters soon; for now, if the name of the reporter is a region of the country, like Pacific or Northeastern, this means that it is a reporter published by West Publishing that contains decisions from state courts in that part of the country.

In addition to the West reporters for state courts, some states also publish opinions issued by their own courts. Washington is one of those states. Just above the case name, *State v. Brown,* is a reference to 50 Wash. App. 405. This is known as a parallel cite, which simply references the volume number, reporter and beginning page where the same opinion is found in another reporter. The parallel cite here references volume 50 of the *Washington Appellate Reports,* beginning on page 405. If the name of the reporter has a specific state in it, this usually means that it is published by the state, not by a commercial publisher like West.

Just below the citation information are the names of the parties involved followed by the docket number of the case in the court that issued the opinion, the title of the issuing court, and the date the opinion was released. (Exhibit IV-N) Following this preliminary information is usually a synopsis or summary of the case and the final disposition of the case. (Exhibit IV-O) This synopsis is usually written by the editors who work for the publisher of the opinion (West Publishing in this case), not by the court.

Next, you will see what are called headnotes. (Exhibit IV-P) Headnotes are a feature of every case that West publishes. An editor (who has a law degree) who works for West reads the opinion and writes a headnote for every point found in the case opinion. In the *State v. Brown* case, the editor identified fourteen (14) different points in the opinion and wrote a headnote describing each one. Every headnote is a brief statement of each point found in the opinion. As mentioned earlier, these headnotes are not written by the court; they are created by the publisher. You will also notice that headnotes are numbered consecutively, with the number appearing at the beginning of the headnote.

Immediately preceding the text of each headnote is a word or phrase in bold type, followed by a number. This is known as a topic and key number. (In the full-text version in Exhibit IV-L, you will see a symbol that looks like a key between the topic and the key; this key symbol is the reason the following number is known as a key number.) For example, headnote 5, located on page 276 of the opinion, is assigned the topic of Constitutional Law, key number 42.2(1). West has created a massive outline of the common law; each main heading in this outline is assigned a name, which is the topic,

[2] The exact name of the commercial database maintained by West has varied over time. For example, it is currently called Westlaw Precision. However, the word Westlaw has always been a part of the name and I will use this when referencing to the online database. The same applies to another major legal database called Lexis.

and each subunit of this main topic is assigned a number, which is known as the key number. So, if you looked at the outline of the law created by West, you would find that one of the large topics is Constitutional Law and within that topic are key numbers, beginning with 1 and numbered sequentially throughout the topic. We will discuss the topic and key number system developed by West and how to use it to locate other relevant cases a little later.

Immediately following the headnotes, you will see the names of the attorneys who represented the parties involved in this litigation before the court. (Exhibit IV-R) Following the names of the attorneys is the name of the judge who wrote the opinion, which is followed by the court's written opinion.

There are several features of the opinion that I want to highlight. Let's assume you are scanning the headnotes in *State v. Brown* and headnote number 6 discusses the exact topic you are researching. You want to read that part of the opinion described by headnote 6. Fortunately, you don't have to read through the entire opinion to locate where the issue referenced by headnote 6 is discussed. There is an easy way to go directly to the relevant part of the opinion. Scattered throughout the opinion you will see brackets with numbers in bold typeface inside. For example, **[6]** is found in the second column of text on page 278 of the opinion. This is a reference to the headnote numbered 6. These bracketed numbers identify the part of the opinion summarized by a headnote. In this example, headnote 6 is based upon the text of the opinion beginning with the language immediately after **[6]** and continuing until **[7]** appears in the text. As you see, using this method makes it easy to identify relevant portions of an opinion by using the headnotes as a guide. (Exhibit IV-Q illustrates this principle using headnote 5.)

I would like to emphasize two things about headnotes. First, the headnotes you read in a reporter published by West are editorial enhancements added by West; they are not a part of the opinion. As a result, you should never cite to language found in a headnote. Second, headnotes can be misleading. Editors occasionally don't do a very good job of writing headnotes and simply misstate what the opinion says. More often, the headnote is ambiguous, either because the author's meaning isn't clear from the words selected or the brief statement doesn't provide sufficient context to understand the meaning conveyed in the opinion. For these reasons, reading a headnote may give the impression that a case is about a specific point but upon reading the opinion it turns out that it doesn't really address what you thought based on your understanding of the headnote. The point is, while headnotes aid in accessing and summarizing opinions, never rely solely upon a headnote for an accurate description of what a case is about; always read the opinion yourself to verify its meaning and, if you choose to cite the case in your writing, cite the language in the opinion, not the headnote.

You will also notice scattered throughout the opinion what looks like an upside-down letter T with a number to the right of the symbol; an example of this is found on page 277 of the opinion, just before the name of the Chief Judge who wrote this opinion. (Exhibit IV-S) This is known as star pagination. As mentioned earlier, some state court decisions are published in more than one reporter: the reporter published by West and a reporter published by the state in which the court is located. When this happens, the case will have a parallel cite. The number just to the right of the upside-down T indicates the number of the page in the parallel reporter. For example, on page 277 in the West *Pacific Reporter* immediately before the judge's name, you will see one of the upside-down Ts with the number 406 next to it. This indicates that page 406 in the Washington Appellate Reports begins with the word Scholfield. Star pagination makes it possible to cite to a case as it appears in a reporter to which you do not have access; in this example, you could cite to the official reporter published by Washington even though you only have access to the West published reporter.

Another aspect of cases we need to discuss are the different types of opinions that you will encounter. Opinions written by a trial court judge have only one author since a single judge sits on a trial court bench. Intermediate courts of appeals typically have 3 judges that hear an appeal and are involved in the opinion. Highest courts of appeals, normally called supreme courts, will have 5, 7, or even 9 (like the U.S. Supreme Court). When you have more than one judge involved, not all judges will necessarily agree, so you may have more than one opinion for the same case. Judges, who did not write the opinion, indicate their acceptance of the outcome and the reasoning in an opinion by signing it. When a majority agree with both the outcome and the reasoning and sign the same opinion, it is known as a majority opinion. Sometimes, a judge agrees with the outcome but not the reasoning and wants to write her own; this is known as a concurring opinion. Finally, if a judge disagrees with the outcome, he may write a dissenting opinion.

In the *State v. Brown* case, you see that a panel of three judges heard oral argument (it is a court of appeals, not a trial court). Judge Scholfield wrote the opinion and Judges Coleman and Williams agreed and signed onto the same opinion.

Below the line in Exhibit IV-T you will see another case issued by the New Mexico Supreme Court, which has five justices. Justice Ransom wrote the opinion; Chief Justice Scarborough, Senior Justice Sosa, and Justice Walters signed onto the opinion written by Ransom. The fifth justice, Stowers, dissented and wrote a dissenting opinion.

You will see several charts representing the different types of opinions in Exhibits IV-U, V, and W. I have used a nine-judge panel, like the U.S. Supreme Court, for illustrative purposes. When at least five of the nine, a majority, sign the same opinion, you have what is known a majority opinion.

Exhibit IV-U

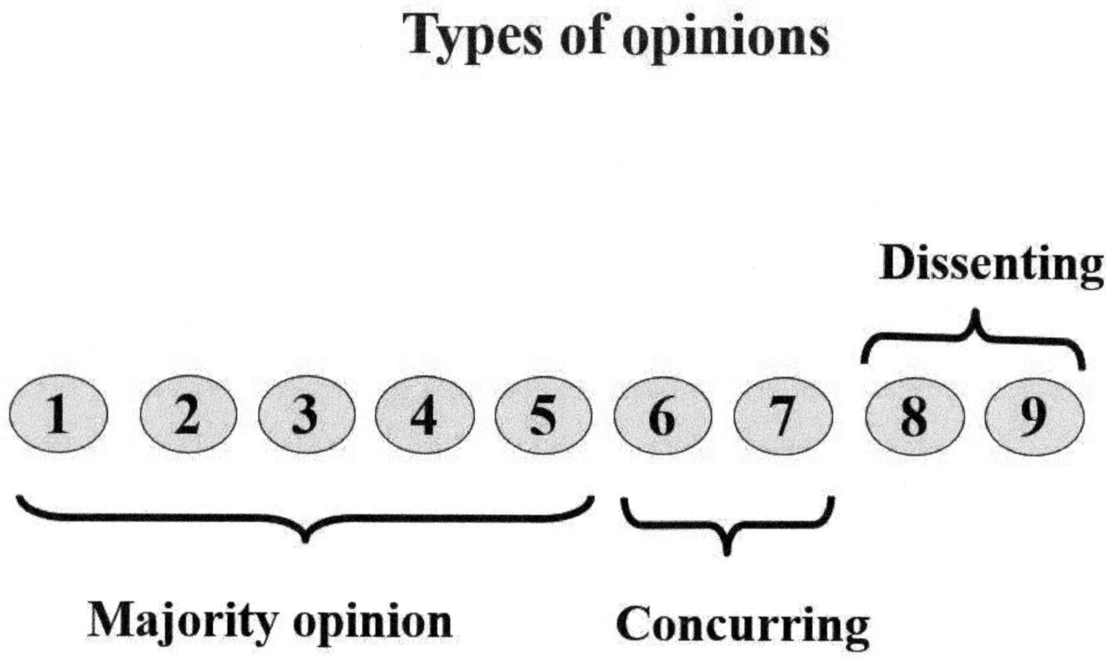

Exhibit IV-V

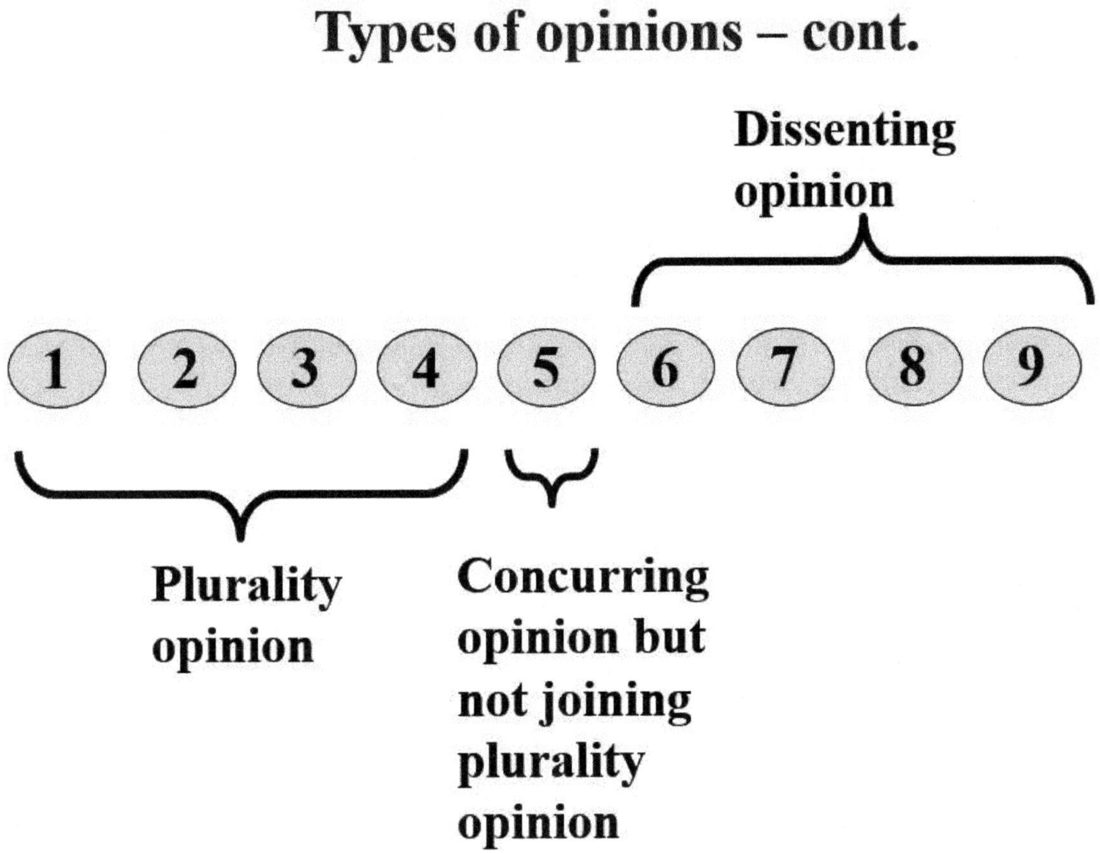

Exhibit IV-W

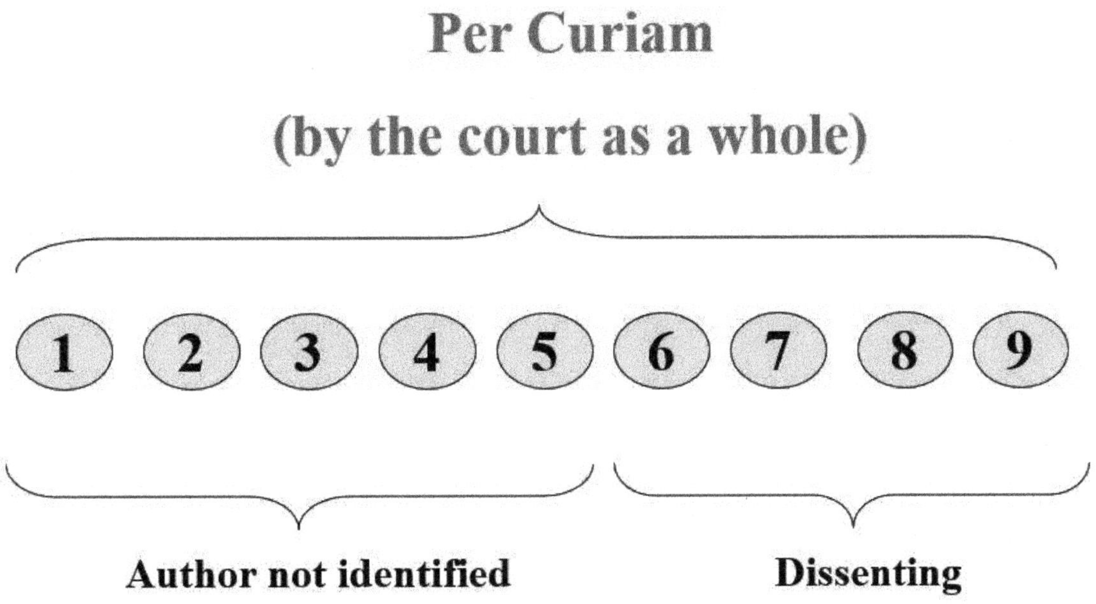

What if you have one opinion that four justices sign, one concurring opinion by a fifth justice, and the remaining four all signing onto another opinion that disagrees with the result of the other opinion that received the support of four justices? (Illustrated in Exhibit IV-V) In this situation, the concurring opinion breaks the tie. Remember, a concurrence means the justice agrees with the outcome but not the reasoning. Five judges agree on the same outcome, so this becomes the position of the court (a.k.a., the court's opinion). However, since no single opinion has the support of the majority, the opinion that represents the winning side with four signatures is known as a plurality opinion.

A plurality opinion can receive less than four votes in a nine-judge court. For example, it is possible that you get three signatures on an opinion, two concurring opinions, and four justices joining a single opinion that arrives at the opposite conclusion. Why isn't the opinion that the four justices agreed upon the plurality opinion? Because the concurring opinions agree with the outcome of the opinion that received three signatures and counts in support of that outcome. This gives you five votes in favor of the same outcome of the case, which is a majority of a court with nine justices. Therefore, the opinion with three signatures becomes the plurality opinion and the four who joined an opinion disagreeing with the outcome becomes the dissent.

There are a couple of questions that arise from this description of different opinions. First, when you have a plurality opinion, does the plurality opinion carry the same weight as a majority opinion? There is no definite, universally accepted, answer to this question. Secondly, you may wonder how you can determine the holding of a case when the plurality opinion only has three out of nine votes with the rest split between various concurring and dissenting opinions. The answer to this question is also not clear.[3] There is a lot of discussion about these questions in the literature, but the answers are well beyond what we have time for in this material.

When you look at a case with multiple opinions of various types, the majority or plurality opinion will be printed first, followed by concurring opinions, and then dissenting opinions. A listing of which justices wrote or joined which opinions is usually printed right before the beginning of the majority or plurality opinion. The justices who joined a specific opinion are also identified at the beginning of the opinion they joined.

Finally, there are per curiam opinions (Exhibit IV-W). This is a Latin phrase which means "for the court as a whole." This is normally used when the case is considered an easy one and all members of the panel agree. Another feature of per curiam opinions is the absence of an identified author; no author's name is attached to the opinion. Occasionally, the court issues a per curiam opinion even though not all justices agreed. The main function of the per curiam opinion in this situation is to keep the identity of the true author from being revealed. There is a famous case decided in 2000 in which the court issued a per curiam opinion when four of the nine justices strongly dissented. Can you identify that case? (Think of the two main contenders for the presidential election that year.)

Summary

1. At the trial court level, a case is litigation between two or more parties.
2. A docket lists all events and documents associated with a court case.
3. Trial judges occasionally write opinions resolving the application of the law to the facts.
4. On appeal, a case only involves certain issues that are appealed. The appeals court considers only those issues and produces an opinion, often referred to as a case, resolving those issues.

[3] The U.S. Supreme Court tried to answer this question in *Marks v. United States*, 430 U.S. 188 (1977) but various courts, along with legal experts, can't agree upon what the Court meant and how it should be applied. The Court has not clarified the issue.

5. Not all opinions are "published" in reporters.

6. Reporters are simply a chronological publication of the opinions that are published.

7. West Publishing prints many of the reporters available today.

8. Some states also publish opinions issued by their courts. When the same case appears in more than one reporter, cites to the same case in the other reporter are known as a parallel cite.

9. When an opinion is published in more than one reporter, the opinion will frequently contain marks indicating where the page breaks appear in the parallel reporter; these marks are known as star pagination.

10. A case published by West contains the following components.

    A. Cite (vol., reporter name, beginning page number).

    B. Names of parties involved.

    C. Docket number assigned to the case.

    D. Date the decision was issued.

    E. Summary of the case.

    F. West headnotes, to which topic and key numbers are assigned.

    G. Opinions of all types related to the litigation.

11. Topic and key numbers are a part of the outline of the law created by West.

12. Headnotes are numbered. Those numbers appear in brackets throughout the opinion to indicate which part of the opinion is related to the numbered headnote.

13. Different types of opinions may exist when multiple judges hear a case and the judges do not agree on the outcome.

    A. Majority (an opinion the majority of the justices sign onto).

    B. Plurality (an opinion that less than a majority of the justices sign onto but gets the most support).

    C. Concurring (an opinion written by a judge who agrees with the outcome of the majority or plurality but arrives at the same conclusion for reasons other than those expressed in the court's opinion).

    D. Dissenting (an opinion written by a judge who disagrees with the court's opinion).

    E. Per Curiam (an opinion that has no identified author and usually represents the thinking of all the justices).

14. Cases appearing in reporters not published by West will display most of the same information except for the case summary, headnotes, and topic and key numbers assigned to the headnotes. Any material written by editors working for West is proprietary information and will not appear in a reporter not published by West.

Assignment 1

The following questions are based on material covered in sections I–IV above. Be sure to read these sections before answering these questions.

Immediately following this assignment are three documents: a docket sheet from the trial court in the case *Ledbetter v. Goodyear Tire*, an unabridged court opinion titled *State v. Burnett*, and the first three pages of another court opinion titled *Ewing v. California*.

1. Answer the following questions based upon the information found in the attached docket from *Ledbetter v. Goodyear Tire.*

A. On what date did this case begin and what event initiated the litigation?

B. Which court tried this case?

C. Who was the plaintiff and the defendant?

D. What docket number was assigned to this case by the court?

E. A verdict was reached on January 24, 2003; did the plaintiff or defendant win the verdict?

F. Did the losing party appeal the case? If so, what docket number was assigned to this case in the court of appeals? (Hint: October 24, 2003).

2. Use the *State v. Burnett* opinion to answer the following questions.

A. What is the docket number of this case?

B. Which court heard this case? Is this court a trial court, an intermediate court of appeals, or the highest court of appeals?

C. Is the copy of the case you are reading from a government published reporter or one published by a commercial publisher? What information did you use to answer this question?

D. Assume you are interested in reading the part of the opinion that discusses whether an earlier ruling by a lower federal court is binding on the court that issued this opinion. Which headnote specifically discusses the general rule on this topic?

E. What topic and key number is assigned to this headnote?

F. On which page(s) in the opinion can you find discussion of this issue?

3. Consult the pages of *Ewing v. California* to answer the following questions.

A. Which court issued this opinion?

B. On page 13 of the case, there is a paragraph that describes which justices joined the various opinions. Based on this information, what types of opinions were written in this case?

C. What type of opinion is the judgment of the court (the one that contains the holding of the case and is binding on the parties involved in the litigation)? Explain how you arrived at this conclusion.

CLOSED,REPORT & RECOMMEND

U.S. District Court
Northern District of Alabama (Eastern)
CIVIL DOCKET FOR CASE #: 1:99−cv−03137−UWC

Ledbetter v. Goodyear Tire & Rub
Assigned to: Judge U W Clemon
Demand: $0
Case in other court: #03−15264−G
Cause: 42:2000 Job Discrimination (Sex)

Date Filed: 11/24/1999
Date Terminated: 01/28/2003
Jury Demand: Plaintiff
Nature of Suit: 442 Civil Rights: Jobs
Jurisdiction: Federal Question

Plaintiff

Lilly M Ledbetter represented by **C Michael Quinn**
LAW OFFICES OF C. MICHAEL QUINN, LLC
2501 Aspen Cove Drive
Birmingham, AL 35243
205−706−8153
Fax: 205−254−1500
Email: mquinn422@gmail.com
ATTORNEY TO BE NOTICED

Jon C Goldfarb
WIGGINS CHILDS PANTAZIS FISHER & GOLDFARB
The Kress Building
301 19th Street North
Birmingham, AL 35203−3204
205−314−0500
Fax: 205−254−1500
Email: jcg@wigginschilds.com
ATTORNEY TO BE NOTICED

Maury S Weiner
WIGGINS CHILDS QUINN & PANTAZIS LLC
The Kress Building
301 19th Street North
Birmingham, AL 35203−3204
205−314−0590
Fax: 205−254−1500
Email: mweiner@wcqp.com
ATTORNEY TO BE NOTICED

Susan W Bullock
FORD HARRISON LLP
420 20th Street North
Suite 2560
Birmingham, AL 35203
205−244−5904
Fax: 205−244−5901
Email: sbullock@fordharrison.com
TERMINATED: 04/03/2002
ATTORNEY TO BE NOTICED

V.

Defendant

Goodyear Tire and Rubber Company, Inc. represented by **Jay D St Clair**
LITTLER MENDELSON PC
420 20th Street North, Suite 2300
Birmingham, AL 35203

205−421−4700
Fax: 205−449−8446
Email: jstclair@littler.com
ATTORNEY TO BE NOTICED

Kelly Estes
BRADLEY ARANT BOULT
CUMMINGS LLP
PO Box 830709
Birmingham, AL 35283−0709
205−521−8000
Fax: 205−488−6437
Email: kestes@babc.com
ATTORNEY TO BE NOTICED

Ronald H Kent , Jr
2790 Saddle Creek Trail
Birmingham, AL 35252
205−218−5073
Email: rhk66@bellsouth.net
ATTORNEY TO BE NOTICED

Date Filed	#	Docket Text
11/24/1999	1	COMPLAINT filed, amount paid $ 150.00, receipt # 200145166 (PGS) (Entered: 11/24/1999)
12/27/1999	2	SUMMONS and complaint returned executed: upon defendant Goodyear Tire & Rub on 12/11/99 filed (PGS) (Entered: 12/27/1999)
01/31/2000	3	NOTICE of appearance for defendant Goodyear Tire & Rubber Co., Inc., by atty Ronald H Kent Jr filed cs (SRJ) (Entered: 01/31/2000)
02/16/2000	4	ORDER reminding parties of their obligations under FRCP 26(f) and LR 26.1(d) filed filed (by Magistrate−Judge John E. Ott) cm (PGS) (Entered: 02/16/2000)
02/28/2000	5	ANSWER by defendant Goodyear Tire & Rub w/appear by atty(s) Jay D St Clair filed cs (PGS) (Entered: 02/28/2000)
03/20/2000	6	Report of Parties (form 35) of compliance with FRCP 26 filed (PGS) (Entered: 03/20/2000)
03/21/2000	7	ORDER (Scheduling) that certain time limits apply as set out in this order; dispositive motions by 1/15/01; intitial disclosure by 4/20/00; discovery cutoff 12/1/00 by Magistrate−Judge John E. Ott entered cm (PGS) (Entered: 03/21/2000)
08/14/2000	8	WITNESS list by plaintiff Lilly M Ledbetter filed cs (PGS) (Entered: 08/15/2000)
11/14/2000	9	MOTION by plaintiff Lilly M Ledbetter to compel production of documents w/exhibits att filed cs (PGS) (Entered: 11/15/2000)
11/22/2000	10	OPPOSITION (Brief) by defendant Goodyear Tire & Rub to pla's motion to compel production of documents [9−1] w/exh att filed cs (PGS) (Entered: 11/24/2000)
12/11/2000	11	ORDER In−court hearing set for 10:00 am on Friday, 12/15/00 filed (by Magistrate−Judge John E. Ott) cm (PGS) (Entered: 12/11/2000)
12/15/2000		COURTROOM NOTES: Hrg before JEO, USMJ re: pla's motion to compel production − arguments − ORDER (oral) submitting the motion − written order to be entered by the Court (Penny Enoch, Rpr 2c86) (DDR) (Entered: 12/18/2000)
01/05/2001	12	MOTION (Joint) by parties to extend dispositive motions ddl (3) weeks to 2/5/01 filed cs (DWC) (Entered: 01/08/2001)
01/09/2001	13	ORDER that dft is ordered to produce the requested information concerning the Area Managers & the Hourly Non−Bargaining Unit Supervisors in the other business center; & denying the motion to the extent pla seeks disclosure of all charges or complaints of discrimination against all supervisors at the Gadsden Plant [9−1] filed (

Case: 1:99-cv-03137-UWC As of: 07/25/2018 08:35 AM CDT 3 of 7

		by Magistrate–Judge John E. Ott) cm (PGS) (Entered: 01/09/2001)
01/09/2001	14	12 – ORDER granting motion to extend dispositive motions ddl (3) weeks to 2/5/01 [12–1] (by Magistrate–Judge John Ott) entered cm (PGS) (Entered: 01/09/2001)
02/05/2001	15	MOTION by defendant Goodyear Tire & Rub for summary judgment filed cs (PGS) (Entered: 02/06/2001)
02/05/2001	16	SUBMISSION of discovery by defendant Goodyear Tire & Rub in support of motion for sj (See separate folder– Vols I & II too large for file) filed cs (PGS) (Entered: 02/06/2001)
02/06/2001	17	BRIEF by defendant Goodyear Tire & Rub in Support of Motion for Summary Judgment filed cs (PGS) (Entered: 02/06/2001)
02/07/2001	18	ORDER (Submission) that the motion for summary judgment [15–1] is submitted 3/7/01; Responsive Brfs Due by 2/21/01, Reply Brfs Due by 3/7/01 , filed (Magistrate–Judge John E. Ott) cm (PGS) (Entered: 02/07/2001)
02/16/2001	19	MOTION by pla Lilly M Ledbetter to extend time (4) days to file a brief in opposition to dft's motion for sumjgm filed cs (DWC) (Entered: 02/20/2001)
02/20/2001	20	19 – ORDER granting motion to extend time (4) days to file a brief in opposition to dft's motion for sumjgm [19–1] (by Magistrate–Judge John E. Ott) entered cm (MAA) (Entered: 02/20/2001)
02/27/2001	21	SUBMISSION of discovery by plaintiff Lilly M Ledbetter filed (Vols I & II) [see separate folder] cs (PGS) (Entered: 02/28/2001)
02/27/2001	22	BRIEF by plaintiff Lilly M Ledbetter in opposition to dft's motion for summary judgment filed cs (PGS) (Entered: 02/28/2001)
03/15/2001	23	MOTION (Joint) of the parties to amend scheduling order filed cs (PGS) (Entered: 03/15/2001)
03/16/2001	24	ORDER granting motion to amend scheduling order [23–1]; that the due dates for the list of trial witnesses, exhibits & any objections from each party will be set by separate order after the motion for summary judgment is decided; filed (by Magistrate–Judge John E. Ott) cm (PGS) (Entered: 03/16/2001)
01/07/2002	25	MOTION by pla's counsel Susan W. Bullock to withdraw as counsel for Lilly M Ledbetter to withdraw attorney filed cs (SNH) (Entered: 01/08/2002)
01/31/2002	26	BRIEF (Reply) by defendant Goodyear Tire & Rubbber in support of the motion for summary judgment w/exhs att filed cs (Received in Judge Ott's chambers on 3/13/01) (PGS) Modified on 01/31/2002 (Entered: 01/31/2002)
04/03/2002	27	25 – ORDER granting motion to withdraw attorney Susan W Bullock [25–1] by Magistrate–Judge John E. Ott) entered cm (PGS) (Entered: 04/03/2002)
04/03/2002		UTILITY event: terminates attorney Susan W Bullock for Lilly M Ledbetter (doc #27) (PGS) (Entered: 04/03/2002)
04/03/2002	28	Report and Recommendation that the motion for summary judgment be granted in part and denied in part as set out filed (by Magistrate–Judge John E. Ott) motion for summary judgment cm (PGS) (Entered: 04/03/2002)
04/03/2002	29	ORDER Case reassigned to Chief Judge U W. Clemon filed (by Magistrate–Judge John E. Ott) cm (PGS) (Entered: 04/03/2002)
04/24/2002	30	MOTION by pla to extend time to w/i (10) days of 4/23/02 to file objection to the RR filed cs (DWC) (Entered: 04/24/2002)
04/25/2002	31	30 – ORDER granting pla's motion to extend time to w/i (10) days of 4/23/02 to file objections to the RR [30–1] (by Chief Judge U W. Clemon) entered cm (DWC) (Entered: 04/26/2002)
05/07/2002	32	OBJECTIONS by pla to RR [28–1] filed cs (DWC) (Entered: 05/07/2002)

Case: 1:99-cv-03137-UWC As of: 07/25/2018 08:35 AM CDT 4 of 7

07/31/2002	33	MEMORANDUM opinion on objections to the Magistrate Judge's Report & Recommendation filed (by Chief Judge U W. Clemon) cm (DWC) (Entered: 07/31/2002)
07/31/2002	34	ORDER, in conformity w/ the Memorandum Opinion on objections to the Magistrate Judge's R&R, SUMMARY JUDGMENT is GRANTED in favor of dft on certain claims as stated & DENIED on other claims [15−1] filed by Chief Judge U W. Clemon) cm (DWC) (Entered: 07/31/2002)
08/26/2002	35	ORDER on pre−trial hearing ; PTC held 1:30 8/19/02 ; jury trial set 12/9/02, Anniston, AL filed (by Chief Judge U W. Clemon) cm (DWC) (Entered: 08/26/2002)
11/07/2002	36	NOTICE of appearance for pla by Maury S Weiner filed cs (DWC) (Entered: 11/07/2002)
11/07/2002	37	MOTION by pla to extend ddl for both parties for witness, exhibit & damage list until 11/12/02 filed cs (DWC) (Entered: 11/07/2002)
11/07/2002	38	37 − ORDER granting motion to extend ddls for both parties to file witness, exhibit & damage list until 11/12/02 [37−1] ; Notice of Compliance ddl 11/12/02 (by Chief Judge U W. Clemon) entered cm (DWC) (Entered: 11/07/2002)
11/12/2002	39	DAMAGE list of plaintiff filed cs (DWC) (Entered: 11/13/2002)
11/12/2002	40	EXHIBIT list by plaintiff filed cs (DWC) (Entered: 11/13/2002)
11/12/2002	41	WITNESS list by plaintiff filed cs (DWC) (Entered: 11/13/2002)
11/21/2002	42	OBJECTIONS by pla to dft's witness list, supplemental witness list & revised exh list filed cs [dft's witlst, supp witlst & revised exhlst not filed w/ the court] (DWC) (Entered: 11/22/2002)
01/21/2003	43	VOIR DIRE questions submitted by plaintiff Lilly M Ledbetter filed cs (DGS) (Entered: 01/21/2003)
01/21/2003	44	VOIR DIRE questions submitted by defendant Goodyear Tire & Rub filed cs (DGS) (Entered: 01/21/2003)
01/21/2003	45	MOTION by defendant Goodyear Tire & Rub in limine filed cs (DGS) (Entered: 01/21/2003)
01/21/2003	46	OPPOSITION by plaintiff Lilly M Ledbetter to defendant's motion in limine number 3 filed cs (DGS) (Entered: 01/21/2003)
01/21/2003	47	OPPOSITION by plaintiff Lilly M Ledbetter to defendant's motion in limine number 1 filed cs (DGS) (Entered: 01/21/2003)
01/21/2003	48	JURY strikes of plaintiff Lilly M Ledbetter , filed (DGS) (Entered: 01/21/2003)
01/21/2003	49	JURY strikes of defendant Goodyear Tire & Rub , filed (DGS) (Entered: 01/22/2003)
01/21/2003		COURTROOM NOTES: JURY TRIAL at Anniston, AL − before the Honorable U. W. Clemon, CUSDJ − opening remarks of the court − juror Inzer and Heacock excused for cause − jury selected and sworn − opening remarks of the court to the jury − opening statements of counsel − plaintiff's testimony − daily adj. − (Penny Enoch, rptr.) (DGS) (Entered: 01/24/2003)
01/22/2003	50	JURY instructions submitted by plaintiff Lilly M Ledbetter filed cs (DGS) (Entered: 01/22/2003)
01/22/2003	51	JURY instructions submitted by defendant Goodyear Tire & Rub filed cs (DGS) (Entered: 01/22/2003)
01/22/2003	52	MOTION by dft in limine #1 prohibiting pla from offering evidence regarding any sexual harassment the pla allegedly experienced while employed at Goodyear filed cs [deemed filed 1/17/03] (DWC) Modified on 01/22/2003 (Entered: 01/22/2003)
01/22/2003	53	MOTION by dft in limine #2 prohibiting pla from seeking to offer evidence regarding a warrant for disorderly conduct against Mike Tucker filed cs [deemed filed 1/17/03] (DWC) Modified on 01/22/2003 (Entered: 01/22/2003)

Case: 1:99-cv-03137-UWC As of: 07/25/2018 08:35 AM CDT 5 of 7

01/22/2003	54	MOTION by dft in limine #3 prohibiting pla from stating her 10/98 retirement was involuntary filed cs (DWC) (Entered: 01/22/2003)
01/22/2003	55	MOTION by dft in limine #4 prohibiting pla from presenting evidence regarding settlement offers filed cs (DWC) (Entered: 01/22/2003)
01/22/2003		COURTROOM NOTES: JURY TRIAL (UWC) – trial resumed – plaintiff's testimony resumed – plaintiff rests – defendant's testimony – defendant rests – daily adj. – (Penny Enoch) (DGS) (Entered: 01/24/2003)
01/22/2003	56	MOTION by defendant Goodyear Tire & Rub for judgment as a matter of law on the plaintiff's pay claim – filed cs (DGS) (Entered: 01/24/2003)
01/22/2003	59	56 – ORDER denying dft's motion for judgment as a matter of law [56–1] (by Chief Judge U W. Clemon) entered cm (DWC) (Entered: 01/28/2003)
01/23/2003		COURTROOM NOTES: JURY TRIAL (UWC) – trial resumed – closing arguments of counsel – court's oral charge to the jury – jury deliberations begin – daily adj. – (Penny Enoch, rptr.) (DGS) (Entered: 01/24/2003)
01/24/2003		COURTROOM NOTES: JURY TRIAL (UWC) – trial resumed – jury deliberations continued – written response of the court to the jury – jury verdict filed this day – written order to be entered by the court – (Penny Encoh, rptr.) (DGS) (Entered: 01/24/2003)
01/24/2003	57	JURY question filed (DGS) (Entered: 01/24/2003)
01/24/2003	58	VERDICT for plaintiff Lilly M Ledbetter against defendant Goodyear Tire & Rub filed (DGS) (Entered: 01/24/2003)
01/28/2003	60	ORDER (Judgment) filed: based solely on the Special Verdict of the Jury, JUDGMENT in the amt $3,843,014.93 ENTERED in favor of pla & against dft; a reasonable atty's fee & costs are taxed against dft (by Chief Judge U W. Clemon) to dismiss case cm (DWC) (Entered: 01/28/2003)
02/06/2003	61	BILL of costs submitted by pla w/exh atta filed (DWC) Modified on 02/07/2003 (Entered: 02/07/2003)
02/07/2003	62	MOTION by pla for attorney fees & expenses filed cs (DWC) (Entered: 02/07/2003)
02/07/2003	63	RENEWED MOTION by dft for judgment as a matter of law , and, in the alternative, for new trial or remittitur filed cs (DWC) (Entered: 02/10/2003)
02/07/2003	64	MOTION by dft to strike the jury's answer to Question 5 in the Special Verdict filed cs (DWC) (Entered: 02/10/2003)
02/07/2003	65	BRIEF by dft in support of its Renewed motion for judgment as a matter of law w/attachments filed cs (DWC) (Entered: 02/10/2003)
02/12/2003	66	64 – ORDER granting motion to strike the jury's answer to Question 5 in the Special Verdict [64–1] (by Chief Judge U W. Clemon) entered cm (DWC) (Entered: 02/13/2003)
02/19/2003	67	OBJECTIONS by dft to pla's motion for attys fees & expenses [62–1] filed cs (DWC) (Entered: 02/19/2003)
02/19/2003	68	OBJECTIONS by dft to pla's Bill of Costs [61–1] filed cs (DWC) (Entered: 02/19/2003)
02/27/2003	69	MOTION by pla to supplement pla's motion for atty's fees & expenses to include an addl expense filed cs (DWC) (Entered: 02/27/2003)
04/24/2003	70	MOTION by pla to continue hearing set for 4/25/03 filed cs (DWC) (Entered: 04/24/2003)
04/24/2003	71	70 – ORDER granting motion to continue hearing set for 4/25/03 [70–1] (by Chief Judge U W. Clemon) entered cm (DWC) (Entered: 04/24/2003)
05/09/2003	72	SUPPLEMENTAL MOTION (petition) by pla for attorney fees, expenses & costs w/exhs atta filed cs [bound filed in expandable folder] (DWC) (Entered: 05/12/2003)

Case: 1:99-cv-03137-UWC As of: 07/25/2018 08:35 AM CDT 6 of 7

05/09/2003	73	OPPOSITION by pla to dft's motion for judgment as a matter of law [63−1], motion for new trial or remittitur [63−2] filed cs [bound filed in expandable folder] (DWC) (Entered: 05/12/2003)
05/30/2003	74	OBJECTIONS by dft to pla's supplemental fee petition [72−1] w/exhs atta filed cs (DWC) (Entered: 05/30/2003)
05/30/2003	75	NOTICE of appearance for dft by Kelly Estes filed cs (DWC) (Entered: 05/30/2003)
06/02/2003	76	NOTICE of compliance (pla's lost wages submission) by pla with the court's 5/30/03 hearing w/exhs atta filed cs (DWC) (Entered: 06/03/2003)
06/03/2003	77	OBJECTIONS by dft to pla's lost wages submission [76−1] filed cs (DWC) (Entered: 06/04/2003)
06/04/2003	78	REPLY by pla to dft's objection to lost wage submission [77−1] filed cs (DWC) (Entered: 06/05/2003)
09/24/2003	79	MEMORANDUM opinion on post−trial motions filed (by Chief Judge U W. Clemon) cm (KWC) (Entered: 09/24/2003)
09/24/2003	80	ORDER on post−trial motions; denying pla's motion for attorney fees & expenses [62−1], without prejudice to its automatic reinstatement in event that pla agrees to remittitur; granting motion for judgment as a matter of law [63−1] solely to entent that jury's award of 328,597.93 in backpay is VACATED; in all other respects, motion for judgment as a matter of law is DENIED; dft's alternative motion for a remittitur is GRANTED; jgmt previously entered in case is hereby REDUCED to $360,000.00 conditioned on pla's filing her assent to remittitur w/in 15 days of this order; denying motion for new trial [63−2] on condition that pla assents to remittitur. Should pla fail to assent to remittitur w/in time fixed, court will reconsider motion sua sponte and GRANT it on issue of damages only; filed (by Chief Judge U W. Clemon) cm (KWC) (Entered: 09/24/2003)
09/24/2003	81	52 − ORDER finding the motion in limine #1 prohibiting pla from offering evidence regarding any sexual harassment [52−1] moot (by Chief Judge U W. Clemon) entered (deemed entered 09/16/03) cm (KWC) Modified on 09/24/2003 (Entered: 09/24/2003)
09/24/2003	82	53 − ORDER finding the motion in limine #2 prohibiting pla from seeking to offer evidence regarding a warrant for disorderly conduct against Mike Tucker [53−1] moot (by Chief Judge U W. Clemon) deemed entered 09/16/03 cm (KWC) (Entered: 09/24/2003)
09/24/2003	83	54 − ORDER finding the motion in limine #3 prohibiting pla from stating her 10/98 retirement was involuntary moot (by Chief Judge U W. Clemon) deemed entered 09/16/03 cm (KWC) (Entered: 09/24/2003)
09/24/2003	84	55 − ORDER finding the motion in limine #4 prohibiting pla from presenting evidence regarding settlement offers [55−1] moot (by Chief Judge U W. Clemon) deemed entered 09/22/03 cm (KWC) (Entered: 09/24/2003)
09/24/2003	85	69 − ORDER denying motion to supplement pla's motion for atty's fees & expenses to include an addl expense [69−1] (by Chief Judge U W. Clemon) deemed entered 09/16/03 cm (KWC) (Entered: 09/24/2003)
09/25/2003	86	NOTICE of compliance (Declaration of intent to accept Remittitur) by pla with [80−1] filed cs (DWC) (Entered: 09/25/2003)
10/14/2003	87	NOTICE of appeal by defendant Goodyear Tire & Rub from District Court decision [80−1] ; notice of appeal, order appealed from and court copy of docket entries w/transmittal letter mailed cm (BST) (Entered: 10/15/2003)
10/14/2003		APPEAL fee received in amount of $ 105 (BST) (Entered: 10/15/2003)
10/24/2003		NOTIFICATION by Circuit Court of Appellate docket number #03−15264−G (KWC) (Entered: 10/24/2003)
10/27/2003	88	Appeal Information Sheet filed by dft [87−1] (KWC) (Entered: 10/27/2003)
11/04/2003	89	Appeal Information Sheet filed by Crtrptr Enoch [87−1] (KWC) (Entered: 11/04/2003)

11/12/2003	90	AFFIDAVIT (supplemental) of C. Michael Quinn regarding motion for attorney fees, expenses & costs [72–1] filed cs (MAA) (Entered: 11/13/2003)
11/24/2003	91	Appeal Information Sheet filed by Penny Enoch [87–1] (DRR) (Entered: 11/24/2003)
11/24/2003	92	TRANSCRIPT of proceedings had before Chief Judge U W. Clemon on 01/21/03, 4 bound volumes = 481 pages (vols 3 & 4 in same binder, in expandable folder) –Court Reporter Penny Enoch (DRR) Modified on 03/10/2004 (Entered: 11/24/2003)
02/25/2004	93	CERTIFICATE of Readiness issued, cm (SRJ) (Entered: 02/25/2004)
02/25/2004	94	72 – ORDER overruling w/out prejudice, motion for attorney fees, expenses & costs [72–1] (by Chief Judge U W. Clemon) entered cm (KWC) (Entered: 02/27/2004)
03/10/2004	95	CERTIFIED RECORD ON APPEAL consisting of Two (2) Volumes of Pleadings, Three (3) Volumes of Transcripts & Three (3) Expandable Folders containing docs. #16, #21, #22 #72 #73 & #92 with certified copy of docket entries and transmittal mailed to US Court of Appeals cm (SRJ) (Entered: 03/10/2004)
11/04/2005	96	USCA JUDGMENT as to 87 Notice of Appeal; It is hereby ORDERED that the attached Opinion is entered as Judgment, the USDC judgement is REVERSED and INSTRUCTED to Dismiss plaintiff Ledbetter's complaint with prejudice, Issued As Mandate 11/03/2005 (SRJ,) (Entered: 11/07/2005)
11/21/2005	97	ORDER OF DISMISSAL with prejudice w/costs hereby taxed against plaintiff consistent with U.S. Court of Appeals–11th Circuit's Mandate 11/2/2005. Signed by Judge U W Clemon on November 21, 2005. (SRJ,) (Entered: 11/21/2005)
12/07/2005	98	BILL OF COSTS by Goodyear Tire and Rubber Company, Inc.. (St Clair, Jay) (Entered: 12/07/2005)
02/13/2006	99	Costs Taxed in amount of $ 3,165.20 against plaintiff, Lilly M. Ledbetter (ECS,) (Entered: 02/13/2006)
11/02/2006	100	A Certified Copy of the Docket Entries, the Original Court File consisting of Two (2) Volumes of Pleadings, Three (3) Volumes of Transcripts, & Two (2) Expandable Folders containing; Expandable #1 contains documents #16, #21, & #22; Expandable #2 contains documents #72, #73, Exhibits, Jury Trial Sheet (1 pg), Courtroom Notes (1 pg) & Venire Report (2 pgs) was Transmitted to the Clerk of the U.S. Supreme Court at their request. (SRJ,) . (Entered: 11/02/2006)
11/02/2006	101	NOTICE of Court's Original Court File mailed to U.S. Supreme Court. (SRJ,) (Entered: 11/02/2006)

93 Ohio St.3d 419

⌊419The STATE of Ohio, Appellee,

v.

BURNETT, Appellant.

No. 00–266.

Supreme Court of Ohio.

Submitted March 13, 2001.

Decided Oct. 17, 2001.

Defendant was convicted in a Hamilton County court of trespass by entering drug-exclusion zone after conviction for drug-related offense. Defendant appealed. The Court of Appeals affirmed. Review was allowed. The Supreme Court, Moyer, C.J., held that: (1) city ordinance which prohibits a person from entering a drug-exclusion zone after arrest for or conviction of a drug-related offense violated defendant's due process right of intra-state travel; (2) the ordinance did not violate the right to freedom of association; and (3) it violated the state constitutional prohibition against municipalities enforcing regulations in conflict with general laws.

Reversed.

Cook, J., concurred separately and filed opinion.

1. Courts ⚷97(5)

Rulings on federal statutory or constitutional law made by a federal court other than the United States Supreme Court are not binding on the state Supreme Court.

2. Constitutional Law ⚷91

The First Amendment right of association encompasses two distinct types of freedoms: the choice to enter into and to maintain certain intimate human relationships, and the right to associate for the purpose of engaging in expressive activity protected by the First Amendment. U.S.C.A. Const.Amend. 1.

3. Constitutional Law ⚷91

Municipal Corporations ⚷721(2)

City ordinance which prohibits a person from entering a drug-exclusion zone after arrest for or conviction of a drug-related offense did not violate defendant's right to freedom of association; the ordinance does not on its face prohibit or interfere with fundamental, personal relationships or infringe the rights of a citizen to associate with other citizens for the purpose of engaging in protected First Amendment activities, but only prohibits access to a particular area of the city. U.S.C.A. Const.Amend. 1.

4. Constitutional Law ⚷83(6)

A constitutional right of intra-state travel exists. U.S.C.A. Const. Art. 4, § 2, cl. 1; U.S.C.A. Const.Amend. 14.

5. Constitutional Law ⚷274(6)

As a fundamental right, the right to intra-state travel is a part of the liberty of which the citizen cannot be deprived without the due process of law. U.S.C.A. Const.Amend. 14.

6. Constitutional Law ⚷274(6)

Any deprivation of the due process right to travel must be evaluated under a compelling-interest test, and the legislation must be narrowly tailored to serve a compelling governmental interest. U.S.C.A. Const.Amend. 14.

7. Constitutional Law ⚷274(6)

Municipal Corporations ⚷721(2)

City ordinance which prohibits a person from entering a drug-exclusion zone after arrest for or conviction of a drug-related offense was not narrowly tailored to serve a compelling governmental interest in dealing with drugs and, therefore, violated defendant's due process right of intra-state travel; the ordinance attacks conduct that is completely innocent and prohibits entry to speak with counsel, visit family, attend church, receive emergency medical care, go to a grocery store, or just to stand on a street corner and look at a blue sky. U.S.C.A. Const.Amend. 14.

8. Constitutional Law ⚷251.3

A statute is "narrowly tailored" for due process purposes, if it targets and eliminates no more than the exact source of the evil it seeks to remedy. U.S.C.A. Const.Amend. 14.

See publication Words and Phrases for other judicial constructions and definitions.

9. Municipal Corporations ⚷592(3), 721(2)

City ordinance which prohibits a person from entering a drug-exclusion zone after arrest for or conviction of a drug-related offense added a criminal penalty for a drug offense and, therefore, violated the state constitutional prohibition against municipalities enforcing regulations in conflict with general laws; the notice of exclusion was delivered by the city's executive branch, and the ordinance added a penalty not imposed by a court and not authorized by statute. Const. Art. 18, § 3.

10. Municipal Corporations ⚷592(1, 4)

An ordinance conflicts with the general laws if it permits or licenses that which the statute forbids and prohibits, and vice versa. Const. Art. 18, § 3.

11. Municipal Corporations ⚷592(3)

A municipality may not, by way of ordinance, add a penalty for violation of a state criminal statute that is not otherwise provided for by the General Assembly. Const. Art. 18, § 3.

Fay D. DuPuis, City Solicitor, Terrence R. Cosgrove, Cincinnati City Prosecutor, and Jennifer Bishop, Assistant Prosecutor, for appellee.

Bruce F. Thompson, Hamilton County Public Defender's Office, for appellant.

Raymond Vasvari, Cleveland, and Bernard F. Wong, Cincinnati, urging reversal for amicus curiae, the American Civil Liberties Union of Ohio Foundation.

MOYER, C.J.

On August 7, 1996, appellee, the city of Cincinnati, passed Ordinance No. 229–1996. The ordinance enacted Chapter 755 of the Cincinnati Municipal Code, which established drug-exclusion zones within the city. In passing the ordinance, the city council stated that certain areas of the city have a higher incidence of drug-related activity, which leads to the degradation of those areas. Ordinance No. 229–1996, Section 1(A). Further, the city council theorized that many people arrested for or convicted of drug offenses frequently returned to these areas. Section 1(B). Finding that its existing laws did not adequately control drug-related activity and that the public interest in "preventing the ⌊420 harmful effects of illegal drug abusers" was great, Sections 1(E) and (F), the city created a drug-exclusion zone under Chapter 755.[1]

The ordinance states, "drug-exclusion zones are those areas of the city as designated by the city council under Chapter 755 of this code, which are areas where the number of arrests for the crimes listed in Chapter 755–5 and other drug-abuse related crimes * * * is significantly higher

1. The enactment initially created only one drug-exclusion zone. It is an area of the city known as "Over the Rhine." See Cincinnati Municipal Code 755–15.

than that for other similarly situated/sized areas of the city." Cincinnati Municipal Code 755–1. Chapter 755 subjects a person to exclusion for ninety days from the public streets, sidewalks, and other public ways in all drug-exclusion zones if the person is arrested or taken into custody within any drug-exclusion zone for any of several enumerated offenses.[2] Cincinnati Municipal Code 755–5. If the offender is subsequently convicted of the crime for which he or she was arrested, the offender is prohibited for one year from the date of conviction from being on any public street, sidewalk, or other public way in all drug-exclusion zones. *Id.* If an excluded person is found within a drug-exclusion zone during the exclusion period, that person is subject to immediate arrest for criminal trespass pursuant to R.C. 2911.21. *Id.*

At the time a person is arrested within a drug-exclusion zone for any of the crimes listed in Section 755–5, the officer making the arrest may, but is not required to, deliver a written notice excluding the person from all drug-exclusion zones. Cincinnati Municipal Code 755–9. If notice is given, it shall specify the areas designated as drug-exclusion zones and it shall provide information concerning the right to appeal the exclusion notice as provided in Section 755–11. *Id.*

If a person is served with an exclusion notice, an appeal of the exclusion may be filed with the director of safety within five calendar days of the issuance of the notice. Cincinnati Municipal Code 755–11. A hearing on the appeal must then be conducted by the director of safety within thirty days. Cincinnati Municipal Code 755–11(1)(a), 755–13(B)(a). During the pendency of the appeal, the exclusion does not take effect. Cincinnati Municipal Code 755–11(1)(b). The city has the burden to show by a preponderance of the evidence that the exclusion is based on conduct outlined in Section 755–5. Cincinnati Municipal Code 755–11(1)(b). 421 A conviction for any of the crimes listed in Section 755–5 or a determination that the arresting officer had probable cause to arrest a person for such crimes is *prima facie* evidence that the exclusion was based on prohibited conduct. Cincinnati Municipal Code 755–11(2)(a).

A variance from an exclusion may also be granted at any time during the exclusion by the chief of police or by a social service agency that provides services within the drug-exclusion zone only for reasons relating to the health, welfare, or well-being of the person excluded, or for drug-counseling services. Cincinnati Municipal Code 755–11(2)(b). The chief of police must grant a variance to any person who can establish that he or she is a bona fide resident of the drug-exclusion zone or a bona fide owner, principal, or employee of a place of lawful employment located in the drug-exclusion zone. *Id.* All variances must be in writing, and the person must keep the variance with him or her at all times within a drug-exclusion zone. Cincinnati Municipal Code 755–11(2)(c). If the person is found to be outside the scope of the variance or is arrested for conduct prohibited by state or federal drug laws, the variance immediately becomes void. Cincinnati Municipal Code 755–11(2)(c) and (d).

2. The offenses include corrupting another with drugs in violation of R.C. 2925.02, drug trafficking in violation of R.C. 2925.03, drug abuse in violation of R.C. 2925.11 (except for minor misdemeanor violations), possessing drug-abuse instruments in violation of R.C. 2925.12, drug paraphernalia in violation of R.C. 2925.14, illegal processing of drug documents in violation of R.C. 2925.23, abusing harmful intoxicants in violation of R.C. 2925.31, trafficking in harmful intoxicants in violation of R.C. 2925.32, and offenses involving counterfeit controlled substances in violation of R.C. 2925.37.

On February 7, 1998, appellant, George Burnett, was arrested for one of the designated drug offenses and was given a ninety-day exclusion notice from the Over the Rhine drug-exclusion zone by the arresting police officer. Immediately upon conviction of the charge, Burnett was served by the city with a notice of a one-year exclusion from the Over the Rhine drug-exclusion zone. On June 23, 1998, Burnett was found to be present in the drug-exclusion zone and was arrested for criminal trespass in violation of R.C. 2911.21.

The trial court overruled Burnett's motion to dismiss, in which he argued that Chapter 755 of the Cincinnati Municipal Code is unconstitutional. Burnett was convicted as charged. Upon Burnett's appeal to the First District Court of Appeals, the judgment of the trial court was affirmed. The case is now before this court pursuant to the allowance of a discretionary appeal.

The issue is whether Chapter 755 of the Cincinnati Municipal Code is constitutional. Burnett argues that the one-year exclusion[3] violates the freedom of assembly and association guaranteed by the First Amendment to the United States Constitution and the right to travel guaranteed by the Fourteenth Amendment to the United States Constitution.

[1] As an initial matter, we consider a question of federalism. After the court of appeals issued its opinion in this case, the United States District Court for the Southern District of Ohio ruled in a separate case, *Johnson v. Cincinnati* ⌊422(S.D.Ohio, 2000), 119 F.Supp.2d 735, that Chapter 755 of the Cincinnati Municipal Code is unconstitutional because it violates rights to freedom of association and freedom of movement.[4] The *Johnson* decision has not been appealed to the United States Court of Appeals for the Sixth Circuit, and counsel for appellant indicated during oral argument that the city has suspended enforcement of Chapter 755 since the *Johnson* decision was issued. The federalism question is whether a state supreme court is bound by an application of federal constitutional law by a federal trial court under the Supremacy Clause of the United States Constitution.[5]

The question of whether a state court is required to follow a federal trial court's interpretation of federal constitutional law is largely unsettled, and the United States Supreme Court has yet to definitively address the subject. Several federal circuit courts and state supreme courts have held that state courts are bound by a decision of a lower federal court, but this rule is not universal. See, *e.g., Yniguez v. Arizona* (C.A.9, 1991), 939 F.2d 727, 736; *Fretwell v. Lockhart* (C.A.8, 1991), 946 F.2d 571, 577, reversed on other grounds (1993), 506 U.S. 364, 113 S.Ct. 838, 122 L.Ed.2d 180; *Busch v. Graphic Color Corp.* (1996), 169 Ill.2d 325, 335, 214 Ill.Dec. 831, 837, 662 N.E.2d 397, 403; *Anderson v. Wagner* (1980), 207 Neb. 87, 91, 296 N.W.2d 455, 458.

Article VI of the United States Constitution provides, "This Constitution, and the Laws of the United States which shall be made in Pursuance thereof * * * shall be

3. Burnett has not challenged the ninety-day exclusion provision of Chapter 755, and, therefore, the constitutionality of the ninety-day provision is not before this court.

4. The constitutional arguments in *Johnson* are the same as those presented by Burnett in the present case.

5. Counsel for Cincinnati addressed this issue pursuant to this court's order to show cause why we should not follow the decision of the District Court for the Southern District of Ohio.

the supreme Law of the Land; and the Judges in every State shall be bound thereby, any Thing in the Constitution or Laws of any State to the Contrary notwithstanding." It has long been settled that the Supremacy Clause binds state courts to decisions of the United States Supreme Court on questions of federal statutory and constitutional law. See *Cooper v. Aaron* (1958), 358 U.S. 1, 78 S.Ct. 1401, 3 L.Ed.2d 5; *Elmendorf v. Taylor* (1825), 23 U.S. (10 Wheat.) 152, 6 L.Ed. 289 (1825); *Martin v. Hunter's Lessee* (1816), 14 U.S. (1 Wheat.) 304, 4 L.Ed. 97. The United States Supreme Court has not, however, indicated whether state courts are bound by inferior federal court decisions.

The language of the Supremacy Clause is sufficiently broad ("the Laws of the United States") to encompass all federal court decisions, and the Supreme Court has stated that state courts are bound by lower federal court decisions in cases involving the Federal Employers' Liability Act ("FELA"). In *S. Ry. Co. v. Gray* (1916), 241 U.S. 333, 338–39, 36 S.Ct. 558, 561, 60 L.Ed. 1030, 1034, the court ⌊423 stated, "As the action is under Federal Employers' Liability Act, rights and obligations depend upon it and applicable principles of common law *as interpreted and applied in Federal courts.*" (Emphasis added.) Likewise, in *Urie v. Thompson* (1949), 337 U.S. 163, 174, 69 S.Ct. 1018, 1027, 93 L.Ed. 1282, 1294–1295, quoting the first appeal to the Supreme Court of Missouri, *Urie v. Thompson* (1943), 352 Mo. 211, 218, 176 S.W.2d 471, 474, the court stated that FELA does not define negligence, leaving that question to be determined " 'by the common law principles as established and applied *in the federal courts.*' " (Emphasis added.)

The holdings in these cases suggest that inferior federal court decisions bind state courts. Scholars have argued, however, that these opinions simply reaffirm the general principle of the Supremacy Clause, or declare only that the federal common law, not state law, applies in FELA cases. See Donald H. Zeigler, Gazing Into the Crystal Ball: Reflections on the Standards State Judges Should Use to Ascertain Federal Law (1999), 40 Wm. & Mary L.Rev. 1143, 1170. Two Supreme Court justices have also opined that state courts are not bound by lower federal court decisions, but that the decisions should be only persuasive. See *Lockhart v. Fretwell* (1993), 506 U.S. 364, 376, 113 S.Ct. 838, 846, 122 L.Ed.2d 180, 193 (Thomas, J., concurring); *Steffel v. Thompson* (1974), 415 U.S. 452, 482, 94 S.Ct. 1209, 1227, 39 L.Ed.2d 505, 528, fn. 3 (Rehnquist, J., concurring).

From a historical perspective, the prospect that states would disregard federal law was the catalyst for the inclusion of the Supremacy Clause in the Constitution. See The Federalist Nos. 27 and 34, at 177, 204–205 (Alexander Hamilton) (Clinton Rossiter Ed., 1961); The Federalist No. 44, at 286–287 (James Madison). The intention of the drafters of the United States Constitution to extend the application of the Supremacy Clause to any federal court that would later be created, however, has not been definitively determined by the United States Supreme Court, and the federal courts of appeals are split on the issue. For instance, *United States ex rel. Lawrence v. Woods* (C.A.7, 1970), 432 F.2d 1072, holds that state courts are not bound by federal district court decisions. In *Woods*, the Seventh Circuit held that a federal district court's ruling that an ordinance was unconstitutional was not binding on that state's supreme court. The court based its decision on several state appellate court decisions and its recognition that finality of determination in respect to the laws of the United States rests in the

Supreme Court of the United States and that the lower federal courts exercise no appellate jurisdiction over state courts. *Id.* at 1075–1076; see, also, *State v. Glover* (1978), 60 Ohio App.2d 283, 287, 14 O.O.3d 253, 255, 396 N.E.2d 1064, 1067 (concluding that Ohio appellate courts are not bound by lower federal court opinions).

⌊424The reasoning in *Woods* reflects the argument that state courts need not follow lower federal court decisions. In cases similar to the one before us, there is a determination on federal law made by a federal trial court in one case and a potential for myriad state court opinions on the same subject. The problem with this approach is that criminal statutes may or may not be enforced depending on which forum, state or federal, in which the subsequent challenge is brought.

Given the uncertainty, we are reluctant to abandon our role in the system of federalism created by the United States Constitution until the United States Supreme Court directs us otherwise. Both inferior federal courts and state courts serve as "laboratories for experimentation to devise various solutions where the best solution is far from clear." *United States v. Lopez* (1995), 514 U.S. 549, 581, 115 S.Ct. 1624, 1641, 131 L.Ed.2d 626, 652 (Kennedy, J., concurring). We therefore conclude that we are not bound by rulings on federal statutory or constitutional law made by a federal court other than the United States Supreme Court. We will, however, accord those decisions some persuasive weight. Cf. *State ex rel. Heller v. Miller* (1980), 61 Ohio St.2d 6, 8, 15 O.O.3d 3, 4, 399 N.E.2d 66, 67. Therefore, the declaration by the United States District Court for the Southern District of Ohio in *Johnson,* 119 F.Supp.2d 735, that the Cincinnati ordinance is unconstitutional does not end our inquiry. We now address Burnett's arguments.

I. Freedom of Association.

[2] The First Amendment provides, "Congress shall make no law * * * abridging * * * the right of the people peaceably to assemble, and to petition the Government for a redress of grievances." From these words, the United States Supreme Court has recognized a right of association. *Roberts v. United States Jaycees* (1984), 468 U.S. 609, 617–618, 104 S.Ct. 3244, 3249, 82 L.Ed.2d 462, 471. This right of association encompasses two distinct types of freedoms.

The first type of freedom of association includes the choice to enter into and to maintain certain intimate human relationships. *Dallas v. Stanglin* (1989), 490 U.S. 19, 23–24, 109 S.Ct. 1591, 1594, 104 L.Ed.2d 18, 25; *Roberts,* 468 U.S. at 617–618, 104 S.Ct. at 3249, 82 L.Ed.2d at 470. These types of associations are those traditional personal bonds that have " 'played a critical role in the culture and traditions of the Nation by cultivating and transmitting shared ideals and beliefs.' " *FW/PBS, Inc. v. Dallas* (1990), 493 U.S. 215, 237, 110 S.Ct. 596, 611, 107 L.Ed.2d 603, 626, quoting *Roberts,* 468 U.S. at 618–619, 104 S.Ct. at 3249–3250, 82 L.Ed.2d at 472. Accordingly, these relationships are protected as fundamental, personal liberties. *Roberts,* 468 U.S. at 618, 104 S.Ct. at 3249, 82 L.Ed.2d at 471.

The second type of freedom is the right to associate for the purpose of engaging in expressive activity protected by the First Amendment. *Stanglin,* ⌊425490 U.S. at 24, 109 S.Ct. at 1595, 104 L.Ed.2d at 25. This includes rights of free speech, assembly, petition for the redress of grievances, and the exercise of religion. *Id.*

[3] Burnett argues that the Cincinnati ordinance is unconstitutional because it impermissibly burdens the right of association by preventing him from entering the

Over the Rhine area of Cincinnati. In this respect, the Cincinnati ordinance is similar to an ordinance we analyzed in *Cleveland v. Trzebuckowski* (1999), 85 Ohio St.3d 524, 709 N.E.2d 1148.

In *Trzebuckowski*, the ordinance forbade minors to enter billiard halls. We held that the ordinance did nothing on its face to burden the creation and development of intimate personal relationships deemed to be fundamental. *Id.* at 529, 709 N.E.2d at 1152. Rather, the ordinance merely prohibited the development of personal relationships within billiard halls, and, thus, there was no violation of a fundamental, personal liberty. *Id.*

We also held in *Trzebuckowski* that the ordinance did not infringe the right to associate for the purpose of engaging in expressive activity protected by the First Amendment. There was no assertion that minors entered billiard halls to engage in protected conduct, merely that they might. *Id.* In quoting the *Stanglin* opinion, we observed, " 'It is possible to find some kernel of expression in almost every activity a person undertakes—for example, walking down the street or meeting one's friends at a shopping mall—but such a kernel is not sufficient to bring the activity within the protection of the First Amendment.' " *Id.*, quoting *Stanglin*, 490 U.S. at 25, 109 S.Ct. at 1595, 104 L.Ed.2d at 25–26.

Similar to the ordinance in *Trzebuckowski*, the Cincinnati ordinance does not burden associational rights. On its face, the ordinance does not prohibit or interfere with fundamental, personal relationships. Nor does the ordinance facially infringe the rights of a citizen to associate with other citizens for the purpose of engaging in protected First Amendment activities. Instead, the ordinance simply prohibits access to Over the Rhine. Furthermore, Burnett has not presented any facts that would indicate that the ordinance, as applied to him, interfered with his First Amendment freedoms. Therefore, because the ordinance prohibits access only to a particular area of the city, and because Burnett has not demonstrated that he personally has been denied his First Amendment freedoms, Chapter 755 of the Cincinnati Municipal Code does not burden the right of association guaranteed by the First Amendment to the United States Constitution. Cf. *Johnson*, 119 F.Supp.2d 735 (declaring that Chapter 755 of the Cincinnati Municipal Code violates the First Amendment on an as-applied basis only); *Trzebuckowski*, 85 Ohio St.3d at 529, 709 N.E.2d at 1152.

II. The Right to Travel.

⌊426Burnett also argues that Chapter 755 of the Municipal Code is unconstitutional because it impermissibly burdens the right to travel. Burnett alleges that the right to travel is a personal liberty protected by the Fourteenth Amendment to the United States Constitution and that Chapter 755 infringes upon this personal liberty by punishing wholly innocent or constitutionally protected conduct. We agree that Chapter 755 of the Cincinnati Municipal Code has impermissibly burdened a fundamental, guaranteed personal liberty by extending its reach further than necessary to advance the public interests it declares.

[4] In all the cases addressing the right to travel, the United States Supreme Court has examined only the right to travel from one state to another.[6] To date, the

6. In its latest case addressing the right to travel, the United States Supreme Court identified three components of the right to travel: (1) it protects the right of a citizen of one state to enter and leave another state, (2) it protects the right to be treated as a welcome visitor rather than as a hostile visitor when temporarily in the second state, and (3) it

court has not expressly recognized a constitutional right of travel within a state. Burnett argues, however, that a right of intrastate travel exists and that the Cincinnati ordinance has impermissibly burdened this right. Precedent of the United States Supreme Court and federal courts of appeals, and our own precedent cause us to conclude that such a constitutional right of travel within a state exists and that the Cincinnati ordinance has unconstitutionally burdened that right.

As suggested by the United States Supreme Court, the right of travel is most likely protected from state interference by the Due Process Clause of the Fourteenth Amendment. See, *e.g.*, *Kent v. Dulles* (1958), 357 U.S. 116, 125, 78 S.Ct. 1113, 1118, 2 L.Ed.2d 1204, 1210 ("The right to travel is a part of the 'liberty' of which the citizen cannot be deprived without the due process of law under the Fifth Amendment"); *Williams v. Fears* (1900), 179 U.S. 270, 274, 21 S.Ct. 128, 129, 45 L.Ed. 186, 188 ("the right to remove from one place to another according to inclination, is an attribute of * * * liberty * * * secured by the Fourteenth Amendment"). When evaluating whether substantive due process protects unenumerated rights, the question, as articulated by Justice Scalia, is ⌊427 whether the asserted right is "'so rooted in the traditions and conscience of our people as to be ranked fundamental.'" *Michael H. v. Gerald D.* (1989), 491 U.S. 110, 122, 109 S.Ct. 2333, 2342, 105 L.Ed.2d 91, 105, quoting *Snyder v. Massachusetts* (1934), 291 U.S. 97, 105, 54 S.Ct. 330, 332, 78 L.Ed. 674, 677 (Cardozo, J.).

We therefore look to those rights that are so deeply rooted in this Nation's history and tradition and implicit in the concept of ordered liberty that neither liberty nor justice would exist if they were surrendered. *Moore v. E. Cleveland* (1977), 431 U.S. 494, 503, 97 S.Ct. 1932, 1938, 52 L.Ed.2d 531, 540. In affording protection to unenumerated rights, however, we must be mindful that a "'careful description' of the asserted fundamental liberty interest" is required. *Washington v. Glucksberg* (1997), 521 U.S. 702, 721, 117 S.Ct. 2258, 2268, 138 L.Ed.2d 772, 788, quoting *Reno v. Flores* (1993), 507 U.S. 292, 302, 113 S.Ct. 1439, 1447, 123 L.Ed.2d 1, 16; see, also, *Michael H.*, 491 U.S. at 127, 109 S.Ct. at 2344, 105 L.Ed.2d at 108, fn. 6. (the relevant traditions must be identified and evaluated at the most specific level of generality possible.) The sole purpose of this limiting function is to provide fundamental protection only to those traditions deeply woven into this Nation's historical fabric without overextending the Due Process Clause.

The right to travel is a liberty interest long enjoyed by every citizen residing within this Nation. As stated by Chief Justice Taney, "For all the great purposes for which the Federal government was

protects the right to be treated like other citizens of a state when the traveler decides to become a permanent resident. *Saenz v. Roe* (1999), 526 U.S. 489, 500, 119 S.Ct. 1518, 1525, 143 L.Ed.2d 689, 702. The court stated that the second component is protected by the Privileges or Immunities Clause of Section 2, Article IV of the United States Constitution. *Id.* at 501, 119 S.Ct. at 1525, 143 L.Ed.2d at 703. Likewise, protection of the third component is grounded in the Privileges or Immunities Clause of the Fourteenth Amendment. *Id.* at 502–503, 119 S.Ct. at 1526, 143 L.Ed.2d at 702–703. Cf. *The Slaughter-House Cases* (1873), 83 U.S. (16 Wall.) 36, 21 L.Ed. 394 (the Privileges or Immunities Clause of the Fourteenth Amendment protects only those rights of citizenship that owe their existence to the federal government, its national character, its Constitution, or its laws, but it is not a source of protection for unenumerated rights). As Roe involved only the second and third components of the right to travel, however, the court declined any further discussion of the first component. 526 U.S. at 501, 119 S.Ct. at 1525, 143 L.Ed.2d at 702.

formed, we are one people, with one common country. We are all citizens of the United States; and, as members of the same community, must have the right to pass and repass through every part of it without interruption, *as freely as in our own States.*" (Emphasis added.) *Smith v. Turner* (1849), 48 U.S. (7 How.) 283, 492, 12 L.Ed. 702, 790 (Taney, C.J., dissenting). The freedom to travel between states and throughout the Nation is one long enjoyed and wholeheartedly cherished. *United States v. Guest* (1966), 383 U.S. 745, 758, 86 S.Ct. 1170, 1178, 16 L.Ed.2d 239, 249; *Williams v. Fears* (1900), 179 U.S. 270, 274, 21 S.Ct. 128, 129, 45 L.Ed. 186, 188. The word "travel" is not mentioned within the text of the Constitution. "Yet the 'constitutional right to travel from one State to another' is firmly embedded in our jurisprudence." *Saenz v. Roe* (1999), 526 U.S. 489, 498, 119 S.Ct. 1518, 1524, 143 L.Ed.2d 689, 701, quoting *Guest*, 383 U.S. at 757, 86 S.Ct. at 1178, 16 L.Ed.2d at 249. Indeed, "the right is so important that it is 'assertable against private interference as well as governmental action * * * a virtually unconditional personal right, guaranteed by the Constitution to us all.'" *Id.*, quoting *Shapiro v. Thompson* (1969), 394 U.S. 618, 643, 89 S.Ct. 1322, 1336, 22 L.Ed.2d 600, 620 (Stewart, J., concurring). Stated succinctly, "[t]he constitutional right to travel from one State to another * * * occupies a position *fundamental* to the concept of our Federal Union. It is a right that has been firmly established and ⊥428 repeatedly recognized." (Emphasis added.) *Guest*, 383 U.S. at 757, 86 S.Ct. at 1178, 16 L.Ed.2d at 249.

In its most specific, careful description, the right of intrastate travel we contemplate is the right to travel locally through public spaces and roadways of this state. Historically, it is beyond contention that being able to travel innocently throughout the country has been an aspect of our national freedom. Likewise, the right to travel within a state is no less fundamental than the right to travel between the states. Every citizen of this state, much like the citizens of this Nation, enjoys the freedom of mobility not only to cross our borders into our sister states, but also to roam about innocently in the wide-open spaces of our state parks or through the streets and sidewalks of our most populous cities. This freedom of mobility is a tradition extending back to when the first settler crossed into what would eventually become this great state, and it is a tradition no Ohioan would freely relinquish.

The United States Supreme Court has stated that in addressing matters of substantive due process, the utmost care must be taken when being asked to break new ground in Fourteenth Amendment jurisprudence. *Collins v. Harker Hts.* (1992), 503 U.S. 115, 125, 112 S.Ct. 1061, 1068, 117 L.Ed.2d 261, 273. Unlike the asserted right evaluated in *Glucksberg* (assisted suicide), for example, recognizing a right of intrastate travel is hardly groundbreaking. Much like the right to interstate travel, the right to intrastate travel has a long, historical recognition in the conscience and traditions of our people. As further observed by the Second Circuit, "[i]t would be meaningless to describe the right to travel between states as a fundamental precept of personal liberty and not to acknowledge a correlative constitutional right to travel within a state." *King v. New Rochelle Mun. Hous. Auth.* (C.A.2, 1971), 442 F.2d 646, 648. Without the one, there would never be the other.

[5, 6] As a fundamental right, the right to intrastate travel "is a part of the 'liberty' of which the citizen cannot be deprived without the due process of law." *Kent v. Dulles* (1958), 357 U.S. 116, 125, 78 S.Ct. 1113, 1118, 2 L.Ed.2d 1204, 1210. Any deprivation of the right to travel, therefore, must be evaluated under a compelling-interest test. See *Shapiro v. Thompson* (1969), 394 U.S. 618, 89 S.Ct. 1322, 22 L.Ed.2d 600, overruled in part on other grounds by *Edelman v. Jordan* (1974), 415 U.S. 651, 94 S.Ct. 1347, 39 L.Ed.2d 662. Accordingly, the legislation must be narrowly tailored to serve a compelling governmental interest. *Reno v. Flores* (1993), 507 U.S. 292, 301–302, 113 S.Ct. 1439, 1447, 123 L.Ed.2d 1, 16.

[7] Cincinnati asserts that the purposes of Chapter 755 are "restoring the quality of life and protecting the health, safety, and welfare of citizens using the public ways" in drug-exclusion zones and "allowing the public to use and enjoy the facilities in such areas without interference arising from illegal drug abuse and/or ⌊429illegal drug abuse related crimes." Ordinance No. 229–1996, Section 1(D). We agree with the city that these asserted interests are compelling. The destruction of some neighborhoods by illegal drug activity has created a crisis of national magnitude, and governments are justified in attacking the problem aggressively. When legislation addressing the drug problem infringes certain fundamental rights, however, more than a compelling interest is needed to survive constitutional scrutiny. The statute must also be narrowly tailored to meet the compelling interest. *Reno,* 507 U.S. at 301–302, 113 S.Ct. at 1447, 123 L.Ed.2d at 16. It is our opinion that while Chapter 755 is justified by a compelling interest, it fails constitutional analysis because the ordinance is not narrowly tailored to restrict only those interests associated with illegal drug activity, but also restricts a substantial amount of innocent conduct.

A person convicted of one of the crimes enumerated in section 755–5 of the Cincinnati Municipal Code is immediately prohibited for one year from being on "public streets, sidewalk[s], and other public ways in all drug-exclusion zones designated in Chapter 755." Cincinnati Municipal Code 755–5. The exclusion is in addition to any criminal penalty for violating the provisions of the Ohio Revised Code. Only if the person is a bona fide resident of the drug-exclusion zone or is legally employed within the drug-exclusion zone does the restriction on travel not apply. Cincinnati Municipal Code 755–11(b)(i) and (ii). The chief of police and social services agencies also have discretion to grant a variance only for health reasons or for drug-abuse-related counseling services. Cincinnati Municipal Code 755–11(2)(b). The ordinance permits no other exceptions.

[8] "A statute is narrowly tailored if it targets and eliminates no more than the exact source of the 'evil' it seeks to remedy." *Frisby v. Schultz* (1988), 487 U.S. 474, 485, 108 S.Ct. 2495, 2503, 101 L.Ed.2d 420, 432; *City Council of Los Angeles v. Taxpayers for Vincent* (1984), 466 U.S. 789, 808–810, 104 S.Ct. 2118, 2130–2132, 80 L.Ed.2d 772, 789–780. The Cincinnati ordinance extends beyond the problems associated with illegal drug activity and attacks any number of potential activities done with an innocent purpose. In this respect, the Cincinnati Ordinance is similar to an ordinance we declared unconstitutional in *Akron v. Rowland* (1993), 67 Ohio St.3d 374, 618 N.E.2d 138.

In *Rowland,* the ordinance prohibited loitering for the purpose of engaging in drug-related activity. In declaring the ordinance unconstitutional, we found significant the fact that "a person does not have to *commit* a drug-related offense to violate the ordinance. The ordinance is prophylactic: it permits police to make an arrest before any crime has occurred. The police do not need to have any evidence that a crime has occurred or is about to occur—

they can make an arrest based on subjective suspicion alone." (Emphasis *sic.*) *Id.* at 386, 618 N.E.2d at 148. The ordinance, we stated, "can easily implicate a person's status, associates, ⌊430mere presence, or otherwise innocent behavior * * * [and therefore] encroach on a 'substantial amount of constitutionally protected conduct.'" *Id.* at 387, 618 N.E.2d at 149, quoting *Houston v. Hill* (1987), 482 U.S. 451, 459, 107 S.Ct. 2502, 2508, 96 L.Ed.2d 398, 410. Without a limit on the intrusions into innocent conduct the ordinance ran afoul of the Due Process Clause. *Id.* at 388, 618 N.E.2d at 149–150; *Columbus v. Thompson* (1971), 25 Ohio St.2d 26, 31–32, 54 O.O.2d 162, 165, 266 N.E.2d 571, 574; *Columbus v. DeLong* (1962), 173 Ohio St. 81, 83, 18 O.O.2d 294, 295, 180 N.E.2d 158, 160.

As the Akron ordinance in *Rowland* did, the Cincinnati ordinance encroaches upon a substantial amount of innocent conduct and is not, therefore, narrowly tailored. A person subject to exclusion is exposed to a criminal penalty by simply being in Over the Rhine. Cincinnati Municipal Code 755–5. The prohibited conduct is not limited to entering a drug-exclusion zone to engage in some type of illegal activity, such as the purchase or sale of drugs or corrupting another with drugs. Instead, the ordinance also attacks conduct that is completely innocent. A person subject to the exclusion ordinance may not enter a drug-exclusion zone to speak with counsel, to visit family, to attend church, to receive emergency medical care, to go to a grocery store, or just to stand on a street corner and look at a blue sky. None of these activities are performed with illegal intention, yet a criminal penalty attaches to them without any evidence of illegality, or improper purpose, or a finding that the person is likely to commit future drug offenses.

"A narrowly tailored ordinance would not authorize the arrest of a grandmother who entered Over the Rhine for the purpose of seeing her grandchildren. A narrowly tailored ordinance would not authorize the arrest of a homeless person who entered Over the Rhine to obtain food, shelter, and clothing from relief agencies. Nor would it prevent any person from meeting with his or her attorney at the attorney's place of business. A narrowly tailored ordinance would not authorize exclusion without, at a minimum, a finding that the particular person to be excluded was likely to repeat his crime in Over the Rhine." *Johnson v. Cincinnati,* 119 F.Supp.2d at 743–744; cf. R.C. 2950.01(E) and 2950.09(B)(1) through (3) (a finding by clear and convincing evidence that a sexual offender is likely to commit future sexual offenses is required before the offender can be classified as a sexual predator). A narrowly tailored ordinance would not strike at an evil with such force that constitutionally protected conduct is harmed along with unprotected conduct. "The Constitution does not permit a legislature to 'set a net large enough to catch all possible offenders, and leave it to the courts to step inside and say who could be rightfully detained, and who should be set at large.'" *Chicago v. Morales* (1999), 527 U.S. 41, 60, 119 S.Ct. 1849, 1861, 144 L.Ed.2d 67, 82, quoting *United States v. Reese* (1875), 92 U.S. 214, 221, 23 L.Ed. 563, 566.

⌊431We hold that Chapter 755 of the Cincinnati Municipal Code violates the constitutional guarantee of the right of travel which is protected by the Due Process Clause of the Fourteenth Amendment to the United States Constitution. Although the Cincinnati ordinance is supported by compelling interests, it is not narrowly tailored to address those interests.

III. Section 3, Article XVIII of the Ohio Constitution.

[9] Burnett further argues that Chapter 755 of the Municipal Code is unconstitutional because it exceeds the local authority granted to the city by Section 3, Article XVIII of the Ohio Constitution, which provides: "Municipalities shall have authority to exercise all powers of local self-government and to adopt and enforce within their limits such local police, sanitary and other similar regulations, as are not in conflict with general laws." We agree.

[10] As stated, Section 3, Article XVIII gives municipalities broad power to adopt laws and regulations that are not in conflict with general laws enacted by the General Assembly. An ordinance conflicts with the general laws if it "'permits or licenses that which the statute forbids and prohibits, and vice versa.'" *Niles v. Howard* (1984), 12 Ohio St.3d 162, 165, 12 OBR 232, 234, 466 N.E.2d 539, 541, quoting *Struthers v. Sokol* (1923), 108 Ohio St. 263, 140 N.E. 519, paragraph two of the syllabus; see, also, *Sheffield v. Rowland* (1999), 87 Ohio St.3d 9, 716 N.E.2d 1121.

Burnett was excluded from the Over the Rhine area of Cincinnati for one year as a result of his conviction for a drug-related offense. This banishment, however, was not imposed by the court that convicted Burnett for his drug crime. Rather, the city (through its executive branch), per the terms of Chapter 755, served Burnett with a notice of exclusion following his conviction. This notice of exclusion authorized by Chapter 755 banished Burnett from Over the Rhine, *adding a criminal penalty for his drug offense that was neither imposed by a court nor authorized by statute.* See *Johnson v. Cincinnati* (S.D.Ohio 2000), 119 F.Supp.2d 735, 748 (holding that Chapter 755 imposed a criminal punishment and not merely a civil penalty); see, also, *Nixon v. Admr. of Gen. Serv.* (1977), 433 U.S. 425, 474, 97 S.Ct. 2777, 2806, 53 L.Ed.2d 867, 910–911 (observing that banishment is historically considered to be punishment).

[11] By authorizing a punishment not provided by statute for violation of a statute, Cincinnati's drug-exclusion ordinance has permitted something that is prohibited under the state criminal code. Cf. *State v. Bilder* (1987), 39 Ohio App.3d 135, 529 N.E.2d 1292 (noting that a court may not pronounce a sentence that is unauthorized by statute). It is true that a municipal ordinance may proscribe the same conduct as a state criminal statute and impose a penalty greater than the state criminal code imposes. *Niles v. Howard*, 12 Ohio St.3d at 165, 12 OBR at 234, 466 N.E.2d at 541. But there is no authority for the proposition that a ⌊432 municipality may, by way of ordinance, add a penalty for violation of a *state criminal statute* that is not otherwise provided for by the General Assembly. The ordinance, therefore, is invalid under Section 3, Article XVIII of the Ohio Constitution.

IV. Conclusion.

For the foregoing reasons, we hold that Chapter 755 of the Cincinnati Municipal Code is an unconstitutional violation of the right to travel as guaranteed by the Fourteenth Amendment to the United States Constitution and a violation of Section 3, Article XVIII of the Ohio Constitution. The judgment of the court of appeals, therefore, is reversed.

Judgment reversed.

DOUGLAS, RESNICK, FRANCIS E. SWEENEY, SR., PFEIFER and LUNDBERG STRATTON, JJ., concur.

COOK, J., concurs separately.

COOK, J., concurring separately.

I agree with the majority that Chapter 755 of the Cincinnati Municipal Code violates the Ohio Constitution and that Burnett's conviction for trespass should therefore be reversed. The majority goes a step further, however, and decides that Chapter 755 also violates the "right to travel," which it finds to be protected by the substantive Due Process Clause of the Fourteenth Amendment to the United States Constitution. I respectfully decline to join the majority's substantive-due-process analysis.

I

The Due Process Clause of the Fourteenth Amendment contains a substantive component that "provides heightened protection against government interference with certain fundamental rights and liberty interests." *Washington v. Glucksberg* (1997), 521 U.S. 702, 720, 117 S.Ct. 2258, 2267, 138 L.Ed.2d 772, 787. This doctrine of substantive due process forbids the government from infringing upon these fundamental liberty interests *at all*, regardless of the procedure provided, unless the infringement survives strict scrutiny; that is, the government's infringement must be "narrowly tailored to serve a compelling state interest." *Reno v. Flores* (1993), 507 U.S. 292, 302, 113 S.Ct. 1439, 1447, 123 L.Ed.2d 1, 16. In this case, the majority concedes that Cincinnati has a compelling interest in addressing the crisis associated with illegal drug activity. It concludes, however, that Cincinnati's drug-exclusion zone ordinance is not narrowly tailored to meet this compelling interest and therefore violates the Fourteenth Amendment.

As established by the United States Supreme Court, substantive-due-process analysis has two primary features. "First, we have regularly observed that the ⌊433Due Process Clause specially protects those fundamental rights and liberties which are, objectively, 'deeply rooted in this Nation's history and tradition,' * * * and 'implicit in the concept of ordered liberty,' such that 'neither liberty nor justice would exist if they were sacrificed.'" *Glucksberg*, 521 U.S. at 720–721, 117 S.Ct. at 2268, 138 L.Ed.2d at 787–788, quoting *Moore v. E. Cleveland* (1977), 431 U.S. 494, 503, 97 S.Ct. 1932, 1938, 52 L.Ed.2d 531, 540 (plurality opinion), and *Palko v. Connecticut* (1937), 302 U.S. 319, 325, 326, 58 S.Ct. 149, 152, 82 L.Ed. 288, 292. Second, substantive-due-process cases require "a 'careful description' of the asserted fundamental liberty interest." *Id.*, quoting *Flores*, 507 U.S. at 302, 113 S.Ct. at 1447, 123 L.Ed.2d at 16.

Although the majority identifies the right to travel as a fundamental liberty protected by substantive due process, *Glucksberg* suggests otherwise. In *Glucksberg*, the court grappled with the question of whether a state statute banning assisted suicide violated substantive due process. The court concluded that there was no fundamental right to assistance in committing suicide. *Glucksberg*, 521 U.S. at 723–728, 117 S.Ct. at 2269–2271, 138 L.Ed.2d at 789–793. Before doing so, however, the court listed several specific freedoms that are subject to heightened scrutiny under substantive due process. *Id.* at 720, 117 S.Ct. at 2267, 138 L.Ed.2d at 787. These include (1) the right to marry, (2) the right to have children, (3) the right to direct the upbringing and education of one's children, (4) the right to marital privacy, (5) the right to use contraception, (6) the right to bodily integrity, and (7) the right to abortion. *Id.* (collecting cases recognizing these fundamental rights). Significantly, however, the court *did not list the right to travel* among these freedoms. This omission strongly suggests that the right to travel is *not* one of the fundamental liberties subjected to heightened scrutiny under substantive due process. Because of the context in which the court listed the fundamental rights—*i.e.*, in a case conducting a searching inquiry as to the existence of a fundamental right to assisted suicide—*Glucksberg*'s list appears to be exhaustive.

The most recent right-to-travel case decided by the United States Supreme Court also calls into doubt the majority's substantive-due-process rationale. See *Saenz v. Roe* (1999), 526 U.S. 489, 119 S.Ct. 1518, 143 L.Ed.2d 689. In *Roe*, the court tested the validity of a California statute that limited the level of welfare benefits available to California residents who had only recently moved to the state. The plaintiffs alleged that California's restriction violated their constitutional right to travel by penalizing their decision to migrate to a new state.

Prior to *Roe*, the court had recognized the right to interstate travel as a basic constitutional right but had been less than clear about the textual source of that right in the Constitution. In *Roe*, however, the court clarified the constitutional sources of the right to travel as recognized in its prior cases:

⊥434"The 'right to travel' discussed in our cases embraces at least three different components. It protects [1] the right of a citizen of one State to enter and to leave another State, [2] the right to be treated as a welcome visitor rather than an unfriendly alien when temporarily present in the second State, and [3] for those travelers who elect to become permanent residents, the right to be treated like other citizens of that State." *Roe*, 526 U.S. at 500, 119 S.Ct. at 1525, 143 L.Ed.2d at 702.

The court then examined which specific provision of the United States Constitution provides the source for each component of the right to travel. The court found that the second right-to-travel component is grounded in Section 2, Article IV of the Constitution, which guarantees that "a citizen of one State who travels in other States, intending to return home at the end of his journey, is entitled to enjoy the 'Privileges and Immunities of Citizens in the several States' that he visits." *Roe*, 526 U.S. at 501, 119 S.Ct. at 1525, 143 L.Ed.2d at 703.[7] A state may not discriminate against citizens of other states " 'where there is no substantial reason for the discrimination beyond the mere fact that they are citizens of other States.' " *Id.* at 502, 119 S.Ct. at 1526, 143 L.Ed.2d at 703, quoting *Toomer v. Witsell* (1948), 334 U.S. 385, 396, 68 S.Ct. 1156, 1162, 92 L.Ed. 1460, 1471; see, also, *Baldwin v. Fish & Game Comm. of Montana* (1978), 436 U.S. 371, 98 S.Ct. 1852, 56 L.Ed.2d 354.

The court also clarified that the third component of the right to travel finds its textual source in the Privileges or Immunities Clause of the Fourteenth Amendment.[8] While acknowledging the existence of "fundamentally differing views concerning the coverage of the Privileges or Immunities Clause of the Fourteenth Amendment," the court concluded that the clause, at a minimum, protects the right of a United States citizen to move to any other state and enjoy the same rights (of state

7. Section 2, Article IV of the United States Constitution states: "The Citizens of each State shall be entitled to all Privileges and Immunities of Citizens in the several States."

8. The Privileges or Immunities Clause of the Fourteenth Amendment provides: "All persons born or naturalized in the United States, and subject to the jurisdiction thereof, are citizens of the United States and of the State wherein they reside. No State shall make or enforce any law which shall abridge the privileges or immunities of citizens of the United States * * *."

and federal citizenship) as any other citizen in that state. *Roe* at 503–504, 119 S.Ct. at 1526–1527, 143 L.Ed.2d at 704–705. The durational residency requirement at issue in *Roe* directly implicated this third component of the right to travel and was therefore subject to a more exacting level of scrutiny. "Neither mere rationality nor some intermediate standard of review should be used to judge the constitutionality of a state rule that discriminates against some of its citizens because they have been domiciled in the State for less than a year." *Id.* at 504, 119 S.Ct. at 1527, 143 L.Ed.2d at 704–705.

⌊435As for the first component of the right to travel, the court declined to identify a textual source. Because the statute at issue in *Roe* "does not directly impair the exercise of the right to free *interstate movement* * * *, we need not identify the source of that particular right in the text of the Constitution. The right of 'free ingress and regress to and from' neighboring States * * * may simply have been 'conceived from the beginning to be a necessary concomitant of the stronger Union the Constitution created.'" (Emphasis added.) *Id.* at 501, 119 S.Ct. at 1525, 143 L.Ed.2d at 702–703, quoting *United States v. Guest* (1966), 383 U.S. 745, 758, 86 S.Ct. 1170, 1178, 16 L.Ed.2d 239, 249.

Roe's search for the constitutional source of the right to travel raises considerable doubt about the majority's analysis in this case. *Roe* conspicuously fails to categorize any aspect of the right to travel as being rooted in substantive due process. When read in conjunction with *Glucksberg*'s omission of the right to travel from its list of fundamental rights, *Roe*'s failure to identify substantive due process leads to the negative inference that substantive due process is *not* the constitutional source of the right. As a matter of federal constitutional law, then, it appears that the majority has either broken new ground in the field of substantive due process or has identified the incorrect source of the right to travel. Neither possibility affords adequate recognition of the Supreme Court's reluctance to expand the concept of substantive due process. See *Collins v. Harker Hts.* (1992), 503 U.S. 115, 125, 112 S.Ct. 1061, 1068, 117 L.Ed.2d 261, 273 (noting that the court exercises "the utmost care whenever we are asked to break new ground in this field").

II

Whatever its source, it is well settled that the right to *interstate* travel is "firmly embedded" in federal constitutional jurisprudence. *Roe*, 526 U.S. at 498, 119 S.Ct. at 1524, 143 L.Ed.2d at 701. But even if I accepted the majority's view that substantive due process provides the source of this right, I still could not join the analysis. The majority's conclusion depends not only on the notion that a fundamental right to interstate travel exists as a matter of substantive due process, but also on the notion that the right to *intra*state travel is included within this right. But this conclusion does not have firm support.

It is true that the United States Supreme Court has suggested the existence of a generalized right to free movement that would logically encompass intrastate travel. See, *e.g., Aptheker v. Secy. of State* (1964), 378 U.S. 500, 505–506, 84 S.Ct. 1659, 1663, 12 L.Ed.2d 992, 997 ("'Freedom of movement across frontiers in either direction, and inside frontiers as well, was a part of our heritage. * * * Freedom of movement is basic in our scheme of values'"), quoting *Kent v. Dulles* (1958), 357 U.S. 116, 126, 78 S.Ct. 1113, 1118, 2 L.Ed.2d 1204, 1210; *Kolender v. Lawson* (1983), 461 U.S. 352, 358, 103 S.Ct. 1855, 1859, 75 L.Ed.2d 903, 910⌊436(noting that a state statute challenged on vagueness grounds "implicate[d] consideration of the constitutional right to freedom of movement"); *Papachristou v. Jacksonville* (1972), 405 U.S. 156, 164, 92 S.Ct. 839, 844, 31 L.Ed.2d 110, 116–117 (identifying "wandering or strolling" from place to place as "historically part of the amenities of life"). But these cases suggesting some broad right of "free movement" have involved either travel across borders (whether state or international) or First Amendment vagueness issues; thus, any comments that can be construed to encompass some generalized right to movement are essentially dicta. See *Hutchins v. Dist. of Columbia* (C.A.D.C.1999), 188 F.3d 531, 537 (en banc; plurality opinion). Moreover, the Supreme Court has specifically *declined* to consider whether the right to interstate travel includes the right to intrastate travel. See *Mem. Hosp. v. Maricopa Cty.* (1974), 415 U.S. 250, 255–256, 94 S.Ct. 1076, 1081, 39 L.Ed.2d 306, 313.

Additionally, the Supreme Court's discussion of the constitutional right to interstate travel in *Bray v. Alexandria Women's Health Clinic* (1993), 506 U.S. 263, 113 S.Ct. 753, 122 L.Ed.2d 34, casts doubt on the proposition that a right to intrastate travel is included. In *Bray*, several abortion clinics sued Operation Rescue under Section 1985(3), Title 42, U.S.Code, which provides a private cause of action for certain types of conspiracy. The plaintiffs alleged that Operation Rescue, through its concerted blockade of abortion clinics, conspired to violate, *inter alia*, the right to interstate travel. The Supreme Court held that the plaintiffs did not have a cognizable claim under Section 1985(3). Justice Scalia's opinion for the court explained one of the reasons:

"Respondents have failed to show a conspiracy to violate the right of interstate travel for yet another reason: Petitioners' proposed demonstrations would not implicate that right. The federal guarantee of interstate travel * * * protects interstate travelers against two sets of burdens: 'the erection of actual barriers *to interstate movement*' and '*being treated differently*' *from intrastate travelers*. *Zobel v. Williams*, 457 U.S. 55, 60 [102 S.Ct. 2309, 2313, 72 L.Ed.2d 672, 677], n. 6 (1982). * * * As far as appears from this record, the only 'actual barriers to ... movement' that would have resulted from petitioners' proposed demonstrations would have been in the immediate vicinity of the abortion clinics, restricting movement from one portion of the Commonwealth of Virginia to another. *Such a purely intrastate restriction does not implicate the right of interstate travel*, even if it is applied intentionally against travelers from other States, unless it is applied *discriminatorily* against them." (First two emphases added.) *Bray*, 506 U.S. at 276–277, 113 S.Ct. at 763, 122 L.Ed.2d at 51.

This explanation of the interstate right to travel, particularly when read in conjunction with the court's later opinion in *Roe*, strongly suggests that a purely [437] *intrastate* restriction does not implicate the right to interstate travel unless the restriction discriminates against *interstate* travelers.

Admittedly, a number of federal cases have declared the existence of a fundamental right to intrastate travel or free movement. See, *e.g.*, *Nunez v. San Diego* (C.A.9, 1997), 114 F.3d 935, 944; *Lutz v. York* (C.A.3, 1990), 899 F.2d 255; *King v. New Rochelle Mun. Hous. Auth.* (C.A.2, 1971), 442 F.2d 646; *Schleifer v. Charlottesville* (W.D.Va.1997), 963 F.Supp. 534, 542–543. These cases, however, were decided before the Supreme Court's clarification of the right to travel in *Roe*. All three components of the right to travel described in *Roe* refer only to *inter*state travel; none of them would seem to include *intra*state travel, casting doubt on the proposition that the right to interstate travel includes a concomitant right to intrastate travel. And in any event, the cases asserting the existence of a fundamental right to intrastate travel do not reflect a consensus view among the circuits. See *Wardwell v. Cincinnati City School Dist. Bd. of Edn.* (C.A.6, 1976), 529 F.2d 625, 627–628 (rejecting a fundamental right to intrastate travel); *Wright v. Jackson* (C.A.5, 1975), 506 F.2d 900, 902–903 (same); see, also, *Townes v. St. Louis* (E.D.Mo.1996), 949 F.Supp. 731, 734–735 (noting split among federal circuits over whether fundamental right to intrastate travel exists and expressing doubt as to whether Eighth Circuit would recognize one), affirmed (C.A.8, 1997), 112 F.3d 514, 1997 WL 210442.

Further, the majority fails to explain why it applies strict scrutiny to the Cincinnati ordinance at issue here. In *Lutz*, one of the leading cases finding the existence of an intrastate travel right, the Third Circuit applied a form of intermediate scrutiny to an "anticruising" ordinance alleged to violate the right to intrastate travel. Rather than follow the *Lutz* methodology, the majority opinion applies strict scrutiny to the Cincinnati ordinance despite the fact that the Supreme Court has applied strict scrutiny *only* to certain impediments to *interstate* travel, such as durational residency requirements. See, *e.g.*, *Shapiro v. Thompson* (1969), 394 U.S. 618, 89 S.Ct. 1322, 22 L.Ed.2d 600; *Roe*, 526 U.S. at 504, 119 S.Ct. at 1527, 143 L.Ed.2d at 705. Moreover, other infringements to interstate travel have not triggered strict scrutiny. *Roe* acknowledged the applicability of something less than strict scrutiny in reviewing state regulations infringing on the second component of the right to travel. *Id.* at 502, 119 S.Ct. at 1526, 143 L.Ed.2d at 703 (Section 2, Article IV bars discrimination against out-of-staters " 'where there is no *substantial reason* for the discrimination beyond the mere fact that they are citizens of other States' " [emphasis added], quoting *Toomer v. Witsell*, 334 U.S. at 396, 68 S.Ct. at 1162, 92 L.Ed. at 1471).

For the foregoing reasons, I cannot join the majority's conclusion that there is a right to intrastate travel protected by the substantive Due Process Clause of the Fourteenth Amendment. That is not to say that the right to intrastate travel ⌊438 does not exist *at all* as a matter of constitutional law. In light of *Roe*, there could be a substantial argument that the Privileges or Immunities Clause of the Fourteenth Amendment protects some generalized right to free intrastate movement that a person may possess as a matter of state citizenship. See *United States v. Wheeler* (1920), 254 U.S. 281, 293, 41 S.Ct. 133, 134, 65 L.Ed. 270, 273 (observing that fundamental rights of state citizenship have historically included the right "to move at will from place to place therein"). Although the clause had been a virtual dead letter since *The Slaughter-House Cases* (1873), 83 U.S. (16 Wall.) 36, 21 L.Ed. 394, *Roe* suggests that the Supreme Court may breathe new life into it. See *Roe*, 526 U.S. at 521–522, 527, 119 S.Ct. at 1535–1536, 1538, 143 L.Ed.2d at 715–716, 719 (Thomas, J., dissenting).

Whether the right of intrastate travel exists as a matter of federal constitutional law, however, is a question we need not reach in order to resolve this case. As the majority correctly holds, the one-year exclusion imposed by Chapter 755 of the Cincinnati Municipal Code is not a valid exercise of the city's power and therefore violates the Ohio Constitution. On that basis, I concur in the judgment.

EWING *v.* CALIFORNIA

CERTIORARI TO THE COURT OF APPEAL OF CALIFORNIA, SECOND APPELLATE DISTRICT

No. 01–6978. Argued November 5, 2002—Decided March 5, 2003

Under California's three strikes law, a defendant who is convicted of a felony and has previously been convicted of two or more serious or violent felonies must receive an indeterminate life imprisonment term. Such a defendant becomes eligible for parole on a date calculated by reference to a minimum term, which, in this case, is 25 years. While on parole, petitioner Ewing was convicted of felony grand theft for stealing three golf clubs, worth $399 apiece. As required by the three strikes law, the prosecutor formally alleged, and the trial court found, that Ewing had been convicted previously of four serious or violent felonies. In sentencing him to 25 years to life, the court refused to exercise its discretion to reduce the conviction to a misdemeanor—under a state law that permits certain offenses, known as "wobblers," to be classified as either misdemeanors or felonies—or to dismiss the allegations of some or all of his prior relevant convictions. The State Court of Appeal affirmed. Relying on *Rummel* v. *Estelle*, 445 U. S. 263, it rejected Ewing's claim that his sentence was grossly disproportionate under the Eighth Amendment and reasoned that enhanced sentences under the three strikes law served the State's legitimate goal of deterring and incapacitating repeat offenders. The State Supreme Court denied review.

Held: The judgment is affirmed.

Affirmed.

JUSTICE O'CONNOR, joined by THE CHIEF JUSTICE and JUSTICE KENNEDY, concluded that Ewing's sentence is not grossly disproportionate and therefore does not violate the Eighth Amendment's prohibition on cruel and unusual punishments. Pp. 20–31.

(a) The Eighth Amendment has a "narrow proportionality principle" that "applies to noncapital sentences." *Harmelin* v. *Michigan*, 501 U. S. 957, 996–997 (KENNEDY, J., concurring in part and concurring in judgment). The Amendment's application in this context is guided by the principles distilled in JUSTICE KENNEDY's concurrence in *Harmelin:* "[T]he primacy of the legislature, the variety of legitimate penological schemes, the nature of our federal system, and the requirement that proportionality review be guided by objective factors" inform the final principle that the "Eighth Amendment does not require strict proportionality between crime and sentence [but] forbids only extreme sentences that are 'grossly disproportionate' to the crime." *Id.*, at 1001. Pp. 20–24.

(b) State legislatures enacting three strikes laws made a deliberate policy choice that individuals who have repeatedly engaged in serious or violent criminal behavior, and whose conduct has not been deterred by more conventional punishment approaches, must be isolated from society to protect the public safety. Though these laws are relatively new, this Court has a longstanding tradition of deferring to state legislatures in making and implementing such important policy decisions. The Constitution "does not mandate adoption of any one penological theory," 501 U. S., at 999, and nothing in the Eighth Amendment prohibits California from choosing to incapacitate criminals who have already been convicted of at least one serious or violent crime. Recidivism has long been recognized as a legitimate basis for increased punishment and is a serious public safety concern in California and the Nation. Any criticism of the law is appropriately directed at the legislature, which is primarily responsible for making the policy choices underlying any criminal sentencing scheme. Pp. 24–28.

(c) In examining Ewing's claim that his sentence is grossly disproportionate, the gravity of the offense must be compared to the harshness of the penalty. Even standing alone, his grand theft should not be taken lightly. The California Supreme Court has noted that crime's seriousness in the context of proportionality review; that it is a "wobbler" is of no moment, for it remains a felony unless the trial court imposes a misdemeanor sentence. The trial judge justifiably exercised her discretion not to extend lenient treatment given Ewing's long criminal history. In weighing the offense's gravity, both his current felony and his long history of felony recidivism must be placed on the scales. Any other approach would not accord proper deference to the policy judgments that find expression in the legislature's choice of sanctions. Ewing's sentence is justified by the State's public-safety interest in incapacitating and deterring recidivist felons, and amply supported by his own long, serious criminal record. He has been convicted of numerous offenses, served nine separate prison terms, and committed most of his crimes while on probation or parole. His prior strikes were serious felonies including robbery and residential burglary. Though long, his current sentence reflects a rational legislative judgment that is entitled to deference. Pp. 28–31.

JUSTICE SCALIA agreed that petitioner's sentence does not violate the Eighth Amendment's prohibition against cruel and unusual punishments, but on the ground that that prohibition was aimed at excluding only certain *modes* of punishment. This case demonstrates why a proportionality principle cannot be intelligently applied, and why *Solem* v. *Helm*, 463 U. S. 277, should not be given *stare decisis* effect. Pp. 31–32.

JUSTICE THOMAS concluded that petitioner's sentence does not violate the Eighth Amendment's prohibition against cruel and unusual punishments because the Amendment contains no proportionality principle. P. 32.

O'CONNOR, J., announced the judgment of the Court and delivered an opinion, in which REHNQUIST, C. J., and KENNEDY, J., joined. SCALIA, J., *post*, p. 31, and THOMAS, J., *post*, p. 32, filed opinions concurring in the judgment. STEVENS, J., filed a dissenting opinion, in which SOUTER, GINSBURG, and BREYER, JJ., joined, *post*, p. 32. BREYER, J., filed a dissenting opinion, in which STEVENS, SOUTER, and GINSBURG, JJ., joined, *post*, p. 35.

Quin Denvir, by appointment of the Court, 535 U. S. 1076, argued the cause for petitioner. With him on the briefs were *David M. Porter*, *Karyn H. Bucur*, and *Mark E. Haddad*.

Donald E. De Nicola, Deputy Attorney General of California, argued the cause for respondent. With him on the brief were *Bill Lockyer*, Attorney General, *Manuel M. Medeiros*, State Solicitor General, *Robert R. Anderson*, Chief Assistant Attorney General, *Pamela C. Hamanaka*, Senior Assistant Attorney General, and *Jaime L. Fuster*, *Kristofer S. Jorstad*, and *David C. Cook*, Deputy Attorneys General.

Assistant Attorney General Chertoff argued the cause for the United States as *amicus curiae* urging affirmance. With him on the brief were *Solicitor General Olson*, *Deputy Solicitor General Dreeben*, *John P. Elwood*, and *Joel M. Gershowitz*.*

**Donald M. Falk*, *Andrew H. Schapiro*, and *Mary Price* filed a brief for Families Against Mandatory Minimums as *amicus curiae* urging reversal.

Briefs of *amici curiae* urging affirmance were filed for the State of Alabama et al. by *William H. Pryor, Jr.*, Attorney General of Alabama, *Nathan A. Forrester*, Solicitor General, and *Michael B. Billingsley*, Deputy Solicitor General, and by the Attorneys General for their respective States as follows: *Steve Carter* of Indiana, *Don Stenberg* of Nebraska,

CHAPTER 2

COURT DECISIONS

V. AUTHORITY OF COURT OPINIONS

The authority of a court opinion in a common law system, like our own, is based on the doctrine of "stare decisis" (also referred to as precedent). The doctrine of stare decisis means that like cases should be decided alike. In other words, the closer the facts of your client's case resemble those of an earlier court decision, the more likely the court in which your client's case is tried will follow the earlier decision by applying the same rule of law. This does not mean, however, that courts will blindly apply a rule of law regardless of the impact; the policy served by and supporting the rule of law is also important. Every rule of law applied by a court serves some purpose and this purpose might evolve over time as other factors change. For this reason, the older a case is, the less likely it is that later courts will follow it.

Technically, the entire opinion of a court does not carry precedential weight, only the holding. The holding consists of the application of the rule of law to the facts of the case. All else in the opinion is dicta (not precedential). Of course, identifying the holding and distinguishing it from dicta is based upon interpretation, which means different parties will frequently disagree about the exact holding of a case. Some will limit the holding to identical facts, thereby reading a case narrowly, while others will read the holding in a more general sense. The court rarely states the holding directly and even if they do, the court's language usually can be interpreted several ways. Identifying the holding of a case and predicting how it will be applied in future cases constitute a major part of your legal education and potentially your practice of law.

Based upon the previous discussion, if an attorney does not want the court to follow earlier decisions, because the holdings of the cases go against her client's desired outcome, she can follow one of two paths: either the facts of the case differ in some legally significant way or the policies supporting the earlier decisions have either changed or differ in some significant way so that blindly applying earlier precedent without consideration of the outcome would not serve justice. Either way, the argument is made that the court should not follow earlier decisions that look, at least on the surface, like they would determine the outcome of the pending case.

The authority of the holding in a case is always persuasive for all other courts. However, some cases go beyond being persuasive and are mandatory. As the terms suggest, a mandatory decision must be followed unless there is a strong reason not to, while a persuasive case may be followed. Whether a case is mandatory or persuasive depends, in part, upon the relationship between the court that issued the earlier opinion and the court hearing your client's case. In other words, the amount of weight carried by a specific court decision is based upon "jurisdiction." Exhibits V-A through C show charts of jurisdiction for courts. Exhibits V-A and B cover federal courts while Exhibit V-C covers state courts.

Exhibit V-A

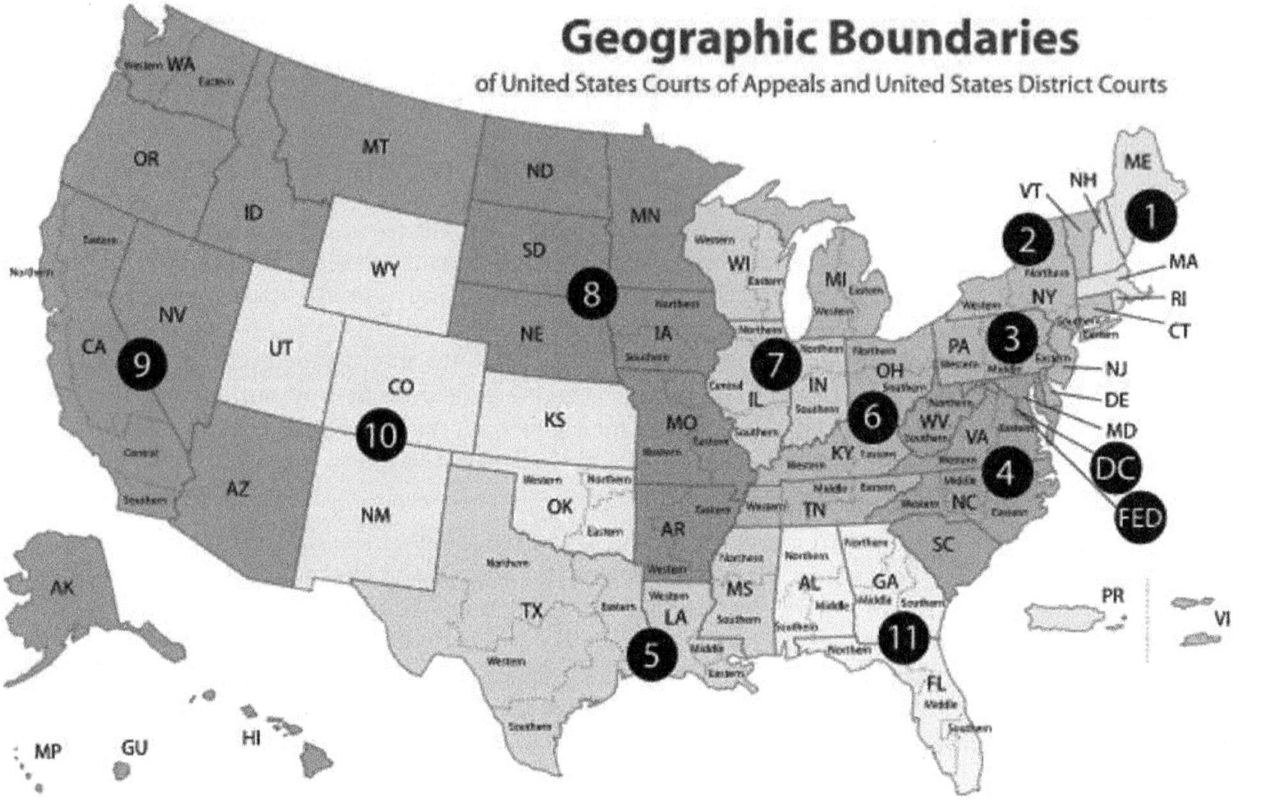

Exhibit V-B

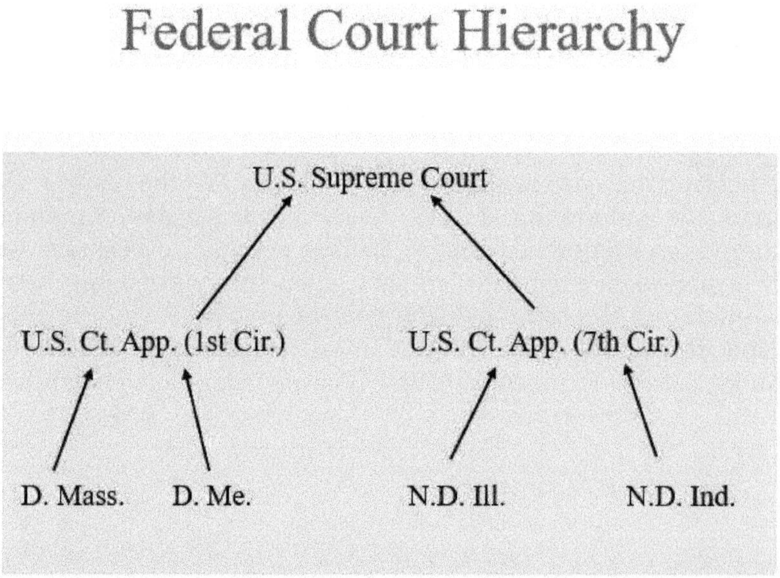

Exhibit V-C

State Court Hierarchy

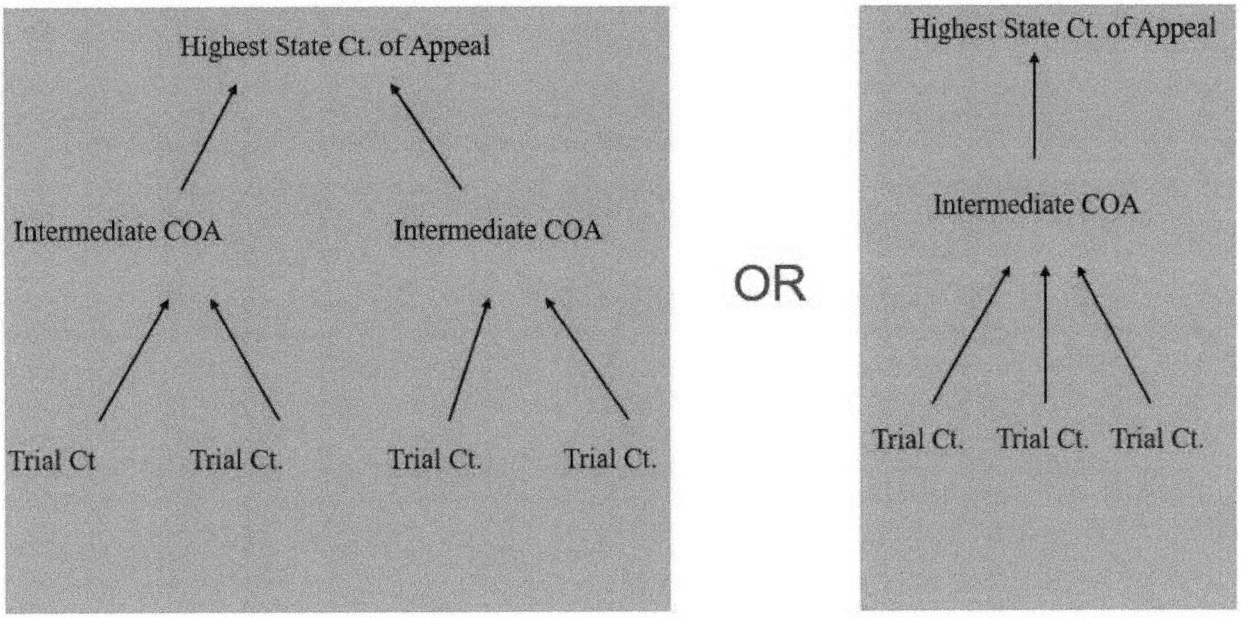

Only per curiam, majority, and plurality decisions (opinions) can be mandatory.[4] All other opinions are merely persuasive. In some instances, however, a good dissenting or concurring opinion has signaled the beginning of a shift in the court's position regarding an issue and ultimately becomes the inspiration for a future majority opinion in a similar case.

There are fifty-one jurisdictions in the United States: a federal court system and fifty different state court systems. The organization of federal and state court systems are very similar. The lowest level of courts, where actual trials occur, are known by various names. Generically, they are referred to as trial courts since this is where most cases begin and where the trials take place. In the federal system they are called district courts while states use varying titles (e.g., superior, district, circuit, etc.).

The next level up from trial courts is known generically as intermediate courts of appeals. This is the first level of appeal from the trial court. At the federal level, these are known as United States Court of Appeals for the # Circuit, where # is either a number or a name. The third, and highest level of courts are known in both the federal and state systems as the Supreme Court or, generically, the highest court of appeal or court of last resort. (Names of these courts differ in one state, New York, where the supreme court is a lower court and the court of last resort is known as the Court of Appeals.)

Within the same jurisdiction, decisions (per curiam, majority, and plurality) issued by a higher court are mandatory authority for any court lower on the hierarchy. Mandatory authority means it must be followed if the facts are similar. Look at the diagram of the federal courts in Exhibits V-A and B; the federal intermediate courts of appeals, referenced as Circuits, are shown. For example, 1st Circuit and D.C. Circuit. In the federal court system, each Circuit Court of Appeals is considered a

[4] Whenever I make a general reference to a court opinion, I am referring to either a per curiam, majority, or plurality opinion.

separate court. Within each circuit are numerous district courts. Any decision issued by the court of appeals from a Circuit Court are binding on all district courts within that Circuit. For example, a federal district court in Indiana is bound to follow relevant cases decided by the 7th Circuit Court of Appeals. However, a district court in Maine is not required to follow decisions of the 7th Circuit because it is part of the 1st Circuit. Put another way, holdings from decisions issued by the 1st Circuit are mandatory law for all federal district courts within the 1st Circuit, like Maine, while only persuasive authority for all district courts in another circuit, like Indiana.

Additionally, any decisions issued by the U.S. Supreme Court are binding on all the federal courts of appeals and district courts. The key to using the chart in Exhibits V-A and B, and deciding what is mandatory and what is persuasive, is to locate the court you are in. If you are in a federal district court in Illinois, the court will be obligated to follow decisions issued by the 7th Circuit and the U.S. Supreme Court. Any court that lies on a direct line in this chart above the court you are in is mandatory for your court.

At the state level, the same general principle applies. Decisions by higher courts are binding on lower courts within the same jurisdiction. The chart I've provided for state courts in Exhibit V-C illustrates two different arrangements; the one on the left is identical to the federal model where each intermediate court of appeals is considered a separate court (some states call them by other names, but the structure is the same). Other states consider the intermediate court of appeals to be one court instead of multiple courts; the diagram on the right represents this model. In this case, a decision by the intermediate court of appeals would be mandatory authority for all trial courts within the state court system.

The discussion above relates to what is known as vertical stare decisis, the authority of a higher court over a lower court within a single jurisdiction. There is also horizontal stare decisis, which deals with whether earlier decisions of a court are mandatory for the same court in later cases. This is a bit more complicated so we will not go into this in great depth, but we need to cover the basics.

The fundamental concept is that earlier decisions of a court should be considered highly persuasive or possibly mandatory for that same court in the future.[5] Take the U.S. Supreme Court, for example. Previous decisions are generally considered mandatory on the court in the future. However, in practice, this is not always the case. Occasionally the same members of the court change their mind and decide that an earlier decision was not the proper course to follow and will overrule the earlier decision. Other times, members of the court change and the new members have a different view and overrule the Court's earlier decision. This does not happen often so, as a rule, one can say the U.S. Supreme Court considers their earlier decisions to be mandatory and binding.

What about the circuit courts of appeals in the federal system; are earlier decisions of the 9th Circuit mandatory for all future litigation in the 9th Circuit? Again, the general rule would suggest it is the same as the rule for the Supreme Court. However, all circuits have court rules (rules adopted by the courts that govern practical matters involving the court's business) that make earlier decisions mandatory within the same circuit in all future cases. The reason for this is a practical one; each circuit has many judges who hear cases. Almost all cases heard by the circuit courts of appeals are heard by a panel consisting of only three out of the many judges on the court. There are many different panels within a circuit. If they didn't make the earlier decisions of one panel mandatory for all other panels within the same circuit, you could potentially have many different outcomes involving the same facts which would make predicting how the court would decide a specific legal issue very challenging, if not impossible. As a result, once a panel decides a legal issue, all future panels in that same circuit are supposed to treat that decision as mandatory.

---

[5] We speak of laws being either mandatory or persuasive as if it is a binary situation. In reality, it is more of a sliding scale with some variation, especially among persuasive authority. In other words, some cases, while not mandatory, are more persuasive than others.

Practically speaking, you can find situations where a panel of three judges fails to treat earlier panel decisions as mandatory. This may be because they either didn't know about the earlier case or maybe they just didn't think it should be followed for some reason.

There are two options available for trying to get a decision issued by a panel of three judges in the federal courts of appeals reversed or modified.

1. An appeal to the U.S. Supreme Court with the hope that the highest court will accept the appeal and reverse the decision, or
2. A petition filed with the circuit court to hear the case "en banc."

En banc means "in full court." In other words, the losing attorney petitions the circuit court that issued the original opinion to rehear it with all judges in that circuit involved instead of a three-judge panel. The circuit court usually only agrees to rehear a case en banc when many of the judges on the court think the panel got it wrong. The court, sitting en banc, can overrule an earlier decision by a panel.

What about horizontal decisis in state courts? Much of the previous discussion applies but, of course, each state is free to establish its own rules on the matter. So, we won't deal with specific states. This is something you will need to determine for the state in which you practice.

VI. AUTHORITY OF COURT DECISIONS IN RELATION TO OTHER FORMS OF PRIMARY AUTHORITY WITHIN A JURISDICTION

Another principle you must understand involves the relationship between a case and other forms of law within the same jurisdiction. In other words, what authority does a decision by a federal court carry compared to the federal constitution, statutes, and agency regulations? The charts in Exhibits VI-A and B show diagrams for both state and federal jurisdictions.

Exhibit VI-A

Hierarchy of Primary Authority

Federal Law

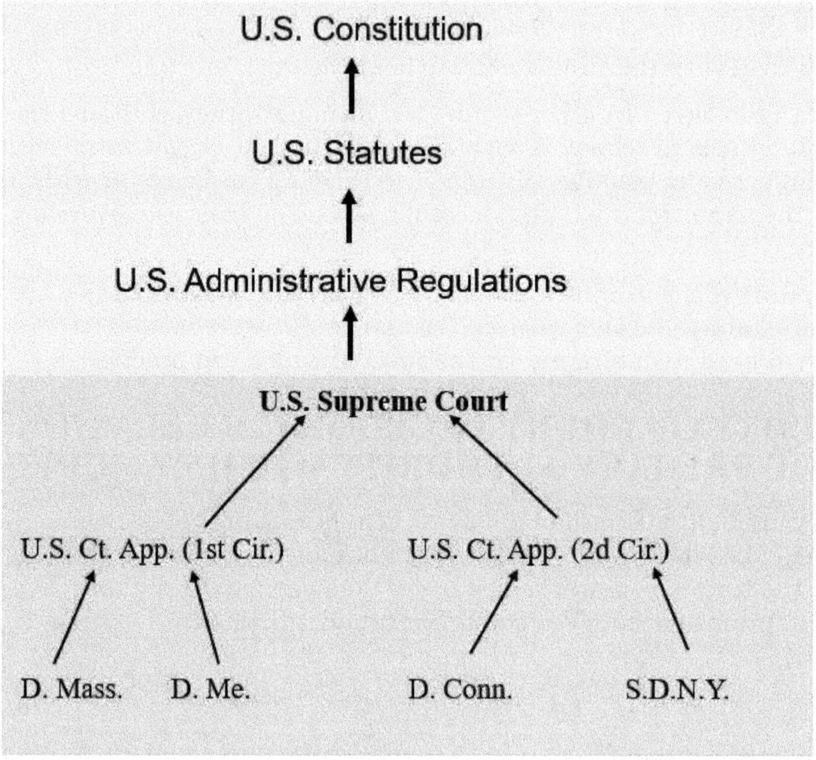

Exhibit VI-B

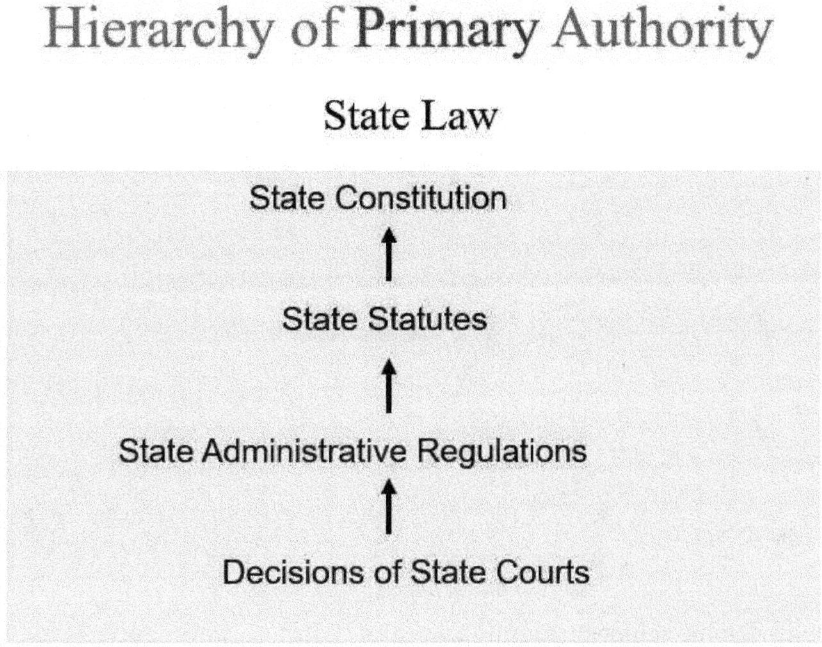

Within a single jurisdiction, such as the federal system of laws, the U.S. Constitution is the highest authority with statutes, administrative regulations, and decisions by courts in descending order. Any form of authority that is higher in the hierarchy takes precedence over any form below. For example, no form of law, statutory, administrative regulation, or court cases, can conflict with the U.S. Constitution. As a result, if any lower form of law, such as a statute, conflicts with the U.S. Constitution, the Constitution takes priority over the lower form and the statutory provision would be considered null, insofar as it conflicts with the Constitution.

The courts are the ones who get to interpret and apply the various forms of the law that are above them so one could argue that court cases are not really at the bottom of the hierarchy. However, the court is theoretically required to follow all forms of higher law. When we discuss statutes later you will see an example where Congress changed the holding of a court by enacting a statute.

The same principle applies to state legal systems; state constitutions, statutes, regulations, and court decisions are in the same order within the hierarchy of authority as those in the federal system. I did not include the structure of the state courts in the diagram.

VII. AUTHORITY OF COURT CASES ACROSS JURISDICTIONS (FEDERAL AND STATE)

So far, so good (and relatively easy). What we've discussed to this point applies when federal courts decide issues involving federal law and state courts decide issues of state law. Reality is frequently not that simple, however.

Federal courts are frequently required to decide or apply state law and state courts are required to decide issues involving federal law. What is mandatory and persuasive in those situations? The charts in Exhibits VII-A and B represent this scenario.

Exhibit VII-A

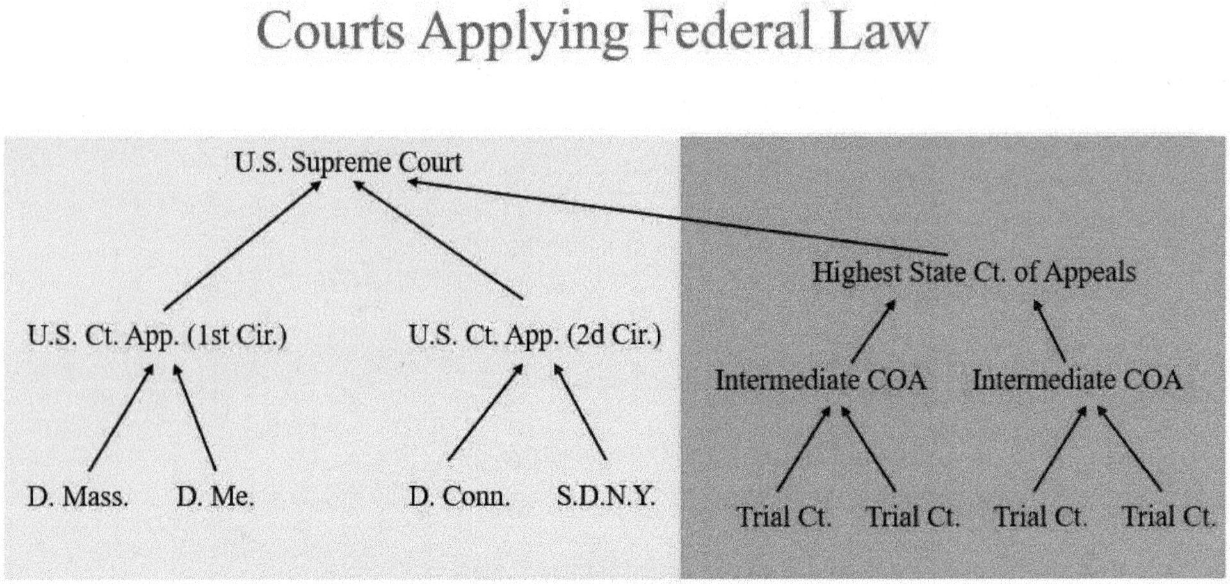

Whenever you must decide what is mandatory and what is persuasive, you must answer two questions.

- Whose law is being applied? (state or federal)
- Which court are you in?

You can answer the first question by doing legal research and locating the various forms of laws, from either federal or state legal systems, that apply to the relevant facts of your case. A case deals with a federal law question if the legal issue involves the application and interpretation of a provision in the U.S. Constitution, a federal statute, an agency regulation issued by a federal agency, or the holding of a federal court opinion. If it is an issue related to any of the various forms of state law, such as a state statute, then it is a matter of state law. It is possible that both federal and state law may apply to the same issue or that multiple issues are involved, some of which involve federal law and others that involve state laws. In a case where the court must interpret both federal and state law, different authorities will be mandatory for each type of law involved.

Once you have determined the source(s) of law involved, you then select the appropriate chart, shown in Exhibit VII-A or B, and locate on that chart the court which is hearing the case. As an example, assume that the law involved is related to the meaning of a phrase in a federal statute. So, we know that federal law is involved. Go to the chart in Exhibit VII-A that is labeled "Courts Applying Federal Law." Let's assume that the court hearing the case is the Federal District Court for the Southern District of New York (S.D.N.Y.), a federal court. Identify that court on the chart. You can now determine which courts' decisions will be mandatory: decisions of the U.S. Court of Appeals for the 2d Circuit and the United States Supreme Court are mandatory for this court on this issue of federal law. If you find any decisions on point that were issued by either of these courts, they are mandatory for the court in which you are litigating the case. Decisions on point from any other court would only be persuasive. The language of the relevant federal statute would, of course, also be mandatory for the trial court.

Now, assume you are researching the same problem involving federal law but this time you are in a state trial court in Illinois. On the same chart, since it involves federal law, locate the state trial court. What would be mandatory authority here? The language of the federal statute, any relevant decisions by the state intermediate court of appeals (COA), the highest court of the state, and decisions of the U.S. Supreme Court would be mandatory authority. All others would merely be persuasive.

At this point many of you may think this can't be completely correct. What about decisions on federal law from the federal circuits? For example, aren't decisions of the 7th Circuit involving federal law also mandatory for state courts in Illinois since Illinois is within the 7th Circuit?[6] Actually, the states are free to decide this issue. The U.S. Supreme Court has never ruled that state courts are required to follow decisions on matters of federal law issued by the federal court of appeals or the federal district courts within the state nor has Congress enacted legislation on the matter. Some state courts of last resort have said that they will consider decisions of the federal circuit in which they reside as mandatory but they are not required to treat them as such.[7]

Just remember that decisions issued by the U.S. Supreme Court that deal with federal law are necessarily mandatory authority for state courts dealing with the same federal issue. Decisions issued by the lower federal courts are only persuasive unless the state has chosen to treat as mandatory the decisions of the federal courts of appeals for the circuit in which they reside.

What about matters of state law? For this you will use the chart labeled "Courts Applying State Law" in Exhibit VII-B. If you are in a federal district court on a matter of state law, mandatory decisions are those issued by the appropriate federal circuit court of appeals, the U.S. Supreme Court, and the highest court in the state whose law is involved. However, wouldn't the U.S. Supreme Court be the highest? Not on matters of purely state law. For example, if the federal court must decide whether a state adheres to the doctrine of contributory or comparative negligence, this is solely a matter of state law and decisions of the highest court of appeal from the state would be used as mandatory authority on that issue.

Exhibit VII-B

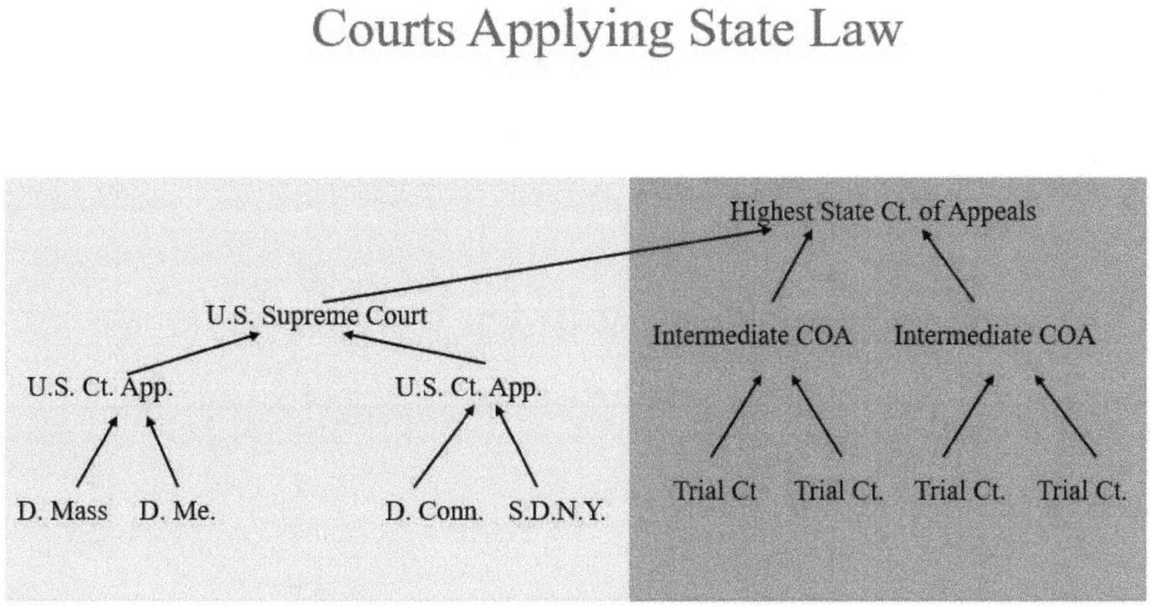

[6] Consult the map shown in Exhibit V-A to confirm that Illinois is geographically located in the 7th Circuit.

[7] If you are curious and want more details, see generally Amanda Frost, *Inferiority Complex: Should State Courts Follow Lower Federal Court Precedent on the Meaning of Federal Law,* 68 VAND. L. REV. 53 (2015) and Colin E. Wrabley, *Applying Federal Court of Appeals' Precedent: Contrasting Approaches to Applying Court of Appeals' Federal Law Holdings and* Erie *State Law Predictions,* 3 SETON HALL CIR. REV. 1 (2006).

On the other hand, if the question is whether a state law conflicts with a federal law, you have two questions to answer, one federal and the other state. The question about what the state law means is a matter of state law; the question about the meaning of a federal law and whether there is a conflict between the state and federal laws is a question of federal law. But on the meaning and application of purely state law, the highest court of appeal in that state would determine what the law of that state is on the subject and the federal courts faced with the issue would look to decisions of the highest court in that state for guidance.[8]

With every rule, such as this one, there are exceptions. It is possible, for example, that a state could have a statute that, on its face, looks neutral but is applied by the courts of that state in a manner that conflicts with federal law. In that instance, if federal law prohibits state law from superseding federal law, the federal courts would likely find a conflict and rule that federal law preempts the state law as it is applied.

VIII. RELATIONSHIP OF FEDERAL AND STATE LEGAL SOURCES OF ALL TYPES

How do the various forms of legal authority in the federal system and the state systems relate to one another? This begins to get complicated; follow along with the chart in Exhibit VIII-A for a graphical explanation of this. First, the federal constitution trumps all other forms of laws, whether federal or state. It lays out the basic framework in which all other laws exist. The basic principle (shown in Exhibit VIII-B) that controls the relationship between federal and state laws is located in Article VI, clause 2, of the U.S. Constitution. It states that the Constitution and other laws of the United States, are "the supreme law of the land and the judges in every state shall be bound thereby, any thing in the constitution or laws of any state to the contrary notwithstanding." In other words, as a rule, federal law preempts state law.

[8] The chart in Exhibit VII-B represents the hierarchy of authority, not the route of appeal. Decisions by the U.S. Supreme Court related to state law are not appealed to the highest court of appeal of the state. Despite this, however, the U.S. Supreme Court, and all lower federal courts, will look to the highest court of appeal in the relevant state for interpretation and application of purely state law.

Exhibit VIII-A

Hierarchy of Primary Authority (Relationship between Federal and State)

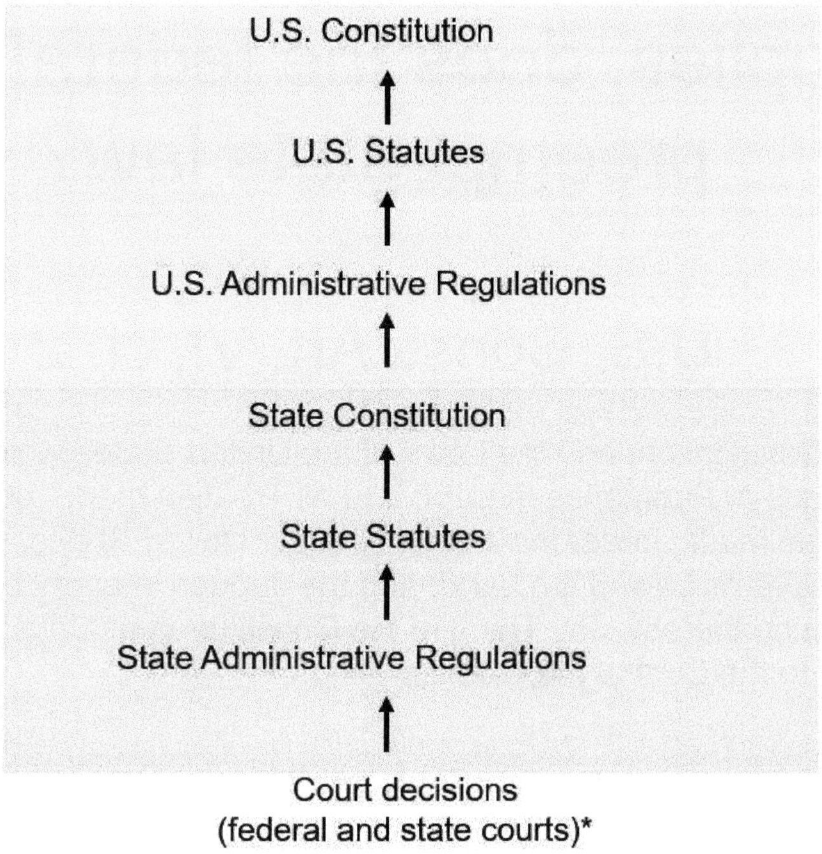

Exhibit VIII-B

If both state and federal law applies, does the federal law preempt state law?

U.S. Const. Art. VI, cl. 2

This Constitution, and the Laws of the United States which shall be made in Pursuance thereof; and all Treaties made, or which shall be made, under the Authority of the United States, shall be the supreme Law of the Land; and the Judges in every State shall be bound thereby, any Thing in the Constitution or Laws of any State to the Contrary notwithstanding.

Federal statutes come next, followed by agency regulations. Then the equivalent forms of state law follow in the same order. Each form of law is subject to the one(s) above on this chart. At the court level, you need to add the discussion in section VII (the previous section) for an explanation of how the different levels of courts relate to one another. This provides a generalized overview of the ways the various laws relate to one another. In those subject areas where the federal government has exclusive authority, the general rule is that state law is below and subject to federal laws; in these instances, state law cannot conflict with federal laws unless Congress allows states to also regulate aspects of the subject.

In some instances, like copyright, states are preempted from enacting laws on the subject; all copyright law is federal. On the other hand, states have the authority to enact laws related to other forms of intellectual property, such as trade secrets. In many instances, the federal government sets a floor of minimum protections and the states can regulate the same subject as long as they offer at least as much or more protection than the federal law. For example, there is a federal law prohibiting sex discrimination in the workplace but states are free to enact similar laws as long as they offer at least the same or additional protection. They cannot override federal law by offering less protection.

The U.S. Constitution also provides that the federal government is limited in the scope of its powers. In other words, the federal government can only exercise authority in those subjects granted to it by the Constitution. For example, Article I, section 8, Clause 8 gives the federal government authority to create laws related to patent and copyright. Clause 3 of the same article and section grants the federal government the authority "to regulate commerce . . . among the several states." Clause 3, commonly known as the Commerce Clause, is used to justify the authority for many federal statutes. There are additional provisions in the Constitution granting various powers to the federal government (and interpreting and applying these powers is the subject of much litigation decided by the courts). However, all other powers not given to the federal government are reserved for the states by the 10th Amendment to the U.S. Constitution. It states that "[t]he powers not delegated to the United States by the Constitution, nor prohibited by it to the States, are reserved to the States respectively, or to the people." So, if a statute enacted by the federal Congress relates to a subject matter reserved for the states, then that federal statute conflicts with the U.S. Constitution and is void.

As a result, many of the subjects you will study in law school and use in practice (contracts, torts, property, etc.) are governed primarily by state law. However, the federal government does get involved in many of these areas through the authority of the Commerce Clause. For example, there is a federal law known as the "Truth in Lending" statute that regulates certain terms in contracts between lenders and debtors when the lenders are involved in interstate commerce.

IX. PUBLICATION OF COURT DECISIONS

A. FEDERAL COURTS

Now that we have discussed the general authority of case law and examined its relationship with other forms of state and federal law, how does one practically go about locating relevant cases?

Long before electronic computers were available, publishers like West Publishing began printing opinions in volumes that were called reporters. Different reporters were created to cover specific courts. For example, the chart in Exhibit IX-A lists the titles of reporters that contain opinions issued by various federal courts. These reporters, with the exception of the Federal Appendix, are still available in print today, though most attorneys access them online through legal databases.

Exhibit IX-A

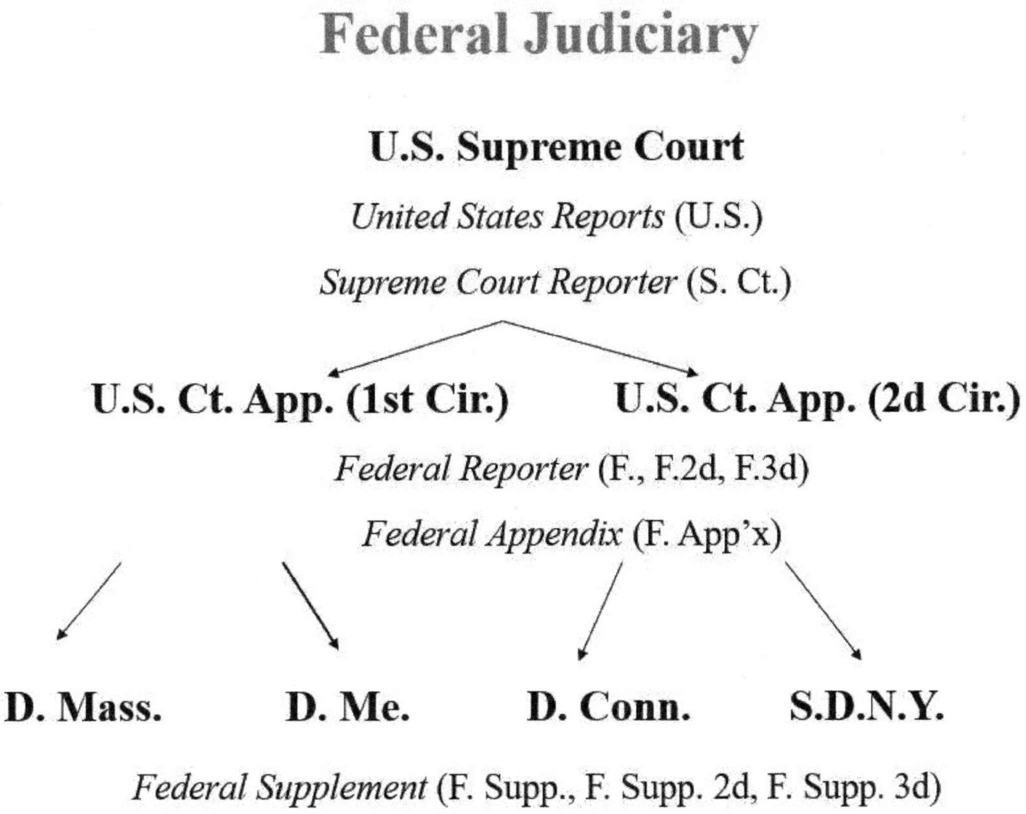

In the federal courts chart, you will notice that two different reporters are listed for the U.S. Supreme Court: United States Reports and Supreme Court Reporter. (The abbreviation in the parenthetical following the title of the reporter is *The Bluebook* abbreviation for that reporter.) The *United States Reports* is an official reporter for opinions issued by the U.S. Supreme Court. Official reporters are those published by the government. The *Supreme Court Reporter* is unofficial and is published by West. The *United States Reports* and the *Supreme Court Reporter* are parallel reporters, both publishing the same opinions issued by the U.S. Supreme Court. Opinions of the intermediate courts of appeals at the federal level are not published by the government; there are no official reporters for opinions issued by these courts. The only reporter for these courts' opinions is published by West and called the *Federal Reporter*. You will notice several abbreviations in the parenthetical following the title of this reporter. This shows that the *Federal Reporter* is currently into the third series (F.3d). Each series contains decisions issued during a specific time period. In Exhibit IX-B you will see that the original *Federal Reporter* covers the years 1880, when this reporter started, through 1924. The second series picks up where the original left off and goes through 1993; the third picks up where the second series left off and continues through today. Each series begins with volume 1; part of the purpose of starting a new series is to avoid four digit volume numbers. You will see this pattern of multiple series repeated in most reporters; many are into the second or third series by now.

Exhibit IX-B

Federal Reporter

First Series	**1880 - 1924**
Second Series	**1924 - 1993**
Third Series	**1993 - present**

The second reporter listed for the federal courts of appeals, the Federal Appendix, is **not** a parallel reporter that prints the same cases. Instead, it includes cases from the same courts of appeals that are not printed in the *Federal Reporter*. To understand why this reporter exists requires some historical background. The federal courts of appeals have never released all written opinions for publication. Those opinions released for publication were printed in the *Federal Reporter* while those not released were, originally, only available to the attorneys representing the parties involved in the litigation and through the docket for the case. Opinions that were not released were generally known as "unpublished" opinions since they were not published in any print reporter. One of the reasons these opinions were not released, and therefore not included in the print reporters, is because the courts thought they were repetitive and didn't add anything new to the common law. They only repeated well established principles of the law and did not need to be published. These unpublished opinions were also known as non-precedential cases because most courts had rules stating that they did not carry precedential authority and forbidding citation to them. Since access was very limited, citation of these unpublished cases was prohibited.

This began to change after electronic databases came along in the late 1970's and early 80's; the publishers who owned the databases began to gain access to these unpublished cases and included them in the database. Inclusion of these cases in the databases meant that they were more readily accessible. The rules still generally limited citing to these cases. However, with access to these cases, it became clear that not all these cases were repetitious of the common law already well established by the published cases. Some, in fact, were breaking new ground. Ultimately, with greater availability, the courts began to relax their rules against citing these cases. At some point, West Publishing decided to begin publishing these "unpublished" cases in a new reporter, now known as the Federal Appendix. When the Federal Appendix began publication in 2001, it didn't really make sense to call them unpublished anymore so they are typically still referred to as non-precedential, although depending on the courts' rules, this may no longer be accurate either as some courts now allow one to cite these opinions. So, the Federal Appendix contains those decisions issued by the federal courts of appeals that are not included in the *Federal Reporter*. West discontinued publication of the *Federal Appendix* in 2021, relying on the databases for access.

Continuing to opinions issued by judges in the federal district courts, you will see on the chart in Exhibit IX-A that opinions written by district court judges in the federal system are published in a reporter entitled the *Federal Supplement*, which is now in its third series. Like decisions by the courts of appeals, there is no official reporter for the district courts. Very few opinions written by district court judges are included in the *Federal Supplement*; approximately 10 to 15% get printed. Some of the nonpublished ones are online in the legal databases but others are not available in either print or online. Those issued in the last fifteen years, give or take a few years, are available through dockets, which we spoke about earlier.

B. STATE COURTS

For reporters that contain state court opinions, West publishes what is known as the regional reporter system. It is composed of multiple titles and each one represents a region of the country. The charts and graphics in Exhibits IX-C and D cover the details. For example, opinions of courts in states located in the western portion of the U.S. are included in the *Pacific Reporter*. (Note: the regions are loosely defined. Kansas and Oklahoma are included in the *Pacific Reporter* even though most wouldn't identify those states as being in the Pacific zone. Decisions of courts in Indiana are in the *Northeastern Reporter*.)

Exhibit IX-C

State Judiciary

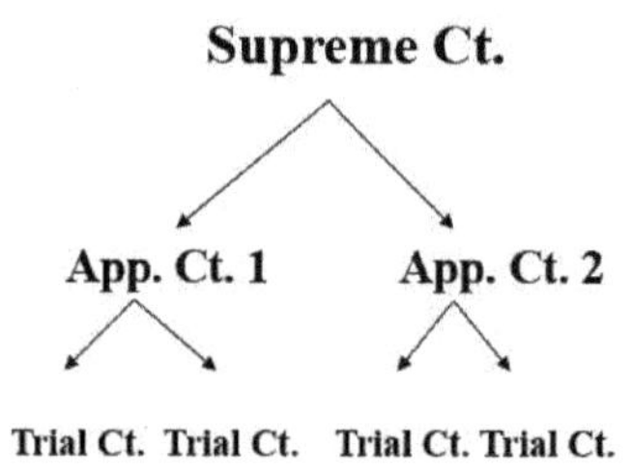

Regional Reporters
- *Pacific*
- *Northwestern*
- *Southwestern*
- *Southern*
- *Northeastern*
- *Southeastern*
- *Atlantic*

Official State reporters
e.g., Michigan Reports

Table 1 in *The Bluebook* indicates if an official reporter is still being published.

Exhibit IX-D

West's National Reporter System – Regional Reporters

West National Reporter System Map © Thomson Reuters, all rights reserved. Used with permission of Thomson Reuters.

Since West Publishing prints these reporters, they are unofficial but everyone uses them. As I mentioned when we discussed star pagination earlier, a few states still publish their opinions in official reporters. Table 1 in *The Bluebook* indicates which states still publish them. For example, look at the entry in Table 1 of *The Bluebook* for Nevada. You will see the following entry:

Supreme Court (Nev.)

Pacific Reporter	1883—date	P., P.2d, P.3d
Nevada Reports	1865—date	Nev.

This table indicates that Nevada still publishes an official reporter, known as the Nevada Reports. If this was no longer published, the date range would indicate the ending date. However, almost no one pays attention to the official reporters anymore, as you will see when we discuss how to cite cases.

The regional reporter system contains decisions issued by the courts of last resort and the intermediate appeals courts of all states, except for California and New York. California has two reporters, the *Pacific Reporter* and *West's California Reporter*. The *Pacific Reporter* contains decisions issued by the California Supreme Court, the intermediate Court of Appeals, and selected decisions from the Appellate Divisions of the Superior Court until 1959. In 1959 West stopped including decisions issued by the intermediate Court of Appeals and the Superior Court in the *Pacific Reporter* and put them in the *California Reporter*. Today, only decisions issued by the California Supreme Court are included in the *Pacific Reporter*. The *California Reporter* contains decisions issued by all three court levels beginning with 1959 until the present.

In New York state, the *Northeastern Reporter* includes only decisions issued by the highest Court of Appeals in the state from 1885 until the present. West also publishes the *New York Supplement*, which contains decisions from the highest Court of Appeals beginning in 1956 until the present, the intermediate court of appeals (known as the Supreme Court) in 1888 until the present, and other lower courts in 1888 until the present.

Most attorneys today access case opinions online in one form or another. However, *The Bluebook*, which specifies the rules for citing to legal sources, requires cites to the print reporters so you will need to be familiar with the reporters discussed here.

Summary

1. The concept of precedent (stare decisis) means that the holding (the rule of law as applied to the facts before the court) in a court's opinion is authority for future decisions by courts.

2. Jurisdiction determines whether this precedential authority is persuasive or mandatory.

3. Only majority, plurality, or per curiam opinions can be mandatory; all other types of opinions can only be persuasive.

4. To determine whether the holding in a majority, plurality, or per curiam opinion is mandatory or persuasive, you must answer two questions.

    A. Is the law being applied state or federal?

    B. Which court will hear and decide the issue?

5. On matters involving interpretation and application of a federal law, the following sources are mandatory.

A. In a federal court:

1. Any decision by a federal court directly above in the hierarchy of federal courts (within the same circuit) will be mandatory.

2. Each circuit court of appeal is separate from other circuit courts.

3. All decisions by the United States Supreme Court are mandatory for all lower federal courts.

B. In a state court:

1. Any decision by a state court directly above in the hierarchy of state courts will be mandatory.

2. Decisions by the federal court of appeals in which the state is located may be mandatory if the state determines they are to be treated as mandatory, otherwise they are merely persuasive.

3. Decisions by the U.S. Supreme Court will be mandatory.

6. On matters involving interpretation and application of a state law, the following sources are mandatory.

A. In a federal court:

1. Any decision by a federal court directly above in the hierarchy of federal courts (within the same circuit) will be mandatory.

2. Decisions by the U.S. Supreme Court will be mandatory.

3. Decisions by the highest court of appeal from the state is mandatory for the federal courts, assuming no conflict with federal law that preempts the state law.

B. In a state court:

1. Any decision by a state court directly above in the hierarchy of state courts will be mandatory.

7. Various forms of laws within a jurisdiction (federal and state) are ordered as follows.

A. Constitution.

B. Statutes.

C. Agency regulations.

D. Court decisions.

8. A law on a lower level cannot conflict with a higher level; if it does, the lower-level authority is void to the extent it conflicts with the higher authority.

9. The relationship between state and federal laws is governed by the following principles from the U.S. Constitution.

A. The federal constitution is supreme and no other laws, whether federal or state, can conflict with it.

B. The federal government's authority is limited to those powers explicitly stated in the U.S. Constitution.

C. Of those powers granted to the federal government, some are exclusive (preempting state laws in the subject area) while others are co-existent with state powers. In this latter case, states may also regulate as long as they do not conflict with the federal laws.

D. All other powers are reserved for the states.

10. Opinions issued by courts are published in reporters.

A. Opinions issued by the U.S. Supreme Court are published in two parallel reporters.

1. *United States Reports* (U.S.) (Official reporter published by U.S. government).

2. *Supreme Court Reporter* (S. Ct.) (Published by West Publishing).

B. Decisions of the U.S. Courts of Appeals are published in the *Federal Reporter* and the *Federal Appendix*; both are published by West Publishing. These two reporters are **not** parallel reporters because opinions found in the *Federal Appendix* are those cases not published in the *Federal Reporter*. The Federal Appendix ceased publication in 2021 and the cases included in this reporter are only available online.

C. Decisions of the U.S. District Courts are printed in the *Federal Supplement,* which is published by West Publishing.

D. Decisions of state courts are published in the regional reporter system which is published by West.

E. Some states publish opinions of their own courts. These are known as official reporters. Table 1 in *The Bluebook* indicates which states still publish their opinions.

X. CITING COURT CASES

You will need to cite case opinions in your legal writing. The rules regarding how to cite case opinions, and other legal sources, are found in *The Bluebook: A Uniform System of Citation.* This publication is currently in its 22nd edition; new editions are released approximately every three years. Hopefully, you already have access to a print copy or the electronic version of *The Bluebook;* if not, get access to either. You will need this resource throughout law school.

First, a brief word about *The Bluebook.* Immediately following the table of contents in *The Bluebook* are rules printed on blue paper which are referred to as the Bluepages. These Bluepages contain the basic rules that apply to citing legal authorities in written memos and briefs, which are the types of documents you will write during your first year of law school. Every rule of citation located in the Bluepages begin with the letter B. For example, Rule B10 covers how to cite cases in a memo or document filed with a court. Immediately following the Bluepages are white pages which contain additional rules that apply specifically to citations in papers and published articles; however, some parts of the rules found here also apply to citation of sources generally so you will need to reference them as well. Rules in the white pages are numbered with the letter R preceding the number; Rule R10 covers citing court opinions (cases). Several tables follow the white pages; any reference to a table in *The Bluebook* begins with the letter T; e.g., table 10 is referred to as T.10.

Below are two sample cites; the top one is for a federal court decision followed by a cite to a decision issued by a state court. Each element of a cite is labeled.

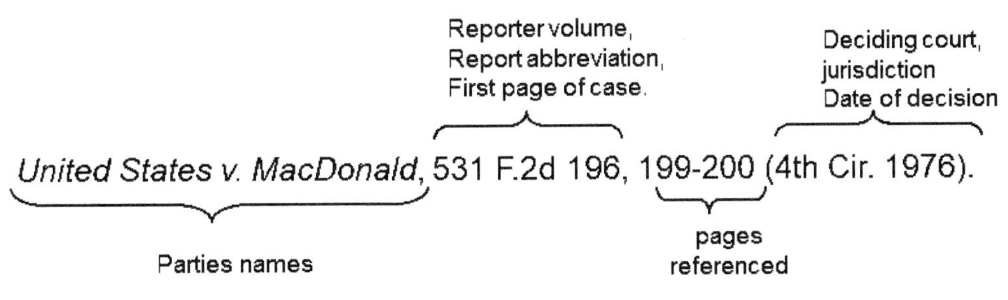

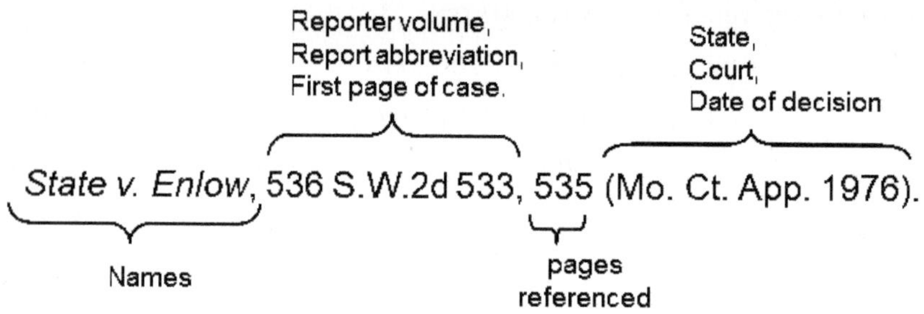

For each element of a cite shown above, the relevant *Bluebook* rule is referenced and explained below.

A. CASE NAMES

1. When a case is referenced in a textual sentence, the names should conform to the rules listed below and should be italicized. For example, "In *Southern Pacific Co. v. Jensen*, 244 U.S. 205 (1917), Justice McReynolds stressed the value of uniform laws."

2. When a case is referenced in a separate stand-alone citation sentence, abbreviate any word contained in T.6 and T.10 of *The Bluebook*. Do not abbreviate words that are part of a state, country, or other geographical unit that is the entire name of the party. Any word over eight letters may also be abbreviated if "substantial space" is saved and the result is clear. For example, *S. Pac. Co. v. Jensen*, 244 U.S. 205 (Pitney, J., dissenting).

3. Use only the first listed party on each side of the litigation.

4. Omit "the" as the first word of a party's name unless it is a part of the commonly known name. E.g., The Civil Rights Cases.

5. Omit words indicating multiple parties, e.g., "et al."

6. Phrases like "on the relation of," "for the use of," and "on behalf of" should be abbreviated as *ex rel.*

7. Phrases like "in the matter of," "petition of," "application of," and similar expressions should be abbreviated as *In re.*

8. Abbreviate widely known acronyms (see Rule R6.1) without periods following the letters, such as NLRB, CIA., etc. Also use the following abbreviations: "&," "Ass'n," "Bros.," "Co.," "Corp.," "Inc.," "Ltd.," and "No."

9. Omit terms like "administrator," "appellee," "executor," and "licensee."

10. When states are parties, the case name will contain one of the following phrases: "People of," "State of," or "Commonwealth of."

   A. If the court deciding the case is a state court located in the named state, then retain the word "People," "State," or "Commonwealth." For example, *Commonwealth of Pennsylvania v. Ferrone* becomes *Commonwealth v. Ferrone* if a Pennsylvania state court decided the case.

   B. If the court deciding the case is not a state court located in the named state, retain the name of the state only and drop the preceding phrase. In the previous example, the title of the case would be *Pennsylvania v. Ferrone* if the U.S. Supreme Court decided the case.

B. REPORTER AND PARENTHETICAL INFORMATION

Federal Cases

Reporter information (volume, reporter name, first page of case, and internal pages if citing to specific pages within the opinion instead of the opinion as a whole)

- Cite federal cases to the reporters listed in T.1 of *The Bluebook.*

Supreme Court—*United States Reports* (U.S.) or *Supreme Court Reporter* (S. Ct.) if not yet printed in U.S.

Courts of Appeals—F.3d, F.2d, F.

District Courts—F. Supp. 2d, F. Supp.

Note: **Rule R6.1** states that spaces between single letters in abbreviations should be deleted. So, if citing the Northwestern Reporter, the abbreviation is N.W., without spaces between letters and periods. Also, whenever you are citing a series which contains a number and a letter, such as 2d (second series), the number and letter are treated as a single character. An example is found above for the Court of Appeals reporter abbreviation, F.3d. As another example, citing to the Northeastern report, second series, the abbreviation would be N.E.2d. All spaces between letters, numbers, and punctuation are deleted. This applies to all abbreviations, not just the titles of reporters.

Parenthetical (court and date)

- Include in the parenthetical:

  1. The name of the court using abbreviations from T.7 and T.10 in *The Bluebook* (omit if decided by the U.S. Supreme Court since the name of the reporter unambiguously indicates which court issued the opinion) and

  2. The year the case was decided.

  Examples:

  Meritor Sav. Bank v. Vinson, 477 U.S. 57 (1986).

  Berry v. Hollander, 925 F.2d 311 (9th Cir. 1991).

  Al-Marri v. Bush, 274 F. Supp. 2d 1003 (C.D. Ill. 2003).

State Cases

Reporter information (volume, reporter name, first page of case, and internal pages)

- If a public domain cite is available, include that cite in addition to the regional reporter.

- If no public domain cite is available, cite to regional reporters only. If the case is not published in the regional reporter, cite to a source in which the case is published.

- Public domain cites and other reporter information is available for each state in T.1 of *The Bluebook.*

Example: *Beck v. Beck*, 1999 ME 110, ¶ 6, 733 A.2d 981, 983 (1999).

- **Public domain cites are not used often so check with your legal writing professor regarding whether to include them.**

Parenthetical (state, court, and date)

- Use the state and court abbreviations listed in T.1.

- Any information about state and court that is clear from the reporter name should be deleted from the parenthetical. Follow the state and court abbreviations from T.1 and T.7 in *The Bluebook.*
- Always indicate the year of decision.

Examples:

Beck v. Beck, 1999 ME 110, ¶ 6, 733 A.2d 981, 983 (1999).

This opinion was issued by the highest court; the abbreviation for this court according to T.1 is Me. This information was already conveyed by the public domain cite so it is deleted from the parenthetical.

DiLucia v. Mandelker, 493 N.Y.S.2d 769 (App. Div. 1985)

This opinion was issued by the Appellate Division of the N.Y. Supreme Court. T.1 lists N.Y. App. Div. as the state and court abbreviation. The state can be deleted from the parenthetical since that information is conveyed by the reporter title.

People v. Cathey, 681 N.W.2d 661 (Mich. Ct. App. 2004)

This opinion was issued by the Michigan Ct. of Appeals; the abbreviation from T.1 is Mich. Ct. App. None of this information is indicated by the reporter so the full abbreviation is included.

C. OTHER INFORMATION THAT MAY BE INCLUDED IN A CASE CITE

Value (weight) of authority in a parenthetical—Rules B10.1.5 and .6, R10.6, R10.7

Examples: per curiam, en banc, plurality opinion, dissenting opinion.

These terms should be included in a parenthetical following the cite.

Example: *Wersba v. Seiler*, 393 F.2d 937 (3d Cir. 1968) (per curiam).

Explanatory phrases in a parenthetical (see Rule R1.5 for further information on explanatory material).

Example: indicating the exact holding.

Prior and subsequent history—Rules B10.1.6 and R10.7

Always indicate subsequent history, except the following instances:

- Omit denial of cert. and comparable rulings if the case was decided over two years ago.
- Omit remand or denial of a rehearing unless relevant to your point.

Indicate prior history only if relevant to your point (prior history goes before subsequent history).

Name changes on appeal—Rule R10.7.2

- Subsequent history: rev'd sub nom. *Leroy v. Great . . .*
- Prior history: just list name.
- Don't include name change in cert. denied.

Indicate significant treatment

Example: *overruled by*

T.8 in The Bluebook contains commonly used phrases for history & weight

Kubrick v. United States, 581 F.2d 1092 (3d Cir. 1978), *aff'g* 435 F. Supp. 166 (E.D. Pa. 1977), *rev'd*, 444 U.S. 111 (1979).

A comma is not used after phrases followed by case citations as their direct object.

D. UNREPORTED CASES—RULES B10.1.4 AND R10.8

Cases available in slip opinion only.

Cite name, docket number, jurisdiction, and full date.

Example: *Groucho Marx Prods. v. Playboy Enters.*, No. 77 Civ. 1782, slip op. at 6 (S.D.N.Y. Dec. 30, 1977).

If online only.

Follow Rules B10.1.4. and R10.8.1.

Depublished cases.

Rule R10.8.1(d)

Mitchell v. Cal. Fair Plan Ass'n, 260 Cal. Rptr. 3 (Ct. App. 1989) (depublished).

Exhibit X-A contains the first page of a case entitled *State of Washington v. Donald Fredric Brown*. Reference this exhibit as you proceed through the steps below, which will demonstrate how to take the information from a case in a reporter and craft it into proper citation form that complies with *The Bluebook*.

E. INFORMATION ABOUT THIS CASE AS IT APPEARS IN THE REPORTER

1. In the regional reporter the case is published in vol. 748 of the *Pacific Reporter*, 2d Series, beginning on page 276.

2. This case is also available in an official reporter, published by the state, in vol. 50 of the Washington Appellate Reports beginning on page 405.

3. The name of the case is *State of Washington, Respondent v. Donald Fredric Brown, Appellant*.

4. The docket number of the case is 18640-0-I.

5. The court that issued the opinion is the Court of Appeals of Washington, Division 1, decided on Jan. 20, 1988.[9]

F. ELEMENTS OF A FULL CITE (RULES B10.1 AND R10)

1. Name of the case.

Rule R10.2.1(f)—Retain only "state" if court deciding case is a part of the named state's court system; if issued by any other court, retain only the name of the state.

Rule B10.1.1(ii)—If an individual, last name only, omit first and middle names or initials of individuals.

---

[9] Relevant Tables and Rules in 22nd edition of *Bluebook* that apply to citing cases:
Rule B10.1
Rule R10—Cases
Table 1—U.S. Jurisdictions
Table 6—Case Names abbrev.
Table 7—Court Names abbrev.

Rule B2—Underline or italicize case name.

After application of the rules, the names appear as follows: *State v. Brown*. (The name could also be underlined instead of italicized.)

2. The source in which the case can be found (usually a reporter).

This case appears in volume 50 of the Washington Appellate Reports, pages 405 through 414, and volume 748 of the *Pacific Reporter* 2nd Series, pages 276 through 282.

Table 1 (T1)—Look up state and cite to the reporter listed for the court.

Rule R10.3.1(b)—In ordinary legal memos, cite to the regional reporter only.

Rule B10.1.2

Use volume number, reporter abbreviation, and first page of case.

If citing to a specific page (pincite) in the case, follow the first page number by a comma and then the internal page number.

Rule R6.1(a) Remove spaces in abbreviations between consecutive, individual letters.

After applying the above rules, the part of the cite that follows the case name appears as 748 P.2d 276.

3. The court and year of decision in a parenthetical.

The issuing court is the Washington state Court of Appeals.

Rule B10.1.3

T.1—State and court abbreviations.

Put this within the parenthetical.

Omit state if reporter clearly indicates the state.

Omit court if decided by highest court within jurisdiction.

After application of the above rules, the first part of the parenthetical appears as

(Wash. Ct. App. ####).

The decision was issued on January 20, 1988.

Rule B10.1.3—Provide year only (do not include month and day).

After application the relevant rules, the parenthetical appears as follows:

(Wash. Ct. App. 1988).

Final citation to this case: *State v. Brown*, 748 P.2d 276 (Wash. Ct. App. 1988).

Assignment 2

The following questions are based on material covered in sections V–X of the reading.

1. Consult *State v. Burnett*, 755 N.E.2d 857 (Ohio 2001), when answering the following questions. You may use the copy of this case that was included with Assignment 1 or retrieve it on Westlaw or Lexis by entering just the cite (reporter volume, reporter abbreviation, and beginning page number) in the query box at the top of the screen. **Do not read the entire case**; begin by reading the abbreviated statement of the facts of the case below and then consult only those parts of the opinion to which the questions direct you.

On August 7, 1996, appellee, the city of Cincinnati, passed an ordinance. The ordinance established drug-exclusion zones within the city. In passing the ordinance, the city council stated that certain areas of the city have a higher incidence of drug-related activity, which leads to the degradation of those areas. Further, the city council theorized that many people arrested for or convicted of drug offenses frequently returned to these areas.

The ordinance states that a person can be excluded for ninety days from the public streets, sidewalks, and other public ways in all drug-exclusion zones if the person is arrested or taken into custody within a drug-exclusion zone for any of several enumerated offenses. If the offender is subsequently convicted of the crime for which he or she was arrested, the offender is prohibited for one year from the date of conviction from being on any public street, sidewalk, or other public way in all drug exclusion zones. If an excluded person is found within a drug-exclusion zone during the exclusion period, that person is subject to immediate arrest for criminal trespass pursuant to Ohio state statutes.

On February 7, 1998, appellant, George Burnett, was arrested for one of the designated drug offenses and was given a ninety-day exclusion notice from the Over the Rhine drug-exclusion zone by the arresting police officer. Immediately upon conviction of the charge, Burnett was served by the city with a notice of a one-year exclusion from the Over the Rhine drug-exclusion zone. On June 23, 1998, Burnett was found to be present in the drug-exclusion zone and was arrested for criminal trespass in violation of the state statute. The defendant filed a motion with the court to dismiss the charges because he argued that the Cincinnati ordinance is unconstitutional. Burnett was ultimately convicted as charged. Upon Burnett's appeal to the First District Court of Appeals, the judgment of the trial court was affirmed. The case is now before this court pursuant to the allowance of a discretionary appeal.

A. Criminal defendants, like the one in this case, frequently claim that the law they were convicted of violating should not be enforced because it conflicts with a higher form of law. This issue involves identifying a hierarchy of primary authority. What higher form of law or laws does the defendant resort to in his defense here? (Hint: there are three different ones relied upon by the defendant in this case. The first begins with roman numeral I at the top of the right column on page 862 of the case. The second begins with roman numeral II half-way down the right column on page 863. The third begins at the top of the left column on page 868, with roman numeral III.)

B. For each of the three defenses raised by the defendant, which ones are based on federal law and which are state law? For each defense, what type of authority does the court rely on in its analysis: federal or state cases? (Hint: any reference to U.S. in a cite, e.g., 493 U.S. 215, means it comes from the United States Supreme Court, the federal court of last resort. Any cite that refers to F.3d or F.2d indicates a case from the federal intermediate court of appeals. If a state name appears in the cite along with a reference to N.E.2d, this is an opinion issued by either a state's court of last resort or intermediate court of appeals.)

C. In January 2000, a federal trial court, in the case of *Johnson v. City of Cincinnati*, ruled on the same issues involved in *Burnett*. *Johnson* is discussed in *State v. Burnett* beginning in the last paragraph in the left column on page 860 through the end of the left column on page 862. The federal trial court in *Johnson* held that the city ordinance conflicted with both the federal constitution's right to travel and freedom of association. The court in *Burnett* had to decide whether it was required to follow the federal court's interpretation or if they could conduct their own analysis and reach their own conclusion, potentially disagreeing with the federal court. What conclusion does the court deciding *Burnett* reach about their obligation to follow the decision by the lower federal court on this issue? What reasons does the court provide in support of this conclusion?

2. Referring to the *Burnett* case:

A. Which justice wrote the court's opinion?

B. Of the types of opinions discussed in the previous reading, what type of opinion is the court's opinion (plurality or majority)?

C. How many justices joined the court's opinion?

D. Did any justice write a separate opinion? If so, what type is it?

E. Do the headnotes in this case describe information from all opinions found in this case? Explain.

3. If a federal district court in Missouri must interpret and apply a provision from a Missouri statute, decisions by which courts would be mandatory authority on this question? (I don't expect you to conduct research beyond the reading materials in the book. If additional information is needed, explain what you would need to fully answer this question.)

4. If a state trial court in Missouri must interpret and apply a provision of a federal statute, which courts' decisions would be mandatory? (I don't expect you to conduct research beyond the reading materials. If additional information is needed, explain what you would need to fully answer this question.)

5. You are appealing a client's case to the state court of appeals in Arizona; the case involves a claim of workplace discrimination. The plaintiff raised claims under three different laws that could apply to the facts before the court: an Arizona state statute, a federal statute, and Arizona state common law (court cases decided by the same court you are in and the highest court of appeals in Arizona). The issue of whether all three laws apply to your client's case are involved in the appeal.

A. Are all three forms of law mandatory for the Arizona Court of Appeals? Explain your answer.

B. The U.S. Supreme Court, in an earlier case, had to interpret and apply the same Arizona state statute that is involved. Would the interpretation given to the state statute by the U.S. Supreme Court be mandatory authority for the Arizona Court of Appeals? Why or why not?

6. You are practicing law in Portland, Oregon. You are writing a memo in support of a motion that will be filed with an Oregon state trial court. In this memo you are citing a decision issued by the Oregon Supreme Court that was decided in 2004. The court in which you are filing the memo requires a citation to the official Oregon Reports if a case is published in this reporter. Does Oregon still publish an official reporter containing decisions issued by the Oregon Supreme Court? If not, when did it cease publication? Where did you locate the information needed to answer this question?

CHAPTER 3

LOCATING CASES AND SECONDARY SOURCES

XI. LOCATING CASES BY SUBJECT

Most of the time, you will need to locate cases by subject. In other words, you will have a legal problem posed by your client and you will need to identify cases that discuss and apply the law relevant to that problem. Many of the tools you will use to accomplish this task are the same tools used when you already know of a relevant case and need to locate other cases on point.

To break you slowly into finding relevant cases and help you be more comfortable using these tools, we will start with a known relevant case and discuss your options for locating additional cases using the known case. This will provide experience using many of the available tools. In the next section of this reading, we will use this knowledge to locate cases in the situation where you don't have a known case and need to start from a subject only.

We will discuss various methods of locating relevant legal authority because not every search option works in all situations. There are certain clues that can help you decide which method to use, and we will discuss some of these, but many times you will not have sufficient information to determine which method is best and you will just have to begin somewhere.

Artificial Intelligence (AI) has become a major player in the search for relevant legal authority. This option will be considered after discussing the traditional methods of locating cases. I am sure the question foremost in your mind at this point is why not skip the traditional methods of locating cases and just use AI. While AI is often a great tool for beginning research, AI has inherent limitations and problems that require the attorney to be actively involved in the research. To be a competent lawyer requires a complete understanding of legal research. AI is one option but it is definitely not the final and only method needed to become competent at legal research. A more detailed discussion on this topic is found in the introduction to AI that follows the discussion of full-text searching later in this chapter.

A. LOCATING CASES STARTING WITH A KNOWN CASE

1. Topic and Key Number Approach

To introduce this option for locating relevant case law, we will use the following situation to illustrate how this method works.

Let's assume that you need to research a question related to labor or employment law. If a person is hired by an employer but has no written contract of employment, this usually means that the person is an employee at-will. This basically means that he or she can be released from the job by the employer for almost any reason, as long as the reason doesn't violate public policy or the law. For example, if the employer fires a worker for refusing to do something that is illegal, the at-will worker could bring a lawsuit against the employer for unlawful termination. However, assuming the employer did not ask the employee to violate public policy or the law, the employer is free to fire the employee.

Sometimes, an employer provides an employee handbook (manual) to each new hire. In this situation, the question arises whether the manual constitutes a contract that places limitations upon when an employee can be terminated. In other words, does an employee manual constitute a "constructive" contract which the employer is obligated to follow. The handbook isn't technically a contract because both parties don't usually sign it, but it might effectively be considered an agreement between the employer and employee, especially if the manual addresses issues related to termination.

A case that deals in part with this question is *Yesudian v. Howard University*, reported at 153 F.3d 731. Log into Westlaw and retrieve this case by entering the cite (the cite consists of just the volume number, reporter abbreviation and first page of the case) into the query box at the top of the initial screen. Hint: when retrieving a document in the commercial databases (Westlaw, Lexis), you don't need to include periods in the citation; just type the numbers and letters without any periods. Also, any reference to the initial screen means the first screen you see after logging into and accessing Westlaw or Lexis. You can return to this initial screen at any time by clicking on the "Westlaw" link in the upper-left part of the screen.

After entering the cite and pressing the ENTER key or clicking on the search button, the case should appear on the screen. Scroll down to headnote 20. (Remember, the headnote numbers are not the same as a topic and key number; the headnote number appears in front of the headnote and is simply a consecutive numbering of the headnotes in a case.) This headnote reads:

> Under District of Columbia law, employee manual overcomes presumption of at-will employment where it sets forth distinction between probationary and permanent employees, providing that the first could be discharged summarily but the latter only after specific preconditions had been met; such manuals generally create factual question for the jury as to existence of a contract.

If we are researching the issue described above and have the *Yesudian* case in hand, we can use this information to locate other cases that discuss this same issue. Hopefully you recall our brief mention of the topic and key number system developed by West. Theoretically, every case that is published in a West reporter and discusses this issue of whether an employee handbook constitutes a contract between the employer and employee has the same topic and key number assigned to the relevant headnote. I say theoretically, because it is always possible that some editor didn't assign the exact same topic and key number that appears with the headnote in the *Yesudian* case. This is a human generated method of locating relevant cases and is subject to error as a result. It isn't foolproof (none of the methods are) but it works well.

Identify the relevant topic and key number that is assigned to headnote 20 in the *Yesudian* case. (If you don't see any headnotes, scroll back to the beginning of the headnotes and click on the down arrow symbol which appears to the right of the "West Headnotes" heading. If you see headnotes but no topic and key numbers, scroll back to the "West Headnotes" heading and select the "Grid View" box located just below the down arrow symbol mentioned above.) The topic and key number appear to the right of the text of the headnote. In this instance, there are three different topics and key numbers assigned to this single headnote. The first topic and key number assigned to headnote 20 is "Labor and Employment 49", the second topic and key number is "Labor and Employment 50", and the third is "Labor and Employment 58."

The three topic and key numbers assigned appear below.

231H	Labor and Employment
231HI	In General
231Hk49	Manuals, Handbooks, and Policy Statements
231Hk50	In General (Formerly 255k2.1 Master and Servant)

231H	Labor and Employment
231HI	In General
231Hk58	Questions of Law and Fact as to Employment Status (Formerly 255k43 Master and Servant)

So, how do you read this? Well, the topic (the broadest heading) always appears first (on the top line). The numbers and letters to the left of the topic are the online numerical designator of the topic; in this example, the topic Labor and Employment has the numerical designator 231H assigned. The key number is the number after the letter "k" that is assigned to the narrowest heading, which appears in the last line. So, the first topic and key number assigned to this headnote are Labor and Employment, key number 49. The letter "k" in front of 49 means "key number." The headings assigned to the numbers that appear between the most general and the most specific are not technically a part of the topic and key number, but they provide insight into organization of the topic.

In this case, this single headnote discusses two different aspects: 1) the nature of employee manuals and handbooks in the context of employment, and 2) which questions involve law and which involve fact in the employment context. The first part of the headnote and the first assigned topic (Labor and Employment) and key numbers (49 and 50) address the issue related to the manuals, which is the subject we are researching.

If you want to see other cases that discuss this same issue, simply click on the topic and key number numerical designator, which looks like this: 231Hk49 or 231Hk50. After clicking on this heading, you will see a list of cases with the names of the parties and the text of the headnote from each case that relates to the same issue as the headnote found in *Yesudian*. Just to be clear, all the cases listed here have at least one headnote which is assigned the same topic and key number as the relevant headnote in *Yesudian* (Labor and Employment k 49 or 50, depending on which one you selected).

Select 231Hk50 and take a quick look at the case and headnote from one of the recent cases in the list, *Vasquez v. Whole Foods Market, Inc.*, by clicking on the name of the case. (Note: by default, cases are shown in reverse chronological order.) Again, these are headnotes written by editors who work for West. They summarize one point from an opinion. Westlaw should take you directly to the headnote on this topic in the *Vasquez* case, which is headnote 31. You will see that the same topic and key number you selected is assigned to headnote 31 in *Vasquez*.

Now, return to the list of headnotes you were viewing before going to the *Vasquez* case by clicking on the left arrow located at the top of the page and to the left of the name of the case you are currently viewing (*Vasquez*).

Note the following features of the display of all cases assigned 231Hk50 on Westlaw.

1. As you just saw, you can retrieve each case by clicking on the name of the case.

2. The court issuing the opinion, the date the case was decided, and the cite to the reporter in which it is found are shown just below the name of the case. If you see dashed lines where the volume and page number should be located, it means this case is too recent to appear in the reporter and the volume/page are not yet known.

3. Near the top of the screen, in a parenthetical immediately following the heading assigned to the key number, it indicates that there are 38 headnotes shown. (This number may be larger if additional cases have been added since the book was updated.) This doesn't mean that there are 38 separate cases because sometimes more than one headnote from a case is assigned the same topic

and key number. For example, you will see that *Howard v. Federal Express Corporation* is listed twice for this very reason.

4. Just below the topic heading and number of headnotes is an indication of the jurisdiction from which the cases are derived. Notice that the jurisdiction here is D.C. Circuit. That means that you are only seeing cases from the federal district court for the District of Columbia and any appeals from this court to the D.C. Circuit or the U.S. Supreme Court. The reason Westlaw defaulted to this jurisdiction is because the case we started with, *Yesudian*, was decided by the D.C. Circuit Court. You can change the jurisdiction to anything you want by clicking on the "Change" link located near the jurisdiction information. Go ahead and select the change link, uncheck the box next to D.C. Circuit, and select Illinois. Now click on the blue "Apply" button. You are now viewing only cases from Illinois state courts that have the same topic and key number assigned to one or more headnotes. They all cover the same issue: employee handbooks.

You now should understand how a topic and key number can lead you to cases from any state or federal courts around the country on this topic.

5. At the top of the left column of the screen you should see the word "Filter." (If you don't see the left column, click on the button with >> symbols located in the top-left corner of the screen.) Here you can select different criteria to further limit the list of cases that are displayed. The following options are available.

- You can search within results. This allows you to limit the cases shown to only those that contain a specific word or phrase. For example, in the *Yesudian* case, you may recall that, according to the headnote, the handbook made a distinction between probationary and permanent employees, suggesting that employees that became permanent had additional protections against being fired than someone who is a new employee on probation. We may want to see if any of these cases from Illinois had the same provision. Type the word **permanent** in the "Search within results" box and select the "apply" link. You should see only one headnote now. Note that entering a word or phrase using this option only searches the text of the headnotes for the word or phrase you entered, not the full text of the opinions. It is possible that a case discusses this issue but the editor writing the headnote didn't include the word "permanent" in the headnote. If this happens, you will not see that case. This is a limitation of this system; you are only searching a human created index system to court cases. (All methods of searching for laws have some type of limitation so this doesn't mean that searching terms found in headnotes is not a valuable option; it is also possible that it will lead to cases that are relevant but that you would not locate by just conducting a full-text search of language in the court's opinion.)

  Now, select the "Remove search" link located directly beneath the "Search within results" box and click the "apply" link to return to the full list.

- You can also limit the list of cases to only those that have the same key number assigned. This is not important for us in this example because the only cases we see in our results are cases with this same key number; however, this option is useful in other contexts where you didn't begin with a topic and key number. For example, when you have done a full-text search and have a list of cases, you can limit to one key number to decrease the total number of cases and increase the number of relevant cases. You will see how this works a little later when we discuss full-text searching.

- You can also further refine your search by jurisdiction here. Since we limited our search to only Illinois cases, clicking on this option only lets you limit to the courts within the state of Illinois (the state supreme court and courts of appeals). You can, however, go back and select other jurisdictions. If you have many different ones selected, you could use this option to limit to a subset of the original list.

- You can limit by dates if you know you only want to see cases decided during a specified time period.

This is a brief look at one method you can use to locate additional cases on a topic once you have a relevant case. As already mentioned, there are limitations to this method; the major one is its dependence upon an editor correctly identifying the issue, writing a headnote that accurately describes a point in the case, and assigning the correct topic and key number to that headnote. As you can see, the topic and key number system is like a subject index to all published case law from all courts, federal and state, in the United States.

Another limitation is that, like any attempt to create an index for information, the user is limited to the categories selected by the indexer to organize the law. The categories used to organize the law may be too broad or too narrow for the user's purposes. In our example, if we were only interested in the legal impact of employee manuals that distinguished between probationary and permanent employees, we would need to limit our results to only cases that discuss this because the assigned topic and key number includes many other cases that involve employee manuals that don't include that distinction. As long as you are aware of its limitations, and use it conjunction with other methods, the topic and key number approach is a very useful tool for locating relevant cases.

So far, we have concentrated on Westlaw headnotes and their topic and key number system; what about Lexis? Lexis also has headnotes and they can be used much like Westlaw's system. However, you should be aware of a few differences in how Lexis works compared to Westlaw.

Sign into Lexis and retrieve the *Yesudian* (153 F.3d 731) case like you did on Westlaw. As you look through this case you will see a section labeled "LexisNexis Headnotes." Like Westlaw, each headnote is a brief statement of a point made in the court's opinion. You will also see that each headnote is numbered. Instead of a topic and key number, however, you will see a trail of subjects that are listed above each headnote beginning with the broadest on the left and going down to the narrowest subject heading at the far right. I will refer to this as the subject trail.

Each of these headings in the subject trail, except for the first, is a link to additional information. For example, click on the most specific heading assigned to headnote 8, "Duration of Employment." A menu of two items will appear: Get documents and Create an alert. The first option, "Get documents," will generate a list of cases that are related to the subject matter of that headnote; select the "Get documents" option. You are now viewing a list of cases, much like you did on Westlaw after selecting the topic and key number.

Practically speaking, this acts much like a topic and key number search on Westlaw; in reality, it doesn't really work like that. Instead, it runs a predefined search, created by editors who work for Lexis, that will locate similar cases on the subject.

Why is this? Well, the company that produces Westlaw has existed and been writing headnotes and assigning topics and key numbers since the 1800's. Lexis didn't exist prior to the 1960's and didn't start putting headnotes with cases until the 1990's. By the time Lexis got started, it would have been a major undertaking to have editors write headnotes for every case that already existed in addition to all those cases just being issued. So, rather than write headnotes, they chose to copy and paste language directly from the opinion to create the headnotes. Instead of creating their own topic and key number outline of the law, they assign headings, but the headings don't really lead to lists of cases on their own like the West system. Instead, editors create searches that run in the background to generate a list of cases, most of which are on topic.

Why didn't Lexis just use the West generated headnotes with topic and key numbers? Because this information is proprietary and subject to copyright law. Lexis could not use the headnotes and topics and key numbers without paying significant amounts of money to West, assuming West would agree to such an arrangement at all. By the way, case opinions issued by federal courts cannot be copyrighted so they are in the public domain and anyone can load them into a database if they want.[10] Keep in mind, though, this only applies to the actual opinion; all other items, like headnotes, are commercial editorial enhancements that are protected by copyright.[11]

The important thing to understand is that subject headings assigned to headnotes on Westlaw and Lexis can be used to locate relevant cases. The methods of generating the list of "relevant" cases differs but looks much the same to the end user.

While looking at the list of cases on Lexis, you will also see on the left side of the screen the option to limit the list of cases by words or phrases that appear in the case, jurisdiction, time, and other options. This is very similar to what you saw on Westlaw with one exception. The "search within results" option on Lexis searches the entire opinion, not just the headnotes.

Now, return to the text of the *Yesudian* case on Lexis by using the back button in your web browser. If you look closely at a headnote on Lexis, at the bottom of the headnote headings you will see a link labeled "View more legal topics." Clicking on this link will open more topics that Lexis thinks is relevant to the legal issue discussed in the related headnote.

Following the text of the headnote you will also see another link labeled "Shepardize—Narrow by this Headnote(#)." This uses another tool which is helpful for locating relevant cases but works on a completely different principle than the one under discussion here; we will discuss it next.

This brief introduction should give you a basic idea of how headnotes and the associated subject index works on Westlaw and Lexis. In addition, however, there is another option for finding similar cases when you begin with a known case.

2. Cases That Cite to the Known Case

Return to the *Yesudian* case on Westlaw. You can do this one of several ways.

- Type the cite in the query box at the top of the screen, just as you did when we started,

Or

- Select the "Westlaw" link in the upper-left part of the screen and enter the cite.

Now, scroll down to the same headnote we worked with before, headnote 20. Immediately below the text of the headnote you will see a line that reads "# Cases that cite this headnote." The # symbol represents a number, which reads 2 as I am writing this but may be higher when you look at it. One quick note before we proceed; the terminology in this line is misleading. As I mentioned earlier, **never** cite to the language of a headnote. When it says "# of cases that cite this headnote," it doesn't literally mean that other cases are citing language found in this headnote. This number indicates how many cases cite to the *Yesudian* case regarding the subject matter of this headnote.

Click on the line under headnote 20 that reads "# Cases that cite this headnote." You will now see links to, and brief descriptions of, several cases. (Refer to Exhibit XI-A, which illustrates this screen.) These cases appear here because they cite to the *Yesudian* case and discuss the subject

[10] While materials created by the federal government cannot be copyrighted, states can legally claim copyright protection for their opinions.

[11] An interesting historical note for the curious; in the late 1980's, West claimed copyright in the page numbers assigned to cases in their reporters. Since most cases are published in a West reporter, it is rather difficult to cite a case without using a page number that was created by West. Obviously, if West successfully claimed copyright in page numbers, this would be a serious blow to anyone who wanted to put cases online; anyone could still post the text of cases but they would not be able to indicate page breaks. West lost this legal battle so other online databases are allowed to display page numbers from West reporters. The decision in this case is *Matthew Bender & Co. v. West Publ'g Co.*, 158 F.3d 693 (2d Cir. 1998).

described in the headnote numbered 20 from the *Yesudian* case. In other words, they cite to the part of *Yesudian* that discusses the issue of employee handbooks.

This method of identifying relevant cases is based upon later cases that cite back to the case you started with. In this resource, known as a citator, the list of cases shown is not based on the topic and key number system but on the citation to a case in an opinion issued later in time. It does, however, use headnotes to limit the results to only those cases that discuss the issue that is covered in the relevant headnote. This method of locating relevant cases is an alternative to the topic and key number approach and may alert you to cases you would not discover using only the topic and key number approach previously described.

Each of the commercial databases has its own citator. Westlaw's citator is called KeyCite and Lexis' is called Shepard's. All citators serve the same function of generating a list of cases that cite the case you started with.

To see how this works on Lexis, retrieve the *Yesudian* case on Lexis, scroll down to the relevant headnote (no. 8), and select the link labeled "*Shepardize*—Narrow by this Headnote (#)." At the time of the last update of this book the number in the parenthetical is 7, which indicates that seven cases cite to *Yesudian* and discuss the topic contained in the headnote. Take a few moments to look at the citator displays in KeyCite on Westlaw and Shepard's on Lexis. On the left side of the screen you will see that you can limit the results displayed by selecting various criteria. We will have more to say about this shortly.

The name of the citator is frequently converted to a verb, as in "Shepardize this case." The process of using the citator on Lexis is known as Shepardizing.[12] Many—especially older attorneys—refer to using any citator as Shepardizing even though they might use KeyCite on Westlaw. One could Shepardize a case long before KeyCite existed, because KeyCite didn't exist until the late 1990's. The term Shepardize has stuck solely because of its usage over a long period of time.

Before we look at the specifics of how citators work, some background information about citators will help you better understand this tool. As you already know, the doctrine of stare decisis results in courts citing earlier decisions. This practice of relying on precedent gave rise to the idea that it would be helpful to create a source that allowed a researcher to begin with the cite of a known case, which I will refer to as the **original case**[13], and generate a list of all later cases that cited the original case. We will refer to the cases citing the original case as **citing cases**. They are also known as **treatment** cases since they discuss the original case; we will discuss this aspect in greater detail later. As you can see, citators are based on a very simple concept; they take a case and generate a list of cases that cited the original case. Citators serve various functions, one of which is to aid in locating other cases discussing the same issue(s) as the original case. The other function of citators will be covered later.

The cases that cite the original case, known as citing cases, are completely unrelated to the original. They involve completely different litigants in a case decided later in time than the original case; the only thing they share is a common issue or rule of law.

a. Limitations and Other Problems Associated with Citators When Used to Locate Additional Relevant Law

Citators are generated by computers today; the computer picks cites of cases out of an opinion and creates a list of the citing cases. This process is very mechanical with little or no human involvement.

---

[12] Shepard's was the earliest citator, dating back the 1800's. As a result, it is the only one to ever be available in print. The online version is much easier to use than the print.

[13] Throughout this section you will see bolded terms or phrases; these are important concepts. A list of these terms, with definitions, is included at the end of this section.

As a result, citators have a few limitations. Additionally, citators have other limitations because they list only citing cases, i.e., cases decided after the original case was decided. What do these limitations mean for the legal researcher?

If the original case you read is not a major case on a topic, it may not be cited by very many, if any, later cases. The important cases on the topic may not cite your original case because they either predate the original case or, if decided after the original case, did not consider it important enough to cite. When beginning your research, you will have no idea whether the case you started with is an important one in the subject area involved.[14] The point here is that sometimes citators will lead to lots of great cases and sometimes they won't. Because of this limitation, **do not Shepardize one case and assume that the list of citing cases is all that exists on the subject**. This problem can only be overcome by following both options listed below:

- Use the citator with multiple cases to locate as many cases as possible.
- Always use citators in conjunction with other methods, such as the topic and key number method discussed previously. You are asking for trouble if you rely solely on one method to locate relevant law and fail to use the alternatives discussed in this book.

Another option that helps alleviate the problem of only seeing cases decided after the original case is the **Table of Authorities**. With a case on the screen in either Lexis or Westlaw, one of the options, in the row of options at the top of the screen, is labeled "Table of Authorities." Selecting this link opens a list of cases that the original case cited. These are cases decided prior to the original case. These might also lead to more important cases on the subject. We will discuss this option in more detail later.

b. Deciding Which Treatment Cases You Must Read

Shepard's and KeyCite listings may contain many citing cases. For example, the 1954 decision in *Brown v. Bd. of Education* has been cited over 2000 times in subsequent cases. However, not all treatment cases listed need to be read.

- The original case likely discusses multiple issues. Since you are not interested in all the issues, you only need to read treatment cases that discuss the issue you are researching. It is a waste of your time to read citing cases which discuss irrelevant issues from the original case. On Westlaw, there are only two cases related to this specific issue that cite to *Yesudian*. Clicking on the link following headnote 20 automatically limits the list of citing cases to only those that cited *Yesudian* regarding the subject matter of headnote 20. However, if you return to *Yesudian* on Westlaw and mouseover the "Citing References" link at the top of the screen, a menu of items will appear. The first item listed is cases with a number inside a parenthetical. This indicates the number of times *Yesudian* has been cited in cases across the United States. Click on the cases link. At the time of this writing, *Yesudian* was cited 313 times in cases. This list includes all issues, not just the issue in which you are interested.

  Out of all the citing cases, how can you identify which citing cases discuss the issue of interest to you? Two options are available; they can be used alone or in combination to limit the cases that must be read. They are:

  1. Identify the headnotes in the original case that discuss the topic of interest and examine only those citing cases that discuss the subject matter covered in those headnotes. As we have already discussed, select the link below the relevant headnote

[14] A recent tool added by Lexis can help you determine how important a specific case is to the subject. We will discuss this later.

like we did when viewing the *Yesudian* case. This method works on both Lexis and Westlaw.

2. Read only those citing cases that include a specific term or phrase in the opinion. You can use this approach on both Lexis and Westlaw by retrieving the full list of citing cases and then entering terms in the "Search within results" box. Don't confuse this with the limiting feature we used earlier with the topic and key number approach. In the citator it searches the full text of all citing opinions for the terms, not just the headnotes assigned to the cases.

- Another tool to help you determine which treatment cases are worth reading is the indication known as **depth of treatment**; Westlaw uses the phrase "depth of treatment" while Lexis labels it "Discussion." These different labels all refer to the same issue, which is how much the citing cases discuss the original case. Many citing cases make only a passing reference to the original case without any analysis or commentary. These are not helpful and can be skipped. Read only cases that include substantive discussion of the original case.

One word of caution here; don't put too much stock in the ranking systems. Lexis and Westlaw appear to attempt to determine how much the original opinion is discussed, not just how many times it's cited. However, if you retrieve the list of citing cases in both services and sort the list by importance, you will frequently see a rather large difference in the ranking of the citing cases.

- Limit citing cases by jurisdiction. If you are only interested in Illinois state law, then limit your search to Illinois state court cases. Cases from Michigan don't matter that much for Illinois law. However, if Illinois has no rule on the issue, you may wish to look at other states as models of what Illinois might adopt.

An efficient researcher will combine these criteria to minimize the number of cases that need to be read while not missing any critical cases.

3. Important Concepts Related to Using Citators to Locate Relevant Cases

Citing case—a case decided later in time that cites or references an earlier case. Also known as a treatment case.

Depth of treatment—how much attention a citing case gives to the case it cites (original case); treatment can vary between a mere cite with no discussion to a detailed discussion of the original case.

Original case—the case you are reading and Shepardizing. When Shepardizing a case, it helps to keep clear who is citing whom by using the phrase "original case" to reference the case that is being Shepardized. Those cases which the original case relied upon and cited are called "**cited cases**" and those that were decided after the original case and that cite to the original case are called "citing cases."

Table of Authorities—a table that lists those cases cited (relied upon) by a case. These cases all precede the original case in time.

Treatment case—see citing case.

Summary

1. Options for locating cases when you know of a relevant case.
   A. Topic and key number approach (human created subject index).
      1. Locate the headnote(s) that describe the relevant issue.
      2. Identify the topic and key number (Westlaw) or subject trail (Lexis) assigned to the headnote(s).
      3. Select the topic link to see a list of other cases that cover a similar subject.
      4. Narrow the list of results by jurisdiction, date, and/or words that appear in the headnotes.
   B. Locate cases that cite to the known case on the same subject you are researching.
      1. This involves using a citator.
         a. Shepard's on Lexis.
         b. KeyCite on Westlaw.
      2. On Lexis and Westlaw, locate the relevant headnote in the known case.
      3. Select the link below the relevant headnote that retrieves a list of cases that cite to the known case regarding the same subject covered by the headnote.
      4. Apply additional filters (jurisdiction, date, words in the citing opinions, etc.) to limit the list as applicable to your problem.
      5. Be aware of the limitations of citators.
         a. The original case (the one you started with) may not be a major case and may not be cited by very many cases.
         b. To overcome this potential problem, Shepardize every relevant case you find to enlarge the universe of relevant cases.
      6. Only read those cases that are important.
         a. Depth of treatment helps you eliminate cases that only mention but do not discuss your case.
         b. Limit by jurisdiction to identify only those cases that are mandatory.
         c. Further limit by specific terms or phrases that appear in the citing cases.
2. *The Bluebook* specifies in its rules how to cite to court decisions.

Assignment 3

The following questions are based on material covered in section XI.A. of the course reading.

1. Your client is a relative of Margot Kidder, a deceased Hollywood actress. The relative tells you that a third-party is selling dolls that look like Margot and he wants to prevent them from making money off her likeness. Margot resided in Tennessee when she died and the company selling the dolls is registered in Tennessee. Another member of your firm found a case on point at 733 S.W.2d 89.

   A. Use Westlaw to answer the following questions until directed to switch to another database. Which headnote in the known case directly addresses the issue of whether a celebrity's right of publicity continues to exist after the death of the celebrity and can be enforced by relatives of the celebrity because the celebrity commercially exploited the right while alive?

B. On which page or pages in the opinion can you read the discussion of the subject matter covered by the relevant headnote you identified above?

C. Cite to this case, including a pincite to the page or pages identified in B. above. (A pincite is a reference to specific pages within an opinion; see B10.1.2 in the *Bluebook* for details.)

D. The reading material identified two different methods you can use with a known case to locate additional cases, one of which is based on the topic and key number.

1. Using the topic and key number approach, how many Tennessee (state and federal) cases does Westlaw identify as related to the subject matter of this case?

2. Assume that you want to see cases from California. How many cases are related in that jurisdiction? (Be sure to check the box in front of the "Include Related Federal" link when you select California to get both federal and California state cases.)

3. Please specify the exact number of federal cases and the exact number of California state cases you found.

4. Look at the California state case decided in 1979. This case was decided early in the historical development of the legal doctrine of the right of publicity. As a result, the court used various terms to refer to the right: right of value, right of publicity, and right of privacy. Which headnote specifically mentions "right of value" and states that it does not survive the death of the celebrity?

5. Why did this case appear in the results you generated? Provide as specific of an answer as possible.

6. Write a cite to the California state case, including a pincite to the pages of the opinion that discuss the subject matter covered by the headnote identified in 5. above.

E. Now, retrieve the case at 733 S.W.2d 89 on Lexis.

1. Which headnote discusses the issue of whether the right of publicity is descendible?

2. Select the link related to this relevant headnote labeled "Right of Publicity" and retrieve the cases (documents). How many California state cases does Lexis list that discuss the same subject as the case you retrieved? Please specify each step you took to locate the answer to this question.

3. Does the 1979 California case found on Westlaw appear in the list found in Lexis?

4. What other method involving a predefined search is available on Lexis for locating relevant cases?

5. Starting with the case at 733 S.W.2d 89, use the option you identified above in 4 to retrieve related cases. Does the 1979 California case appear in the list of cases using this option?

F. The other method of locating additional cases on the same subject is the citing cases method.

1. Return to Westlaw and retrieve the case at 733 S.W.2d 89. How many cases cite to this case on the topic of whether a celebrity's right of publicity survives their death?

2. Which jurisdiction(s) are these from?

3. Can you have Westlaw locate related cases from other jurisdictions that are different than the ones shown in the initial list you retrieved? Why or why not?

4. One of the cases in the list was decided by a Missouri state court? Why did this case appear in this list?

5. Write a cite for the Missouri state case from 4 above. (No pincite is needed in this cite.)

2. There is a third method of locating cases on the same subject when you have a known case. Give it some thought and identify this third method if you can. (Hint: think about what other types of information you find in a case opinion and how it might help you locate other related cases.)

B. LOCATING CASES BY SUBJECT WITHOUT A KNOWN CASE

So far, we have discussed two different methods of locating relevant cases when you have a known case. What if you don't know of any case on point and need to locate cases purely by subject? How can this be accomplished?

If you have no other information than the general subject matter, the following options are available.

- Locate an article or book that discusses the subject and provides cites to relevant cases or any other laws that are applicable.
- Locate the relevant topic and key number and use it to locate relevant cases.
- Search the full-text of cases in the legal databases.

The first method, locating an article or book that discusses the subject and cites to relevant sources, is an excellent way to begin and one that I highly recommend. We will discuss this option in greater detail when we talk more about locating articles and books, which we refer to as "secondary" sources.

You can also use the topic and key number system, or the comparable approach on Lexis, to locate cases even if you don't have a relevant case to start with.

Lastly, we will discuss details about conducting a full-text search of court opinions using the legal databases.

1. Subject Index Approach to Locating Relevant Cases

We discussed earlier the topic and key number system and how to use it when you already have a relevant case. However, you don't need a case already in hand to use the topic and key number system. You can begin your search by looking for relevant topics and key numbers on Westlaw (or the equivalent on Lexis) and then examine the cases to which the topic and key number are assigned.

Return to the main search screen on Westlaw; this is the screen you see when you first log onto Westlaw. Under the search box near the top of the screen, you will see several links; one is labeled "Content types." Select this option.

Select the link labeled "Key Numbers." You should now see an alphabetical list of topics. The numbers immediately prior to each topic is the numerical designation for that topic on Westlaw. Don't confuse this number with the key number. Key numbers are assigned to subtopics within a topic.

As we begin our search for relevant cases, take note of the jurisdiction. Just below the search box at the top of the list of topics and key numbers is a line that reads "Jurisdiction selected: #######." This will default to whatever jurisdiction you last selected. So that we are all seeing the same cases, let's limit our search for Illinois cases only. If the Jurisdiction label doesn't read Illinois, click on the "Change Jurisdiction" link, deselect whatever jurisdiction was already selected (by clicking on the jurisdiction with the check mark in front of it) and then select Illinois. Be sure to also check the box next to the line that reads "Include related federal," which is located below the list of state jurisdictions. This will include decisions from federal district courts located in Illinois, any cases decided by the 7th Circuit Court of Appeals that originated in a federal district court in Illinois, and any cases from a federal district court in Illinois that were successfully appealed to the U.S. Supreme Court. Finish the selection of jurisdiction by clicking on the "Apply" button at the bottom.

You have three options for locating topic and key numbers that are assigned to relevant cases.

1. Browse through the topics looking for one that may be relevant,
2. Search the terms associated with topics and key numbers, or
3. Search the text of headnotes.

Let's see how each option works while searching for a relevant topic and key number related to the issue of whether employment manuals constitute contracts between employees and employers. To use the browsing method (#1 above), you must think about which larger subject would include your issue. In our problem, one option is contracts and it seems logical that it might include relevant cases. Labor or employment law is the legal context for the issue so this is also a possible subject heading. If you aren't sure which topic is relevant, you would need to click on each potentially relevant topic and browse the subheadings within that topic.

To save time, the topic of Labor and Employment is the right one for our search. Select this topic and browse the subheadings. Key number 49 covers "Manuals, handbook, and policy statements." This looks promising and, as we already know, is in fact relevant. Click on the plus symbol in front of 49. Now click on key number 50; you will see a list of cases and headnotes from those cases. A quick scan of the headnotes confirms this is the right topic and key number.

Now, let's search the terms used to describe a topic and/or key number (#2 above). To do this, go back to the first screen that lists all the topic and key numbers. You will see a search box located at the end of the list of topics that is labeled "Title Search." For your search, enter the term "handbook" in this box. The results will display a list of topics and key numbers that contain the word handbook. You will see Labor and Employment, key number 49, listed among the results. If you select key number 49 you will then see a detailed list of key numbers; selecting key number 50 will display a list of cases.

Remember, this is only searching terms that occur in the descriptions assigned to the topic and key numbers. It is not searching either the text of headnotes nor the full text of the opinion. A search for "employee handbook" returns no results because that phrase does not appear in the terms assigned to the topics and key numbers. However, just searching for handbook does work in this search. When searching only the terms associated with a topic and key number, you must use more general terms.

Finally, let's search the text of the headnotes (#3 above). To do this, go back to the first screen that lists all the topic and key numbers. You will see a search box located at the very top of the screen that contains the words "Search for Key Numbers relevant to your issue." Enter the search "employee handbook" in this box. After entering the phrase, including the quotes, check that Illinois (state and federal) is the selected jurisdiction. Now, click on the search button. You should see a list of relevant topics and key numbers. Select key number 50 under the topic Labor and Employment. You will see a list of cases; somewhere in this list should appear a case entitled *Dawson v. City of Geneseo*. Selecting this case will take you directly to the headnotes in the *Dawson* case to which the topic of Labor and Employment is assigned. As a reminder, this option searches the text of the headnotes for your search terms.

The search we just ran is looking for any occurrence of the phrase "employee handbook" in the text of headnotes. Searching for just the term "handbook" would also work when searching the text of headnotes but will get you many more results than searching for the phrase "employee handbook." Just keep in mind that the narrower the universe of terms you are searching, the more selective you must be in your search terms. The smallest set, a list of terms used to describe a topic and key numbers, requires more general terms than when searching the text of headnotes.

Regardless of which of the three methods you used to identify the topic and key number that is relevant, once you get to the page where cases and headnotes are listed, you can select the case to retrieve the full text. When you retrieve the text of a case, the database will automatically take you to the headnote that is assigned the relevant topic and key number.

Also, remember that we are only seeing cases from the jurisdiction you selected (or was selected by default). You can always see cases from any jurisdiction to which the same topic and key number is assigned by changing the jurisdiction at the top of the screen.

The list of cases, with the text of the headnote, you are viewing here is also available in printed volumes called Digests. If someone references a print version of a West Digest, it is simply a printed list of cites to cases, along with relevant headnote(s), organized by topic and key number. A printed digest is many volumes organized alphabetically by topic and within each topic by key number. It is unlikely that you will have to use the printed Digest but some firms may still have them.

This is how one uses the topic and key number system to locate cases purely by subject. Lexis has a similar system of locating relevant cases, though it isn't directly tied into their subjects assigned to headnotes. Instead, Lexis runs a predefined search that is designed to locate relevant cases. Log into Lexis and let's see how this works.

Once you are logged into Lexis and are looking at the main search screen (click on the "Lexis+" link at the top left if you don't see the main search screen), locate the section labeled "Explore." This is located about half-way down the screen. Select the tab labeled "Topics." You should see a list of various topics, one of which is "Labor & Employment Law." Select this subject.

If you scan down the list, you will see a heading "Employment Handbooks." Expand this subject by clicking on the + symbol in front of it and then select the subheading labeled "Employee Benefits." Lexis generates this list by running a predefined search. It doesn't work exactly like topic and key numbers on Westlaw but it looks the same. You can then limit by jurisdiction using the "Court" filter, which is available on the left side of the screen.

Once you find a relevant case, you can proceed as we did in the previous section. Enough about subject indexes to cases using the major legal databases. Let's turn our attention to another option, searching the full text of cases.

2. Full Text Searching of Court Opinions

The major legal databases (Westlaw, Lexis) permit the searching of the full text of cases. While these databases offer many advantages, full-text searching is probably one of the biggest. Searching by topic and key number using the print digests has been around for about 150 years but full-text searching was not possible until the advent of computerized databases.

Let's look for cases in Illinois state involving the same issue: whether an employee handbook is a constructive contract. Log into Westlaw, or if you are already in the database, click on the Westlaw icon in the upper left corner of the screen. Either way, you should be at the initial screen. To search the cases of a specific state, Illinois in this case, select the "State Materials" tab near the top of the screen, select Illinois, and then select the link labeled "All Illinois State cases." Now, in the search box at the top of the screen, enter the words "employee handbook constructive contract" **without** the quotes. Press the enter key or click on the search button to the right of the search box.

There are approximately 90 cases that satisfy this search. You should once more see a list of case names with court and citation information followed by an excerpt from the case with the search terms highlighted. This looks much like the lists we have seen before. However, this time, the list shows all cases that contain the words you included in the search anywhere in the headnotes or the opinion itself, not just the headnotes only.

Retrieve the *Duldulao v. Saint Mary of Nazareth Hosp. Center* case by clicking on the name of the case. You will see the beginning of the case and multiple occurrences of the words you searched for, which are highlighted. After the preliminary information about the case and a synopsis of the case, you will see the headnotes assigned by the editors. Headnote number 2 has the same topic and key number we have seen before related to this subject (Labor and Employment k 50).

Let's look at the options you have when viewing a case on the screen. At the top-left part of the screen is a label that reads "# of ## results" with a back and forward arrow on either side. This allows you to go to the next or previous case in the list of cases your search retrieved. If you want to start over and run a different search, you can delete the search you just ran and type a new search in the search box, which is located at the very top of the screen.

If you want to see other cases assigned the same topic and key number, you can click on the topic and key number assigned to headnote 2 (231Hk50). Recall we did this earlier when we talked about using a known case to locate other cases. Just below the text of the headnote is the link that says "### Cases that cite this headnote." This is the citator link we spoke of earlier, yet another way to locate additional relevant cases.

You can now begin to see that you have several different methods available to locate a relevant case by subject and, once you have a relevant case, several ways to locate additional cases on point. Not every method of locating a case will generate useful results but you should be able to find relevant cases by using one or more of the methods discussed here.

a. Natural Language

When searching Westlaw, you can search the full text of the case by just entering words, just like we did in our previous search. When you type words and run the search, Westlaw will automatically run what is known as natural language search. In other words, it takes the words (and phrases if you place quotes around two or more words) and runs them through an algorithm that West has developed.[15] When running a natural language search, you won't know exactly why you got the results you received. However, the key is that you will hopefully find some that are relevant which you can then use to find others.

Return to the screen of results generated by the search we just ran on Westlaw. If you look near the top of the screen, you will see a box labeled "Sort." The world "Relevance" should appear in this box. In other words, the algorithm has ordered the results with the most relevant case listed first and the least relevant last. Relevance here is determined by the algorithm. Hopefully, its analysis of what is relevant corresponds to your own. The natural language search engine will also drop terms, so some of the cases that appear later in the list will not contain all your search terms. Terms that were dropped are listed after the synopsis of the case; you can tell it that the dropped term must be in the results if you wish. In this situation, we don't need to use this option since the cases it has retrieved are relevant to the issue.

Another advantage to natural language searching is that the algorithms are sufficiently smart to pick up variations of the terms you enter in your search (plurals and other variations of the terms). This feature allows retrieval of cases that use synonyms of the words in your search, providing greater flexibility in searching. The algorithms are getting better (smarter?) with time and usage based in part upon the cases previous searchers looked at that were retrieved by similar searches.

[15] The exact criteria used by the algorithm is a trade secret so we can't know the exact search that was run by Westlaw. The same is true for natural language searches on Lexis.

Lexis works very much like Westlaw; it offers basic natural language searching using proprietary algorithms developed by Lexis. Running the same natural language search on Lexis that you ran on Westlaw will get you some of the same cases and some new ones that you didn't see on Westlaw. Try running the same search on Lexis and compare the results.

b. Terms and Connectors Searching

If you know the exact terms you want to search for in the database and you want it to search only for those terms, you can use an advanced search. Return to the list of cases from your last search on Westlaw and scroll to the top of the list; you should now see, to the right of the search box, the word "Advanced." Click on this. You will now see a template that allows you to enter specific terms. This is also known as a terms and connectors search because it allows you to use connectors to specify the relationship that must exist between words. For example, if we were doing this same search using terms and connectors, you could enter the same words in the search box labeled "All of these terms." After entering your terms, look at the search box at the top of the screen; your terms have automatically been placed in the search box and the connector (& or and) has been placed between each word. The "and" (& on Westlaw) will require that all four words appear in the same document.

On the right side of the screen you will see a list of connectors that can be used. The & (and) connector is quite broad; a search run with the & connector requires all the words to appear in the same document but they can be anywhere in the document. On the other hand, use of the /s (same sentence) connector requires all terms to appear in the same sentence. You should keep this in mind when formulating a terms and connectors search.

Terms and connectors searching also offers truncation; an exclamation mark (!) at the end of a word allows for automatic truncation, which will retrieve any occurrence of the letters you entered followed by any number of letters.

Lexis also offers an advanced search feature that allows you to specify the exact terms to be searched and the exact relationship between those terms much like Westlaw.

A terms and connectors search does not drop terms and does not look for alternatives; it is very literal and retrieves only those cases that match exactly your search query. You must be careful in formulating this type of search because of the nature of human language. The same idea can be expressed using various combinations of words and a single word often has multiple meanings. Terms and connectors are best used when you have familiarity with a subject. If you are new to the subject and don't know how courts might refer to the issue, it can be quite challenging. Natural language searching can help with this, as you have just seen. However, it doesn't work miracles and if the terms you use in your search are not close, you may get nothing that is relevant. In the situation where you are not familiar with the terminology used in relevant cases, consulting a secondary source (book or article) is a good option before searching for cases directly online.

Frankly, instances where you need to use the terms and connectors method of searching are diminishing as the algorithms improve with time. This previous sentence may be somewhat controversial for some but I believe this is an honest appraisal of the options available for searching the full text of case law.

c. Working with the Results of a Search

Once you have a list of results from a search, you have several options to customize the list and see only those cases that are likely most important for your research. For example, you can limit by date, limit by jurisdiction, retrieve only cases that contain an additional term or phrase, etc. Both Lexis and Westlaw offer these options for limiting results on the left side of the page.

For example, return to Westlaw and the results you found when using the natural language search engine for cases discussing employee handbook and constructive contracts. If we are only interested in those cases that also contain the word permanent, simply enter that word in the "Search within results" box and search. Recall, this will find cases in which the employee manual makes distinctions between a new employee and permanent employees.[16]

d. Full-Text Searching: The Good and Bad

As already discussed, full-text searching provides much power but it also has its limitations. When the searcher isn't familiar with the subject, much time and money can be wasted using full-text searching. For this reason, if you are researching an area of the law that is unfamiliar to you, I highly recommend consulting books, articles, and other sources, such as AI, that discuss the law and cite to relevant cases and other forms of the law. As a matter of fact, the most common complaint by law firms about summer associates and new attorney hires is that they are too quick to jump online and start searching full text instead of learning as much as they can from secondary sources (books, articles, any source that is not a law) first. Running full-text searches without knowing the subject can be very expensive, depending upon the type of contract your firm has with Westlaw, and all law firms frown on this for obvious reasons. This is also frequently a waste of your time, which is also money.

e. Features to Assist in Searching

The databases now have search assist features that make searching easier. Return to Westlaw once more and be sure you are limited to Illinois only cases. Begin typing the following search: employee handbook. You may have noticed earlier when we ran this same search that a suggested search drops down. In this case it reads "Does an employee handbook create a contract?—Illinois." Selecting this option will generate a list of results.

After running a search, a couple of cases appear at the top of the list and the database asks if this case was helpful. By clicking yes or no, you are helping the algorithm learn what individuals who type those words in a search are looking for and will help provide more relevant cases for future searchers.

If you want to learn more about online searching, tutorials are available online. You can access these tutorials on Westlaw by scrolling to the bottom of the first screen you see after you log-in; you should see a link labeled "Training and Support." On Lexis, there is a "Help" link in the upper right portion of the initial screen after log-in.

Summary

1. These options are available when you need to locate cases on a topic.

   A. Locate an article or book (secondary source) that discusses the issue.

   B. Use the subject index approach and locate the relevant topic and key number (or comparable arrangement on Lexis).

   C. Search the full text of cases.

2. On Westlaw, you can access the topic and key number index system using several methods.

   A. Browsing the topics for relevant key numbers.

   B. Searching the terms assigned to the topic and key numbers.

---

[16] This will actually search for the occurrence of the word permanent anywhere in the opinion, so it won't be limited to only those cases where the word permanent appeared with or near the word manual. You just must look at the results to determine which cases are relevant.

C. Searching the text of headnotes and using the topic and key numbers assigned to the relevant headnotes.

3. Lexis works much the same way except when you select a topic assigned to a headnote it runs a predefined search which generates the list of cases.

4. Full-text searching can be accomplished using either natural language or terms and connectors.

A. Natural language takes the terms you enter and runs them through an algorithm to produce the list of results.

1. The algorithms are proprietary information so you can't know exactly why the results you see were found.

2. Natural language will drop terms so not all terms will appear.

B. Terms and Connectors allows you to specify the exact terms and the relationship between those terms.

1. This option is known as advanced searching.

2. Only those documents that satisfy the exact requirements of your search will be retrieved.

3. No terms are dropped, as may happen when running a natural language search.

5. Full-text searching can be a challenge and you may get cases you never expected because:

A. The same idea can be expressed using different words and phrases.

B. The same word can have multiple meanings.

6. When you have a list of results from a search, you can use several options to limit the results.

A. Jurisdiction.

B. Date.

C. Word or words that appear in the opinion (this option can be used to further narrow the search).

7. Lexis and Westlaw databases are now suggesting searches as you type. Be sure to watch for this as it may save you considerable effort if others have run similar searches before you.

Assignment 4

The following questions are based on material covered in sections XI.B.1 and .2 of the reading.

1. You are working on a case involving an employee who was terminated from his job because he refused an order from a supervisor to drive a company owned truck for which he did not have the proper license as required by the state. This took place in Milwaukee, Wisconsin. The employee did not have a written contract of employment and was not provided with an employee handbook that might be considered a constructive contract. As a result, this is a true case of employment-at-will. Such employees normally can be released for almost any reason and have no legal recourse available when released from the job. Can the employee in this case bring a lawsuit for wrongful discharge?

A. Search for a relevant topic and key number on Westlaw, following one of the three methods listed in section XI.B.1. Use the terms provided in the problem for your search. Which topic and key number(s) is (are) relevant?

B. Identify the easiest way to limit the list of results to cases decided by a Wisconsin state court (excluding federal courts in Wisconsin)?

C. How many cases were decided by a Wisconsin state court?

D. With the list of cases under a specific key number on screen, look at the top of the screen. You should see a trail that shows you where you are in the topic and key number system. The beginning of this trail looks like this: Home>West Key Number System>. In this trail you should see the heading "Adverse Employment Action" followed by a range of key numbers. Click on this link. This will display the surrounding key numbers under the topic you selected.

By glancing at the headings assigned to the key numbers in this part of the topic, do they cover only adverse employment action regarding at-will employees or do they cover all employees generally, regardless of whether they are at-will or not? (Hint: we haven't discussed this but look at the list of key numbers and make your best educated guess.)

E. How could you limit the list to only those cases that specifically discuss at-will employees? Explain.

F. Using Lexis, select the "Topics" option on the main screen. Select the "Labor & Employment" link. Which heading on the screen looks relevant to your research?

G. Under the "Public Policy" heading. limit your search to only Wisconsin cases. Approximately how many do you find?

H. If you were filing a case involving this subject in a Wisconsin state trial court, decisions from which court(s) would be mandatory? I'm not asking for specific cases; just identify the courts whose decisions would be mandatory. Explain your answer.

2. Time to research on your own with minimal guidance from me. You are practicing in California and represent a client who has come to you regarding malpractice by her previous attorney. She discussed this issue with the previous attorney and he told her that, even if he did commit malpractice, the statute of limitations had already run out and would prevent litigation about the matter. She knows that the clock for bringing a legal malpractice has run out if it began when she suffered the actual injury caused by the act constituting malpractice. However, she didn't realize the malpractice happened until later. If the clock began when she discovered the malpractice, she still has time to bring the suit within the time allowed. You must answer the question of when the clock for the statute of limitations on professional malpractice begins to run. Is it when the act is committed or when the person harmed learns of the act? California law applies and you will file, if litigation is warranted, in a California state trial court.

Using either Lexis or Westlaw and the methods we have discussed, please identify two cases on point. Describe the steps you took to identify the cases and what is the relevant topic and key number on Westlaw or topic on Lexis?

f. Artificial Intelligence in Legal Research

Now that we have covered the basics of locating relevant cases, let's turn our attention to the use of AI in locating cases. A brief introduction to the use of AI in legal research is necessary since AI differs significantly from the traditional methods of legal research. AI is proving to be a revolutionary tool for the legal profession; it is currently used to perform several functions, including legal research, document review, and drafting of legal documents to name a few. There is little doubt that AI will continue to make attorneys more efficient in various aspects of the practice of law and will have a major impact on the profession.

Since this book is an introduction to the fundamentals of legal research, I will deal exclusively with the use of AI for legal research. The popular conception is that AI will conduct legal research for the user, thereby eliminating the need to learn the details of research discussed in this book. This is a dangerous misconception. Relying exclusively on AI as the final source of information will leave the researcher open to many issues, including charges of malpractice and incompetence. It no doubt is a great place to begin legal research and can save much time when beginning to understand an unfamiliar area of the law. However, it should only be used as a place to begin and does not relieve the attorney of the duty to continue research using the various tools to find all relevant laws.

Answers generated by AI, depending on the query, usually provide a brief discussion of the topic and cites to various legal authorities. The discussion may be relevant and the legal authorities cited may be useful for the issue. However, it is imperative that the legal sources are verified. The verification of which I speak involves two components. The first part involves verifying that the legal authorities referenced by AI exist. AI can sometimes be deceptive by referencing cases and other legal authorities that do not exist. AI will sometimes hallucinate and create something out of thin air. As a result, the existence of every source that AI references must be confirmed. We will concentrate in this book on the use of the AI chatbots created by Westlaw (CoCounsel) and Lexis (Protégé). Since Protégé and CoCounsel have been trained using primarily legal sources, one would expect they would be less prone to hallucinating than the general chatbots that have been exposed to a much broader universe of information. While they are less prone to hallucinate, they are not exempt from this problem. One study has found that these specialized models hallucinate as often as one-third of the time.[17]

After verifying that each authority referenced actually exists, the user must also verify that the sources referenced actually support what AI claims. AI's description of what a legal authority supports can be misleading if not outright wrong. Additionally, in situations where the common law has evolved, such as being superseded by a statute, AI will often discuss the earlier common law as if it remains valid.

Because of these issues, lawyers who relied exclusively upon output generated by AI without locating and reading cases cited have been fined and sanctioned by courts. The traditional tools described in this book should be used to verify the existence of relevant legal authority referenced by AI and lead to a complete understanding of the subject. Legal competence demands the use of all available tools and your analytical skills when determining the state of the law on an issue.

It is always helpful to remember how AI functions. It is easy when reading the output generated by AI to feel like you are having an exchange with an "intelligent" being. However, we know the answers generated by AI are based upon how often words appear near each other in the documents scanned by AI. Continually remind yourself of this when working with AI to avoid being lulled into a false sense of security.

Trying to teach the art of query formulation for AI is rather challenging. There are so many variations in how a specific question can be asked and the output from AI will obviously vary based upon the exact query used. Sometimes AI will even generate different answers to the exact same query. Despite this issue, I will try to point out the most efficient use of AI when searching for each of the different sources of information, including searching for court opinions, statutes, administrative law, and secondary sources. I will make suggestions about how to formulate the best query to generate the most useful information given the information known to the researcher. Just like searching the databases using the other tools discussed in this book, it can be challenging to determine the best terms to include in a search, especially when one is unfamiliar with the subject. AI does appear to be good tool for finding relevant information even when using very general terms. For example, explaining the situation in the query without use of specific legal terminology will often provide useful results. We will see how this works when searching for specific types of legal authority.

The important thing to learn is how AI can assist in performing legal research while also remaining aware of its limitations. AI is best thought of as a customizable secondary source, such as an article.

---

[17] Varun Magish et al, *Hallucination-Free? Assessing the Reliability of Leading AI Legal Research Tools*, 22 J. Empirical Legal Stud. 216, 240 (2025).

Just as in any online searching, the terms you select to represent the concepts of your issue and how you organize those terms in your query will impact the results you obtain from AI. However, always remember that when AI generates an answer to your query, it is not a subject specialist. The report generated by AI will at best be incomplete and possibly inaccurate, at least in part.

Links to the AI component of both Westlaw (CoCounsel) and Lexis (Protégé) are located in the upper right portion of the main search screen. Beginning with the *Yesudian v. Howard University* case mentioned before, you could enter a query similar to this: Starting with *Yesudian v. Howard University*, 153 F.3d 731, find other cases that discuss whether an employee handbook can be considered a constructive contract.

You can also just ask AI the general question without mentioning a specific case; this method seems to generate similar results, so it isn't clear that mentioning the case in your query makes much difference to the final report. This is part of the issue with using AI; you never know with certainty how varying the terms in the query will change the results. You will need to experiment to determine what produces the best results for your query. You can also follow up an initial query with additional questions designed to focus on specifics.

Note that Westlaw will conduct the search in the jurisdiction you have selected on the main search screen unless you specify a different one in your query. On Lexis, if the query asks about the law in a specific jurisdiction and it differs from the one selected on your main search page, it will ask which jurisdiction you want to use for the query.

As mentioned earlier, a general question can be asked to specifically locate cases. AI seems to be good at suggesting areas of the law that correlate with facts. For example, run the following query: According to Tennessee law, can an heir of a celebrity prevent use of the celebrity's picture. This query will generate cases that deal with the legal doctrine of the right of publicity even though you did not include the specific legal phrase in your query. You can include the legal phrase in your query if you know it. For example, in this query you could include the phrase right of publicity. You could also increase precision by asking whether the heir can control the commercial use of the celebrity's likeness. The simple query I posted above illustrates the power of AI. You generally want to include all relevant information that you know in your query but just including facts will often retrieve information that is useful and will often identify the legal doctrine(s) related to the facts.

When formulating queries, the most efficient query will contain as much about the legal problem as possible. You should still consider using books and articles when beginning to research a new topic. AI does not make secondary sources obsolete when you are unfamiliar with a subject area, but it does offer greater flexibility. Beginning with AI and then going to a good law review article will be most beneficial. A more general query may return a lot of information in which you are not interested, depending on the subject matter. The more specific you are in the query, the more likely the results will be relevant.

Ai will also generally reference other types of legal authorities if they are relevant. Even though you may ask for cases on a subject, you will likely get a reference to a relevant statute if one exists. This is not guaranteed so looking for statutes using the traditional search methods discussed later in this book is necessary. Asking AI for the laws that apply in a certain jurisdiction, instead of asking for cases only, will increase the chances of finding statutes and other forms of law besides cases.

As you use AI on Lexis and Westlaw, you will notice that CoCounsel takes considerably more time than Protégé to generate an answer to a query. However, it also seems to provide more information about background and related issues than Protégé. If you have access to both, it is useful to compare the results obtained.

3. Types of Secondary Sources Available and Tools Used to Locate Relevant Information

We just discussed how important it is to use explanations of the law (secondary sources in the form of books, articles, etc.) if you are researching a subject with which you are not familiar. Not only can these secondary sources explain the law and the terminology used in the area, but they will also cite to primary sources that can help you get started in your research.

Remember, secondary sources include everything that is not primary. Secondary sources are **not** the law; they discuss and cite to various types of laws. They can be very useful for background information, especially if you are not familiar with the subject area. They can also provide detailed analysis of a subject and cites to primary sources.

There are several types of secondary sources, some of which have counterparts in the non-legal world while others are unique. Below is a list of the different types of secondary sources along with the tools that allow you to search them for relevant information on a subject.

- Journal and Law Review Articles[18]
    1. Journals and Law Reviews (Lexis and Westlaw)
    2. HeinOnline (available if your school subscribes to this service)
    3. Google Scholar (scholar.google.com)
- *Restatements* (Westlaw and Lexis)
- Legal Encyclopedias
    1. *American Jurisprudence 2d* series (Am. Jur. 2d) (Westlaw and Lexis)
    2. *Corpus Juris Secundum* (CJS) (Westlaw)
- *American Law Reports* (Westlaw or Lexis)
- Treatises (Nutshells, Hornbooks, books)
    1. Law School Library online catalogs
    2. Google Books (books.google.com)
    3. Secondary sources on Westlaw and Lexis

Exhibits XI-B through P are illustrations of the various types of secondary sources. In the following pages we will cover these aspects of secondary sources.

1. Information about the level of authority (a.k.a. weight) each secondary source possesses.
2. A description of each with reference to the appropriate illustration so you can see how it looks in print and/or online.
3. Discussion of the options available for locating relevant information in the various types of secondary sources.
4. Information about citing the various secondary sources according to *The Bluebook*.

Let's begin by discussing the relative weight each source carries compared with other secondary sources. Not all secondary sources are equal in value; some are intended only as a general introduction while others are intended to provide in-depth analysis of a very specific legal topic.

---

[18] Many law schools have multiple journals. One journal usually has the words "Law Review" in the title while the others usually have "Journal of" in the title. In this reading, any time I reference law reviews, I am using that phrase broadly to reference all articles published in all journals, regardless of the name of the journal.

Additionally, there may be times when you wish to cite a secondary source in a memo or brief to support a point. When deciding which secondary sources to cite, you must be aware of the level of authority carried by a specific source.

The following test may be used to determine the level of authority assigned to a particular secondary source.

1. Who wrote it?

   When it comes to secondary sources, some list no author, others are written by editors who work for a company, some (quite a few, actually) are written by law professors, and others are written by an individual (may or may not be a law professor) who is a recognized authority in the subject matter. Most recognized authorities in this field are law professors but it is possible for someone to be an authority who is not a law professor. Materials written by identified authors who are recognized authorities carry the most weight. Materials which have no identified author or are written by editors carry the least weight.

2. Level of analysis.

   Some are written as a general overview only (with no in-depth analysis) while others go into detail on all aspects of an issue. A secondary source that provides detailed analysis can be of two types: those that cover a very narrow topic while others aim to cover a large, expansive subject. For example, law review articles are often detailed analysis of a very specific topic while multi-volume treatises (books) cover broad subjects in detail. Sources offering detailed analysis typically carry the most weight regardless of whether they focus on a narrow subject or deal with a much larger area of the law.

3. How much documentation is provided to support the material presented?

   Are many resources cited to support the information or are few to none cited? Those that extensively cite sources in support of the argument are usually considered to carry more weight.

We will discuss these elements as we look at each source. Only the more authoritative ones will be worth citing; the others, while possibly helpful in understanding an issue or leading to relevant primary sources, are not worth citing.

There is another matter we should cover before looking at specific sources. Any source that is organized by subject (books, *Restatements*, and legal encyclopedias) will have a Table of Contents (TOC) that can be useful for a couple reasons. First, you can browse the TOC to locate relevant information instead of conducting a full-text search. Second, once you locate relevant information, you can use the TOC to quickly determine if nearby parts or sections of the source might also be relevant to your research.

Legal encyclopedias, books (treatises), and *Restatements* are organized by subject and have TOCs. *American Law Reports* (ALR) and law review articles are published in random order, so they do not have a TOC that is useful for your research. Occasionally, an issue of a law review might publish numerous articles related to the same subject; in this situation, the TOC of the issue might be worth consulting.

When you are using secondary sources online that have a TOC, it is usually displayed on the first screen after you have selected the database from the main menu or through the link that appears while you type the name of the source in the main search query box. Once you are viewing a specific page or section within the source, a link to the TOC will appear somewhere on the screen. If you are using a print version of the source, you can simply flip pages to quickly see how the section you are reading relates to the other aspects of the same subject. It isn't as easy when viewing the same source online. When online, the TOC can provide helpful context for your search.

a. Legal Encyclopedias (Exhibits XI-B and C)

Legal encyclopedias are very much like regular encyclopedias, except they cover legal subjects exclusively. There are two legal encyclopedias that are national in scope, both published today by West Publishing: *American Jurisprudence 2d* (Am. Jur. 2d) and *Corpus Juris Secundum* (C.J.S.). (Some publishers produce legal encyclopedias that are specific to the law of a single state.)

Like most regular encyclopedias, they provide general background information about a very broad topic. Individuals who authored the articles are not normally identified. Cases are cited but not many other sources. So, this is a good source if you are looking for very general background information on a subject about which you know very little. As you might have guessed, articles in a legal encyclopedia are almost never cited in documents filed with courts or in academic literature; they do not carry much weight.

Both encyclopedias are available on Westlaw. To access CJS, log into Westlaw and begin typing *Corpus Juris Secundum* in the search box and it will open a link to this resource which you can select. Once you see the screen that displays the TOC, you can either search the full text of the encyclopedia or browse through the article headings using the TOC. Follow the same process to access *American Jurisprudence 2d.* When entering this title in the search box you will also see links to other titles than begin with the words American Jurisprudence. These other titles are not the encyclopedia; they are books that contain forms of documents and other aids that an attorney can use in practice. *American Jurisprudence 2d* is also available on Lexis; follow the same procedure as described on Westlaw.

b. **American Law Reports** *(ALR) (Exhibits XI-D Through F)*

This resource began as a case reporter a long time ago. The intent was to publish only those cases that broke new ground and were considered important by the original publisher. An editor would write an article about the case; this article was published alongside the case in ALR. The article would discuss other cases from other jurisdictions on the same topic. This product was ultimately not competitive as a reporter in the marketplace and today is no longer used as a reporter; however, the articles are valuable guides to the laws on the subject. The information found in the articles is the only thing of value. The articles are called annotations, a term we will encounter later in reference to a completely different source. Just remember that an annotation in ALR is an article.

This resource has been published in several series. Just like with the reporters, each series begins where the previous series ended and begins with volume 1. The main set of ALR is currently in its 6th series. At some point in time, the publisher decided to separate state law issues from federal law issues and started an ALR Federal set.

The author of an annotation is usually, though not always, identified. However, these are editors who work for the publisher and not academics or recognized experts. The articles tend to be very general (an overview) and usually only deal with case law from all the states along with some statutes. While considered a good source for an overview of a subject area, these are not generally cited.

ALR annotations are available on Lexis and Westlaw; just type the full title of the set (*American Law Reports*) in the search box and the database will provide a link to the source. Since the annotations are published in random order, there is no TOC available that can assist in locating relevant annotations. You must search the full text of the annotations, although Westlaw has created lists of relevant annotations by subject.

c. *Books (Treatises) (Exhibits XI-G Through I)*

I assume that you are familiar with the basic book. A book is also known as a treatise (not to be confused with a treaty) and you will hear both terms used to refer to the same material. Legal books are no different from regular books; they have (at a minimum) a table of contents, substantive content, and an index. Sometimes they have tables of cases, which lists alphabetically, by the first named party, all the cases discussed in the book. Books may also have a table that lists all statutes discussed in the book.

There are three different types of books commonly found in the legal world. The first is a series published by West which is known as a Nutshell. The example shown in Exhibit XI-G is *Products Liability in a Nutshell*. These books are short works on a general subject. They are mainly written for use by law students and anyone else interested in a brief introduction to a rather large subject area. A nutshell is usually written by someone who is an acknowledged expert on the subject, but they are very brief and introductory in nature. They are not cited as an authoritative source.

The second type of book is usually a single volume work. Again, West publishes a series of these. Each work covers a rather broad subject area but since there is an entire volume dedicated to the subject, the treatment has some depth to it. Also, most authors are usually, though not always, considered to be recognized experts in the subject area. Several other publishers also publish works similar in nature. The West published series is commonly referred to as hornbooks. In case you are wondering where the name hornbook comes from, it has a long history which isn't important for our purposes.

The third common type of book is the multiple volume work. These provide more in-depth treatment of a subject than the single volume. Otherwise, they are like a single volume.

How do you find relevant books? There are several sources, some of which you probably already know. Google has a specialized website called Google Books (books.google.com) which can be used to locate some. This site searches the full text of books but not all pages will be available for viewing on this site for copyright reasons. Still, it can be a useful tool to identify relevant books on a subject.

Other useful sources are online catalogs created by academic law libraries across the country. Every law school in the United States has a law library with an online catalog which allows you to search for books in their collection. These catalogs usually do not allow searching of the full text of books, but you can search titles and assigned subject headings using the keyword or title options. Some catalogs do allow for full text searching but this will vary by institution. All law school library catalogs are open for anyone to search so you do not have to be a student at an institution to search its catalog. There will be other functions available that require you to be a student at that institution, but basic searching is available for anyone. A Google search will provide you with links to any institution's catalog. If you locate a relevant book that your institution does not own, you can request a copy through interlibrary loan; enquire about this with the law library at your law school.

Many books are available on Lexis and Westlaw. These are full-text searchable and 100% of the text is available online. Online books have useful TOC's which can be used to track down relevant information. A list of treatises available in a database are available under the link to secondary sources, which is located on the main menu.

You will not always find a book that covers only the exact, specific, topic you are researching. You may, instead, need to know the broader subject matter that includes the specific topic you are researching. For example, you are unlikely to find a book that only discusses the liability of a doctor who exposes patients to HIV but this subject matter will most likely be examined in a book discussing laws related to the medical profession. It will most certainly be a part of books that discuss torts, since this is a type of tort involving injury to the person.

Most books are considered authoritative. Again, the depth of treatment and the reputation of the author(s) of a book will influence the amount of weight it carries and influence the ultimate decision whether to cite the source.

d. Law Review Articles (Exhibits XI-J Through N)

Articles published in law reviews are another frequently used secondary source. Most legal journals, unlike journals in other professions, are published by law students at American law schools. Many articles are written by law professors or other academics involved in some way with the legal profession.

There are two major types of law review articles: those written by law students who are on the law review staff at a law school and articles written by non-law students (faculty, lawyers, etc.). The latter group writes most of the articles. Articles tend to be a very detailed analysis of a narrow subject and are extensively documented with footnotes. As a result, law review articles are probably the most cited secondary source in case opinions and documents filed with courts. Articles by students, however, are rarely cited unless it is an exceptional article that covers a subject not written about by anyone else.

Several sources are available for locating articles on a subject. HeinOnline is a major source of law review articles today. (Shown in Exhibits XI-K and L) It is a full-text, searchable, database that contains almost all law reviews published. Access to this database is by subscription only but most, if not all, law schools in the United States subscribe to this service. A search by name or a list of available databases in your law school's online catalog will provide the url for accessing this resource at your institution.

Lexis and Westlaw (see Exhibit XI-J) also have selected journals online which are searchable much like case opinions. Like books, links to these will be found under the heading of secondary sources. Many journals are also searchable through Google Scholar (scholar.google.com). In Google Scholar you can search but may not be able to retrieve the full text of all articles. However, most law schools today have repositories in which articles written by their faculty are available in full text. You can locate these through a general Google search.

Exhibits XI-M and N show the beginning of a typical law review article, the first written by a non-student (law faculty, etc.) and the second by a law student.

e. **Restatements** *(Exhibits XI-O and P)*

This is probably the most unique secondary source in the legal profession. It began, historically, as an attempt to codify the common law. That is, subject matter experts, mostly law professors, attempted to distill rules of the common law from cases and formulate those rules in brief summaries. The American Law Institute (ALI) is the organization that started this work and is still involved today. Exhibit XI-O displays a list of the *Restatements* that exist today. As you can see, not all subjects are covered. Some subjects are now in their second or third series. Once the law has evolved sufficiently, they will decide to close off a series and start a new series. Each series is numbered consecutively just like reporters.

As you can see in Exhibit XI-P, *Restatements* are divided into sections. This example displays section 19 of the third series of *Restatement of Torts.* The bold text is the statement of the principle that has been extracted from numerous cases; this is frequently referenced as the "black letter" rule of law. This phrase basically means a well-established principle of law. Following the statement of the rule is information about the general history of that rule. This source may also contain cites to cases from which the rule is derived. These black letter rules express the view of a majority of jurisdictions around the country; the *Restatements* will often mention a minority view if some jurisdictions follow a different rule.

In print, the *Restatements* also have separate appendix volumes that list cases from around the country that cite to sections of the *Restatements.* The full text of the main volumes, along with the appendix of citing cases, are also available on both Lexis and Westlaw. You can search them full-text or browse through them.

Restatements are highly authoritative and courts cite them frequently. No rule has a single author but the expertise of the panel working on a subject is extremely high.

f. Levels of Persuasiveness of Secondary Sources Compared to Some Primary Sources

Throughout this book we have talked about how primary sources, the laws themselves, are either mandatory or persuasive. Secondary sources can only be persuasive. What about the situation where your jurisdiction has no mandatory law but you find a persuasive case from another jurisdiction and a persuasive secondary source? Do court cases that are not mandatory (i.e., persuasive) always carry more weight than secondary sources?

Your first instinct might be to answer this question in the affirmative; it intuitively makes sense that a primary source, though only persuasive, would carry more weight than a secondary source. However, this is not always true. For example, a black letter rule from a *Restatement* might carry more weight than a lower court opinion from a state court outside your jurisdiction. In other words, don't automatically assume that all primary sources will carry more weight than an authoritative secondary source. Normally, only *Restatements* and law review articles or books written by a well-known expert will carry more weight than some lower court opinions. This is true of *Restatements* because they are written by panels of experts that carry much weight in the legal world. Regarding law review articles and books, the weight they carry depends upon who wrote them and the level of detail and originality contained in the work.

g. Citing the Various Secondary Sources According to The Bluebook

In the Exhibits referenced in this section on secondary sources, you will see the citation format specified by *The Bluebook* with a reference to the appropriate rule. As you may have noticed, *The Bluebook* still prefers cites to print sources. As a result, the dates used in the parenthetical of a cite are usually the copyright from the printed source.

However, you will frequently access these secondary sources online today. The database copyright date, which is always the current year, is usually what you will see when viewing the source online. This date is not what *The Bluebook* wants for the year in the parenthetical; it wants the copyright on the original printed source. How do you cite to these sources when accessing them online? Some online sources may provide the actual copyright date of the printed version, such as the *Restatements* on Westlaw and Lexis; in this case, Rule 18.2.1(a) permits citation to the online version just like you were accessing it in print. Also, some sources will provide a pdf of the original which will enable you to cite it according to Rule 18.2.1(b)(ii). In this case, you cite to it as if you were accessing the print version but with the url of the pdf after the year in the parenthetical. If the database doesn't provide enough information to cite to the print version, then use the modifications stated in Rule 15.9 for books and legal encyclopedias and Rule 16.8 for journal articles and ALR Annotations.

You may have noticed that some of the secondary sources are organized by section. (For example, *CJS.*) *The Bluebook* states in Rule B3 that you may cite the section number instead of the page for those that are organized by sections. (Interestingly, Rule 3.3 indicates that if a source is organized into sections, you should use sections in a cite.) As a rule, I think most people cite to sections instead of pages if section numbers are assigned. However, law review articles and some books do not assign section numbers.

There are instances where you may want to provide a page cite in addition to the section number. For example, when a section is several pages in length and you are citing a specific point found on one page, you may cite the section and then the page number. See the following cite to a treatise (book) from *The Bluebook*:

Laurence H. Tribe, *American Constitutional Law* § 15–4, at 1314 (2d ed. 1988).

h. AI

CoCounsel on Westlaw does not directly search for secondary sources at this time. It will generate a list of cases that cite to secondary sources but this is not the best way to search for relevant secondary sources. However, it is useful if you are interested in only seeing those secondary sources that courts have cited. These sources may carry more weight because courts have cited them. A good query on the subject of whether the right of publicity survives the death of the celebrity might look like this: locate secondary sources that discuss the descendibility of the right of publicity. This search includes specific terminology that courts tend to use when discussing this issue.

Protégé on Lexis will find some secondary sources on a subject. It does not currently locate law review articles but does cover selected treatises. Both AI apps will no doubt expand to search more secondary sources in time.

Summary

1. Secondary sources are helpful for:
   A. Providing background information and analysis about a specific subject.
   B. Providing cites to relevant primary sources.
2. Secondary sources are not the law (only primary source are the law); they only discuss the law.
3. Secondary sources include legal encyclopedias, books, articles, annotations in *American Law Reports*, and *Restatements*.
4. The weight carried by each type of secondary sources depends upon the following factors.
   A. Who wrote it; are they considered an expert by others?
   B. The depth of analysis; how extensive is the treatment given to the subject?
   C. Amount of documentation supporting the information.
5. You generally want to cite materials written by recognized experts who have provided in-depth analysis and extensive documentation. (The one exception for documentation requirement is *Restatements*, which carry great weight based upon the expertise of the multiple authors.)
6. Sample pages illustrating each secondary source and *The Bluebook* rules covering how to cite the source are shown with each illustration.
7. In some instances, a very authoritative secondary source, such as a black letter rule from a *Restatement*, carries more weight than an opinion that is only persuasive from a lower court.
8. If a source is organized into sections, you should cite to the section numbers rather than page numbers. However, you may also include a cite to page numbers when it assists in identifying the exact location of the material being cited.

Assignment 5

The following questions are based on material covered in section XI.B.3 of the reading.

Let's continue searching for information about whether the right of publicity survives the death of the celebrity using various secondary sources.

1. Examine the legal encyclopedias, beginning with Corpus Juris Secundum (CJS).

A. Access CJS first on Westlaw, using the method described in the reading. (Note: if typing the title of a source doesn't work, you can always click on the link to Secondary Sources found on the main menu and find links to the various secondary sources.) Using the table of contents that you see on the first page after selecting CJS, which article (or topic) heading looks relevant to our issue? You may need to scroll through the TOC or use the search button (Ctrl+F on a Windows computer, Command+F on the Mac).

B. Once you locate the relevant article, click on the + symbol before the article title to see the subdivisions within that article. What is the number (a roman numeral) assigned to the subunit of the article that specifically discusses the right of publicity?

C. After clicking on the + symbol in front of the subunit you just identified, you should see a selected list of sections in this article. To identify which section or sections discuss whether the right of publicity survives the death of the celebrity (or is descendible), you could browse each section. However, a faster way to accomplish this task is to check the box located in front of the roman numeral; this automatically selects all sections within this unit. You can now search only those sections for the words survive or descendible.

Once you select this box, go ahead and type the following search in the query box:

Survive descendible

Which section did your search identify as the relevant section?

D. Please provide a complete cite to the relevant section of CJS according to *The Bluebook*. (Use Rules B15.1, 15.9(a), and Table 12 to create your citation.)

E. Provide a cite to an Arizona case referenced in this section of *C.J.S.* that discusses whether the right of publicity is descendible.

2. Using Lexis, locate the encyclopedia known as American Jurisprudence 2nd. The TOC will appear. However, let's use a different method this time: a full-text search.

A. After you have selected American Jurisprudence 2d, run the following natural language search, including the quotation marks where indicated: "right of publicity" descendible. Scan the list of results; based upon the results, most of the results appear in the same article. Which article in this encyclopedia discusses this right?

B. One of the results you see refers to § 15 of the relevant article; retrieve this section. Based on the text of this section, have the majority of states, which have addressed the issue, held that the right of publicity survives the death of the celebrity?

C. Immediately following the article is a section entitled "Reference." It provides references to other resources you could use to locate relevant information on this topic. There are five listings under this heading; which resources are identified in the first and fifth listings?

3. Let's move on to books available on Lexis.

Return to the initial search screen by clicking on the heading at the top-left part of the screen labeled "Lexis+." In the second column of resources under the "Content" tab, you will see a link to "Secondary Materials." Select this link. The next screen displays various types of secondary sources; under the heading of "Content Type" is a link to "Treatises, Guides." Select this.

In the search box at the top, enter the same search we just ran: "right of publicity" descendible.

A list of various books should appear; the total number of results, shown inside a parenthetical near the top of the results, is quite large. Scroll down to the first link to an A.L.R. annotation. Retrieve this document.

Provide a full cite to this annotation according to *The Bluebook*. (Use Rules R16.7.6 and R16.8) (Hint: As mentioned in the reading, not all annotations have an identified author; if the author is listed, their name will appear near the link to the "Jurisdictional table of statutes and cases." If no name is indicated, skip it in the cite. Also, the Bluebook doesn't provide an example of citing an A.L.R. annotation found in a commercial database, so just make your best guess based upon the cite to C.J.S. on Westlaw.)

4. Now, let's use Google Books (books.google.com) to locate relevant treatises on the subject.

Enter the same search we did on Lexis in Q. 3 above. You should see a book by Rothman that is number one or near the top of the list of results. Provide a full citation to this book. (Hint: when citing a book as a whole without a pincite, no page number is needed. Every book begins with page 1 so no need to include that information in the cite.)

5. Let's look at the Restatements on Westlaw. Return to the main search screen on Westlaw. We need to locate the relevant section on the same topic we have been working with throughout this assignment. How would you proceed with this search? I'll leave it to you. All I ask is that you identify the exact title of the relevant Restatement and the section number. **You do not need to cite according to *The Bluebook*.** (Hint: your search will retrieve numerous sections found in the Restatements. Only one of them contains extensive discussion of whether the right of publicity survives death and is descendible. Remember, after running a natural language search the results are ordered by relevance. One aspect of relevance is the number of times the words you searched for are found in the document. Therefore, the first item listed in the results will normally contain more references to the search terms than documents further down the list.)

6. Of all the secondary resources we have looked at in this assignment, which one(s) would you cite in a brief you are writing that will be filed with a court. Explain your answers. Be sure to consider the criteria I discussed in the reading in your answer.

7. Another form of secondary source that you may use will be web pages retrieved by searching Google. Run the following search on Google: **statute of limitations professional malpractice begin to run against an attorney figuring out the statute of limitations**.

In the first several results should be a website with the title "Figuring Out the Statute of Limitations for Legal Malpractice." Retrieve this page. This page cites a case. How would you use this case to locate relevant cases in Illinois? List each step you would take to accomplish this task.

Assignment 6

OVERVIEW

At this point you have been introduced to:

- the concept of authority.
- dockets.
- secondary authorities which, depending on their nature, can provide general explanations or in-depth analysis of specific legal problems as well as references to governing primary authorities.
- various types of opinions issued by courts.
- locating cases using the topic and key number system on Westlaw or the subject headings assigned by Lexis.
- using citing cases to identify relevant cases.
- full-text searching of case law online.
- *Bluebook* citation rules.

OBJECTIVE

Your task is to find cases that are relevant to the issue raised in the problem below. In doing so, you should at least think about how to use all the materials discussed thus far. Keep in mind that the purpose of this assessment is to review and practice working with the sources and methods of research we have covered in this book. For this reason, don't just locate one secondary source and use it to identify all the cases you cite below.

PROBLEM

Eighteen months ago, your client underwent major surgery at a hospital in his hometown of Springfield, Illinois. The surgery went well and he has recovered completely. Last week he received a letter from the hospital informing him that one of the surgeons who participated in his surgery recently tested HIV positive. The letter explained that it was highly unlikely that he was exposed to the AIDS virus during the surgery and offered free testing and counseling.

Since receiving this information, your client has suffered from emotional distress and insomnia. He wants to know if he can recover damages for negligent infliction of emotional distress based on his fear of contracting AIDS.

Your law firm has asked you to research this issue in preparation for possible litigation in an Illinois state trial court. Assume that Illinois considers the state Appellate Court to be a unified court; decisions of any state Appellate Court are considered mandatory authority for all state trial courts.

Use Westlaw or Lexis for case finding.

TASK

Follow the instructions below.

A. Using the information covered to this point, locate each type of source listed below that is relevant to your problem.

B. Create a list of cites to relevant sources and write a brief, no more than one paragraph, summary of the law on this issue.

C. You are expected to cite **all** authorities in *Bluebook* form as much as possible. Provide cites to relevant sources as instructed below under each type of source.

D. Question 7 asks for cites to three cases, at least one of which is mandatory authority. I suggest following the steps listed below, which uses the three major methods of locating cases we have discussed in the readings. Following these steps will provide you the opportunity to experience again how each option works.

1. Locate the first case by consulting a secondary source.
2. Locate another case by using the topic and key number, if using Westlaw, or the subject headings, if using Lexis, found in the first case.
3. Locate another case through the citing case method using either the first or second case.

SOURCES

1. **Legal encyclopedias**—Cite one using *Bluebook* form. If citing to *Am. Jur. 2d*, be sure it is the encyclopedia and not a form book with a similar title.

2. **Treatises**—Cite one using *Bluebook* form. Skim the table of contents or index (if available) to locate relevant pages. Provide a pincite to those pages that look relevant to the topic.

3. **Legal periodical articles**—Cite one article using *Bluebook* form (try to locate and cite a nonstudent written article in a regular law school journal).

4. **Restatements**—Cite using *Bluebook* form.

5. **American Law Reports**—Cite one annotation using *Bluebook* form.

6. **Subject headings from relevant cases**

   A. If you used Westlaw, which topic(s) and key number(s) were most relevant?

   B. If you used Lexis, which topics (the subject headings assigned to the headnotes) were pertinent?

7. **Primary sources**—Cite three (3) cases in *Bluebook* form; at least one should be a mandatory case. For each case indicate whether it is mandatory or persuasive.

8. **Provide a brief statement (no more than one paragraph) about the controlling law you located.**

TIME

You should be able to complete this assignment in approximately two or three hours.

CHAPTER 4

USING CITATORS

XII. MAKING SURE THAT THE CASE LAW YOU FOUND REPRESENTS THE CURRENT STATE OF THE LAW[19]

A. CITATORS

Now that we've looked at the various ways to locate court opinions, let's turn our attention to another task the legal researcher must perform to fully research an issue. Having found one or more relevant cases, how can you determine whether the rule of law in the case you are reading is still valid or was valid when the events involved in the litigation occurred?

Citators, which we looked at briefly when discussing how to locate additional cases on point, also serve a critically important additional function: identifying whether a rule of law applied in a past case remains valid today. Like everything else, the rules of law applied by courts evolve and change over time. For various reasons, courts often decide to change the rules they applied in previous cases. When a court decides to no longer follow the previous rule of law, how can they notify everyone that the rule of law has changed? They don't (and could not) go back and rewrite earlier opinions. They can only state and discuss the modified rule in the opinion in which they announce the change and in subsequent opinions until the rule changes again. The challenge, then, is to locate cases that discuss the same issue as, and were decided after, the case you are reading (which we will refer to as the **original case**). You must do this to determine whether the later cases apply the same rule or have modified it in some way.

In other words, once you locate a relevant case, you only know the rule of law at the time the opinion was issued. If that case was issued many years ago, the rule applied by the court today to the same facts may be different. Part of your job as an attorney is to determine whether the rule of law applied in the case you just read is still valid or if it has changed.

Using a citator for this purpose is a little more challenging than using it to locate additional relevant cases. To understand how a citator helps determine if a rule of law from a case is still valid, it is helpful to first think about events that may modify a rule of law found in a case.

1. The case may be reversed or modified on appeal. These cases result from the same litigation at different stages of the appeal process; they are known as **history** cases.

2. Cases decided later in time, involving different parties (**treatment cases**), may cite to and discuss an earlier case. If these later cases are issued by the same or a higher court within the same jurisdiction, they may overrule, criticize, or modify the earlier rule of law. To use a well-known example, the U.S. Supreme Court in *Brown v. Bd. of Education* effectively overruled the rule of law applied by the Court in its earlier decision in *Plessy v. Ferguson*.

3. The legislature, in the same jurisdiction (or a **superseding jurisdiction**), may enact a statute that changes the common law rule. In the hierarchy of laws in the U.S., statutes take priority over the common law within the same jurisdiction and, in some circumstances involving both state and federal law, statutes enacted by Congress will take priority over

[19] Throughout this section you will see bolded terms or phrases; these are important concepts. A list of these terms, with definitions, is included at the end of this section.

state laws. In this situation, any cases that conflict with a statute will be superseded and the new statute will control future litigation.

4. An administrative agency, in the same jurisdiction (or a superseding jurisdiction), may enact an administrative rule changing the common law rule. Just as with statutes, administrative agencies usually have the authority to change the common law.

Citators can help you determine whether any of these events happened. However, as I already mentioned, citators are computer generated products based solely on cases citing other cases; they are not the result of human effort to determine the current status of a specific case. As a result, Shepardizing or KeyCiting a single case does not provide sufficient information to conclude with certainty whether a rule of law from a case remains good law even when no negative history or treatment is indicated. Citators are merely one tool available to legal researchers in their quest to locate relevant and up-to-date information about the status of the law. We will discuss this limitation and how to work around it later in this section.

Let's use an example to illustrate how citators provide the information necessary to determine the status of a rule of law from a case. Assume you are reading a relevant case decided by the Seventh Circuit Court of Appeals. With few exceptions, this case did not originate in the Court of Appeals; it began in a federal district court somewhere within the Seventh Circuit, such as the district court for the Northern District of Illinois. If a written opinion was issued by the district court, a cite to the district court opinion will be found when Shepardizing the Seventh Circuit case; this is known as **prior history** since the district court opinion was the result of the same litigation involving the same parties but was issued prior to the Seventh Circuit decision. If this case goes on appeal from the Seventh Circuit to the U.S. Supreme Court and the Supreme Court issues an opinion, a cite to the Supreme Court decision will be found when Shepardizing the Seventh Circuit case; this is known as **subsequent history**. However, don't assume that subsequent history cases will always consist of decisions from a higher court; it can include decisions from a lower court if the case is remanded (sent back) by the higher to the lower court and the lower court issues another opinion. The important point is to determine if the relevant holding in the case has been adversely affected by any court on appeal or on remand. Citators provide complete **history** information so you can know with certainty that you are seeing everything that happened to the case on appeal.

On appeal, the court can do many things to the lower court's opinion. A few of the more significant actions a court can take regarding a case on appeal include:

- **affirm** (higher court agrees with the lower court's decision)
- **modify** (higher court modifies the lower court's decision)
- **reverse** (higher court disagrees with the lower court's decision)

If the case is remanded (sent back) to a lower court, the higher court will frequently instruct the lower court to reconsider the case within the parameters established by the higher court. The lower court may then issue another opinion that trumps the lower court's earlier decision.

When using citators to check the history of a case, watch especially for cases that indicate reversed, modified, or affirmed. Also, determine whether the action taken by the court hearing the appeal affects the specific issue that applies to your issue. Many cases contain multiple holdings and the court may reverse or modify one holding only, leaving the holding that matters in your situation intact. This will determine whether you can still use the case and, if the appellate court did modify the holding relevant to your research, the nature of the arguments you will have to make if you want to use the original case.

As previously discussed, citators also indicate how the rule of law from the original case has been treated in subsequent litigation between other parties (treatment cases).

Treatment in **citing cases** can vary widely. Selected types of treatment include:

- **overrule** (the rule of law in the original case has been changed; only an opinion issued by a court at an equal or higher level in the same jurisdiction as the original case can overrule a previous decision. For example, if you are reading an Illinois Court of Appeals case about a matter of state law, only the Illinois Court of Appeals or the Illinois Supreme Court can overrule the original opinion. A court in Iowa, or any other state, cannot overrule an Illinois state court case. **Don't confuse overruled with reversed; reversed is what a higher court does on appeal, which is part of the history of the original case. Overrule is something a court from the same or higher level, within the same jurisdiction, does to a specific rule of law from the original case in a later case involving different litigants.**)
- **question** (the citing case questions the validity of the rule of law)
- **criticize** (citing case disagrees with some part of the original decision)
- **distinguish** (citing case is determined to be different either in law or fact)
- **explain** (case you are Shepardizing is interpreted in a significant way, rather than just a brief or passing mention)
- **follow** (citing case refers to the case as controlling authority)

When using citators to determine if a treatment case has adversely affected the rule of law in the original case, be sure to watch for and read any cases that treat the original case negatively, such as overruled, criticized, etc. For those cases that are critical, you must also pay attention to the jurisdiction and level of the criticizing court. If your original case was decided by the Illinois Court of Appeals but the court criticizing it is in Michigan, the Michigan case doesn't mean much in Illinois. However, critical treatment by the Illinois Court of Appeals or Illinois Supreme Court would be very important to read. We will discuss this in greater detail later in this section.

Don't assume that negative treatment is the only type of treatment that can have an impact on a rule of law. Sometimes cases that follow an earlier case will make slight changes that may become significant later in time. In other words, don't completely ignore cases that treat the issue of interest to you in a positive manner.

B. LIMITATIONS OF CITATORS WHEN USED TO DETERMINE THE STATUS OF A RULE OF LAW AND HOW TO OVERCOME THESE LIMITATIONS

If you Shepardize a case and find no negative history or negative treatment, you cannot assume that the point of law for which it stands is still valid. (Please memorize, read and reread this section until you completely understand this idea, and never forget it!) This is true because citators do not cover all possible events that can negatively affect a rule of law in a case. To help explain this, let's revisit the list of ways a rule of law can be changed and determine, for each possible scenario, whether Shepardizing alone is sufficient.

1. A case reversed or modified on appeal: Citators handle this very well.

2. A case overruled or criticized: Citators will always indicate if the original case is overruled or criticized. However, as discussed earlier, your real interest is in whether the rule of law from the original case has been criticized or overruled. It is possible that a later case overruled the relevant rule of law but did not cite your original case. If this happens, Shepardizing the original case will not notify you of the overruling. It is possible the overruling court had several cases to choose from when overruling. If the case you are Shepardizing is not a major player among all cases on the topic, the overruling or criticizing

case may mention only the major cases and neglect your original case. You simply do not know when you first begin your research whether the case you read is significant in the larger scheme of things.

Lexis now has a feature known as "Ravel View," which helps one work around this problem. Ravel View helps put the cases on a subject into perspective. As an example, log into Lexis and run a search for the phrase "right of publicity" (including the quote marks) in California cases. Be sure to also check the box in the upper right part of the screen next to the "include related federal content" line. Your search should retrieve approximately 572 cases. Now, look in the upper right part of the display on the page showing a list of results; you should see a group of icons.

Select the icon on the far right of the display; the phrase "Ravel View" will display when you mouseover the icon. Select the Ravel View icon. This takes the top seventy-five cases from your results and shows them graphically. The graph indicates several things. The size of the circle associated with a case is based on how often it is cited; this usually gives you an idea of how important a case is on the subject. The graph also indicates the level of court; federal courts are listed at the top in order from Supreme to district court. State courts are shown at the bottom of the graph. Within the same level of court, the higher the circle the more relevant the case is for your problem. For example, all federal courts of appeals will be listed in the same band on the graph; the higher ones supposedly are more relevant. The graph also shows cases through time, from left to right. Cases to the left of another case are ones that were decided earlier in time. If a line connects the two cases, this means the later case relied upon and cited the earlier one. When you click on the circle representing a specific case, that case will appear at the top of the list on the right side of the screen. With a specific case selected, you can then mouseover other cases and see the relationship between them and the case you selected. The features of Ravel View are demonstrated in a video available at https://www.youtube.com/watch?v=avZyA8BFToM.

While this feature can be very helpful, it does have limitations. First, the number of times a case has been cited tends to correspond to its importance, but this is not a guarantee that it is the most important case. A recent case that hasn't been cited much yet because it is so new may in fact be more important than the others. Second, if your issue involves state law, federal courts may mean little or nothing on the topic. Third, Ravel view doesn't narrow in on just one issue, so you still must contend with the multiple issue problem. In other words, the citing cases may be citing one another about an issue other than the one you care about. Fourth, Ravel View is only available when you have a list of cases generated by a search on the screen; it is not available when you have a single case displayed on the screen in Lexis. This is a bit of a problem since often you are starting with a single case and want to know how it relates to other cases on the same subject. To remedy this problem, you must run a search that generates the case you started with in its results.

You can overcome the latter problem by following these steps.

1. With the original case on the screen, select the "More like this Headnote" link located at the end of a headnote that is on point for your research. (Recall that this link runs a predefined natural language search.)

2. Selecting "More like this Headnote" will retrieve a list of cases on the subject with your original case included in the list. (Don't use the subject links associated with the headnote; your case will not usually be among those results.)

3. You can now select "Ravel View" and see how your original case compares to others on the subject.

Using Ravel View is basically helping you Shepardize more than just the original case. It helps you Shepardize the cases that cite (**citing cases**) your original case. By Shepardizing the citing cases, the bigger picture should begin to emerge and provide insight into which cases are important and what has happened to the rule of law over time. However, don't stop with the first level of citing cases, i.e., cases that cited your original case. Be sure to continue Shepardizing all relevant cases that you locate. Ravel View can assist in implementing this option.

In addition to Shepardizing the citing cases and cases that cited to them, you should also (and Ravel View assists with this) check on the cases relied upon and cited by the original case; these are known as **cited cases**. It is possible that the rule of law applied in one of the cases relied upon by your original case (cited case) was treated negatively by a case decided after your original case but that did not cite your original case. For example, refer to Exhibit XII-A. Citing case A might have overruled a holding from Cited case 1 that your original case relied upon; you would not see this when Shepardizing the original case because Citing case A didn't cite your original case so it is not technically a citing case of the Original case. However, Shepardizing Cited case 1, which was relied upon by your original case, would provide a clue about this change. So, you need to be sure and Shepardize the cases upon which your original case relied to help identify any changes to the rule of law which the court is applying.

Exhibit XII-A

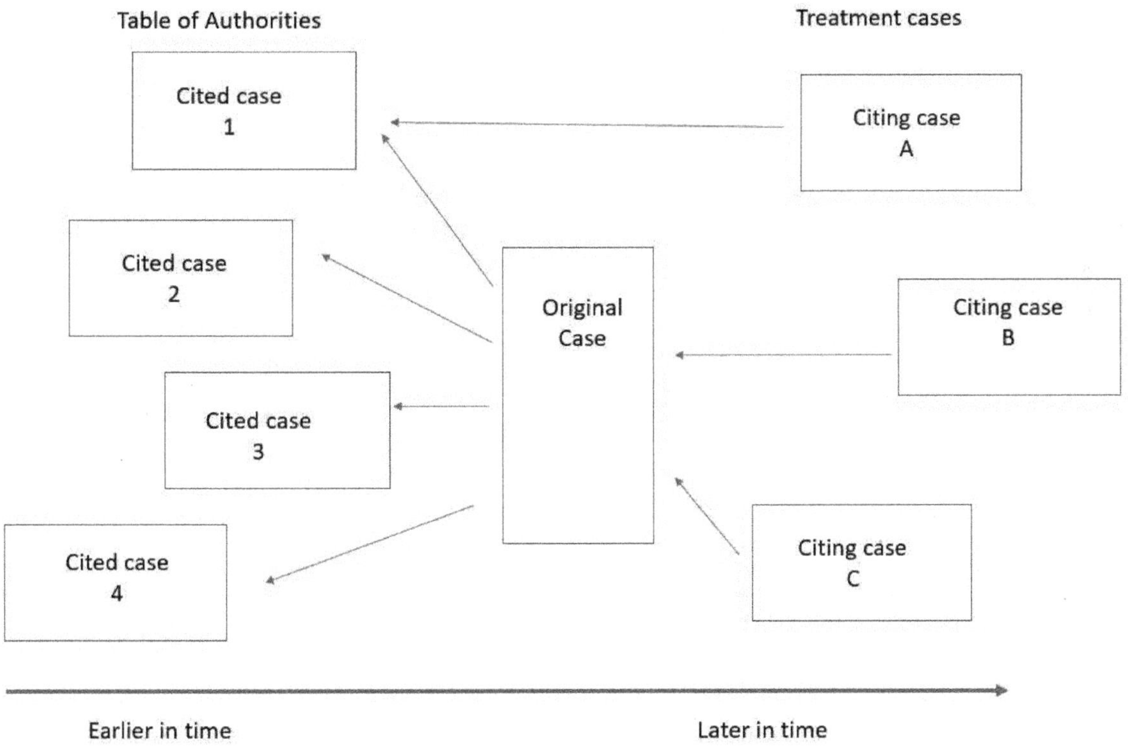

While you could read the original case and note all the cases it cites to identify cited cases, a far easier way of getting this information involves using the **table of authorities**. This table lists the cases that the original case cited. Westlaw and Lexis both provide a link to the table of authorities when viewing a case. Don't confuse this with the cases that cite your original case. The table of authorities indicates those cases decided prior in time to the original case and that were cited by the original case. The cases that cite the original case (citing cases) are those decided after the original case was issued.

Westlaw has recently devised a method of alerting you to the occurrence of overruling where the original case itself was not specifically overruled by name. When you view a case which Westlaw thinks has been overruled, they include a signal with the case labeled "Overruling Risk." This reflects a judgment of an algorithm, so you need to follow up and verify for yourself whether the rule has been overruled. For an example of this label on Westlaw, retrieve *Childress v. Heckler*, 616 F. Supp. 563 (E.D. La. 1985).

There is another possible situation that you should always keep in mind. Some cases are never overruled or directly criticized even though the rule of law in the case is no longer good law. They die a slow death without much fanfare. This is known as implicit overruling or overruling by implication. In this instance, Shepardizing the original case will not help; Ravel View will not necessarily help either. KeyCite might, but not always, pick up on the implicit overruling and provide an overruling risk indicator. Shepardizing multiple relevant cases **may** provide insight, but not always. If the rule of law you are following has not received much attention by the courts since the original case, then citators will be of no use. A good law review article or treatise (book) might be the most helpful in this situation.[20]

3. The legislature enacts a statute changing the rule: Citators may help in this situation, but you can't count on them. **Citators will only identify a later statutory change when all the following statements are true.**

   1) A later case cites your original case,

   2) The same citing case mentions the statutory change, and

   3) The statutory change and the original case are explicitly discussed together in the citing case.

By Shepardizing the major cases you increase the chances of finding cases that mention the statute. However, this alone may not be sufficient. Consulting indexes to statutes and other sources that reference statutes is the only way to determine for sure if this scenario has occurred. Once again, a good law review article or book may also assist.

This scenario can happen when the legislature from the same jurisdiction as the court that issued the opinion enacts legislation that supersedes the court made law. In the case of state law, Congress may also be able to alter state law when the subject involved is one which both states and the federal government share jurisdiction. In other words, if the federal government has the authority, Congress could enact a rule that would supersede state common law on the matter.

4. An administrative agency issues a ruling that changes the rule; this is identical to a statutory change in 3 above.

C. DETAILS ABOUT USING CITATORS

Some of the information described here is presented in YouTube videos; information about locating links to relevant videos are provided below. **You should still go through the description in this reading since the videos do not discuss everything covered here.** Also, be sure to only view

[20] An example of this is the case *Beauharnais v. Illinois*, 343 U.S. 250 (1952). Illinois at that time had a criminal libel statute. The defendant had been convicted under this statute. The Illinois and U.S. Supreme Court both upheld the defendant's conviction. Neither KeyCite on Westlaw nor Shepard's on Lexis directly indicate that this case is no longer good law. However, when you examine the citing cases from later lower courts you will see that most of them recognize that the U.S. Supreme Court effectively overruled this holding in *New York Times v. Sullivan*, 376 U.S. 254 (1964). *New York Times* did not cite the *Beauharnais* case.

videos created in the last twelve to eighteen months. Older videos may no longer reflect the current version of the citators and how they function.

Lexis Shepard's YouTube videos: Search YouTube for Lexis Shepard's tutorials.

Westlaw: Search YouTube for Westlaw KeyCite tutorials.

Now let's look at the citators that are available and see how they work. To use a citator you must already know of a relevant case. As an example, log into Westlaw and Lexis, and retrieve the *Memphis Development Foundation* case located at 616 F.2d 956. Now, look at Westlaw. Near the top of the screen you should see tabs labeled "Negative Treatment," "History," and "Citing References." (There are others but we will concentrate on these for now). On Lexis, you should see an orange box with the letter "Q" next to the case name. A link to "Citing Decisions" and "History," among others, are near the top of the screen. Other ways to get to this information are available but these are the easiest ways when you have a case on the screen.

D. CASE STATUS INDICATORS

Case status indicators are symbols used by the databases to quickly indicate whether they think a case is still good law based upon all history and treatment cases; they are located near the case name when viewing the case. The most important status indicators are those that reflect something negative. The negative ones use either red or yellow markers to caution the legal researcher about the validity of the case. The symbols used by Lexis and Westlaw vary but the use of colors is pretty consistent. The most important status indicators are listed in the table below.

The meaning of any given status indicator, when viewing a case, is displayed when you mouseover the symbol. When viewing a case online, the status indicator for that case is located in the upper left part of the page, immediately before the name or title of the case.

Always keep in mind that these **case status indicators are judgment calls** made by computers and editors working for Westlaw and Lexis. Use the status indicators as guides but be sure to read the cases to determine the status of the original case for yourself. A good illustration of this principle is shown in the *Memphis* case. The same case gets an orange Q on Lexis but a yellow flag on Westlaw. Also, remember that negative treatment can be related to any rule of law in the original case. If a citator indicates that a case has treated your original case negatively, and there are multiple issues in your original case, you cannot know for sure whether the negative treatment relates to the rule of law in which you are interested without reading the citing case.

Case Status Indicators

Westlaw	Lexis
Red flag—no longer valid on at least one point of law	*Red stop sign*—negative treatment or history
	Orange box with a Q—Questioned
Yellow flag—some negative treatment or history	*Yellow caution sign*—possible negative treatment

E. PRESENTATION OF INFORMATION

Lexis and Westlaw databases separate history from treatment cases. Westlaw has a separate list of negative treatment; they do this to highlight and draw attention to negative treatment cases. These negative treatment cases are also included in the citing references list.

The cases listed under history are the previous and subsequent history of the case you Shepardized. They always mark the case you Shepardized, the original case, so you can see which are prior and which are subsequent.

You should also note that Westlaw offers the option of presenting history in a graphical format, which can be useful when the history of a case is complex. After selecting the "History" tab you will see either a list of the history cases only or a list on the left and a graphic of the history cases on the right. If you don't see the graphic, look at the top of the KeyCite display; you will see a heading labeled "Graphic." Clicking on "Show" will display the history graphically. If you already see the graphic, you can turn it off by selecting the "Hide" option.

As we already discussed, the citing cases are known as treatment cases. Let's begin by looking at the list of citing cases in KeyCite on Westlaw in the *Memphis* case, called "Citing References." Select "Citing References" and view the list of cases. Exhibit XII-B shows a KeyCite display. Going from left to right, you see **treatment indicators** are written out; these indicate how this citing case treated *Memphis*, the original case. Any treatment case deemed to be negative by the editors at Westlaw will display the word "negative" in red letters immediately below the treatment indicator. Positive treatment cases are assigned a treatment indicator only; these consist of cited by, discussed by, etc.

Treatment indicators express how that specific citing case treated the original case; for example, KeyCite on Westlaw indicates that, in their analysis, the *Reeves* case treated the *Memphis* case negatively by distinguishing itself from *Memphis* in some way. **Be careful and don't confuse treatment indicators with status indicators; the former indicates how a specific citing case treated the original case while the latter indicates how the history and citing cases, as a whole, have treated the original case.** So, in this example, the status indicator assigned to *Memphis* is a yellow flag because several cases have treated it negatively in some way. The treatment indicator tells you which cases treated *Memphis* negatively. *Reeves* and *State ex rel. Elvis Presley* are assigned negative treatment indicators ("Distinguished by" and "Disagreed With by") whereas *Factors* and *ETW Corp.* have positive treatment indicators.

Now, looking once again at the display of treatment cases (Exhibit XII-B), the treatment indicators are followed by the status indicator associated with the citing case. The case name, some of which have quotation marks immediately following, appear next. The quotation marks indicate that the citing case quotes exact language from the original case. Following this is the date the citing case was decided and the type of document (case, law review article, etc.). Depth of treatment follows next and is indicated by the number of green boxes. Four green boxes indicates that the citing case provides a good deal of discussion on at least one point in the original case; one green box indicates the citing case probably only cited the original case without discussion. Finally, you see the headnotes from the original case that are discussed in the citing case. In other words, when *Reeves v. United Artists* discussed *Memphis*, the discussion revolved around the subjects covered by headnotes 1, 2, and 4 from the *Memphis* case. The text of the headnote in the original case (*Memphis* in this case) appears if you mouseover the headnote number. We will see shortly how this can be used to your advantage as you Shepardize cases.

In KeyCite on Westlaw, treatment cases can be sorted by either depth of treatment or date. A "Sort By:" option is located just above the first treatment case near the center of the page.

The "Citing Decisions" link in Shepard's on Lexis shows similar information as KeyCite. After selecting the "Citing Decisions" tab, you will notice a table that summarizes information about which jurisdictions the citing cases are in and how they treated the original case. Scroll on down to the listing of each citing case. Exhibit XII-C illustrates the Lexis Shepard's display. You will see a small box of various colors. These boxes attempt to communicate the same information as the written treatment indicator, which immediately follows the colored box. Lexis provides status indicators for the citing cases immediately after the case name. Depth of discussion is shown by bars below the citing case name. Just as on Westlaw, the legal issue the citing case discusses is indicated by referencing the number of the headnote from the original case. In Exhibit XII-C, Reeves cited to and discussed the original case about the topic found in headnote 2 of the original case.

At first glance, you might think that the treatment indicator "Cited by" in Shepard's specifies depth of treatment. However, this is not the case. Shepard's uses "cited by" as an alternative to followed, overruled, and all the other treatment indicators. "Cited by" is used regardless of whether the treatment case simply provided a cite to the original case with no discussion or discussed it extensively. You must use the Depth of Discussion indicator to determine the extent of treatment.

Lexis organizes the display of treatment cases by jurisdiction. Federal courts of appeals and district courts are presented in numerical order starting with the 1st Circuit. These are followed by state courts, which are presented in alphabetical order by state name. Lexis allows you to sort by analysis, depth of discussion, court, and date; these options are under the "Display Settings" pull-down window.

F. CUSTOMIZING THE CITATOR DISPLAY

In the earlier section about "Deciding which treatment cases you must read," we discussed ways of reducing the number of cases that must be read without missing crucial information. Lexis and Westlaw include the ability to limit and customize the citator display, using the criteria previously discussed, so you see only the important cases for your research.

You may customize the Shepard's display on Lexis by clicking on the "Citing Decisions" link. The column on the left side of the screen is headed by the phrase "Narrow By." So, for example, if you wish to see only those cases that questioned the validity of *Memphis*, you can click on the "Questioned" link. If you want to incorporate multiple factors into your customization, you need to click on the "Select multiple" link at the bottom of each section.

You can limit the display by treatment indicators, court, headnotes, and by terms or phrases that appear in the text of the cases. By using these methods of limitation, you can avoid reading cases that do not deal with your issue. For example, you can limit the list of cases to only those that cited the original case on a specific subject matter by selecting the headnote or headnotes that cover the exact topic of interest. Remember, the headnotes referenced on Lexis are the headnotes found at the beginning of cases on Lexis; you can view the text of the headnotes by clicking on the "View text of headnotes" option directly below the Headnotes heading on the left side of the screen. Another way to narrow your search is to limit by the appearance of a specific word or phrase in the box with the phrase "Enter search terms" inside.

The KeyCite display on Westlaw can be customized in a similar fashion. Be sure you are looking at the list of citing references and then click on the "Filters" option near the top of the left column. All the options will appear; if you wish to use multiple filters, select each one you wish to impose on the data. You may select the method(s) by checking the name of the option or the + symbol after each option. To view the text of the headnotes, click on the "Headnote Topics" link and select the appropriate subject. For example, if you want to see all headnotes related to "Torts" in the *Memphis* case, select Torts in the pop-up that appeared after selecting "Headnote Topics." If you wish to limit to those cases that contain specific terms in the text of the opinion, include them in the "Search within results." Once you have selected all the limits you wish, click on the "Apply" button at the bottom of the list.

Practice Point: *As we previously discussed when we talked about locating other cases using information in a case, when you are reading a case on Westlaw or Lexis and you find a relevant headnote, you can immediately see all cases that discuss the subject covered by that headnote and* *that cite the case you are reading without going to the full KeyCite/Shepard's display and using the headnote feature. On Westlaw, click on the "Cases that cite this headnote" link; on Lexis, click on the "Shepardize—Narrow by this Headnote" link located at the end of each headnote. (The language used by Westlaw, "Cases that cite this headnote," is a little misleading; cases don't cite headnotes and you shouldn't either. Westlaw is identifying those cases that have cited to the original case regarding the subject covered by the headnote.)*

As mentioned earlier, Shepard's and KeyCite allow you to customize the display of citing cases by specifying the presence of selected words or phrases in the citing case. In the right situation, this is a good alternative to use when customizing by headnotes. Remember, many times a topic and key number are broader in scope than what you need. If there is a term or phrase that consistently appears in relevant cases, include it. However, don't use this feature unless you are quite sure the word or phrase is used by the courts and has a precise meaning; improper use of this feature will likely cause many relevant cases to drop out of the results.

The citators provide references to secondary sources, such as law review articles, ALR Annotations, etc. that cite the original case. The scope of secondary sources covered in the citators varies but, for our purposes, just remember that they provide references to selected secondary sources.

G. TABLE OF AUTHORITIES (TOA)

I mentioned earlier that it is important to consult the table of authorities for a case; this is a table that lists all the cases the original case relied upon. These cases were decided earlier than the original case and thus are not captured by citators when you Shepardize a case. As we discussed earlier, if one of the cases relied upon by the original case was overruled or otherwise changed by a case that was decided after the original case, you need to know about it. Lexis and Westlaw provide access to a table of authorities. Both include a link to the TOA for a case when you are viewing the original case or when you are in Shepard's/KeyCite.

H. INCLUDING SIGNIFICANT HISTORY AND TREATMENT IN CITES TO CASES

When citing a case, *The Bluebook* indicates (Rules B10.1.6, 10.7.1, and Table 8) that you should include citations to subsequent history cases under certain circumstances. If the case you are citing was decided more than two years ago, you should not include denials of certiorari or similar discretionary appeals unless the denial is particularly relevant to your point.[21] Rule 10.7.1(c) states that cites to certain types of treatment cases (such as overruled, abrogated, or superseded by statute) should also be included. Table 8 lists the possible explanatory phrases.

I. IMPORTANT CONCEPTS RELATED TO CITATORS

Affirm—something a higher court can do to a lower court opinion on appeal. The higher court leaves the lower court opinion unchanged if they affirm. This is part of the history of a case.

Case status indicator—symbols used by the databases to indicate the status of the law from a case based on all the history and treatment cases.

[21] When citing a newer case (decided less than two years ago), it is helpful for the reader if you specify whether the case is being appealed to a higher court and, if so, the status of that appeal. If the losing party has filed for an appeal (or a petition for certiorari to the U.S. Supreme Court), the appeal will either be granted, denied, or pending. For a case decided less than two years ago, if the cite contains nothing about the subsequent history, the reader is left wondering whether an appeal is in process. If the appeal has been granted or denied, this information should be included with a cite to the case. However, once two or more years have passed since the case was decided, the status of an appeal will have been long settled and then you are only concerned with what happened if the appeal was granted. In this situation, you do not need to indicate that a case was denied appeal. However, if the denial of appeal carries some other significance for the writer when citing the case, reference to the denial may be included.

Cited case—a case that is referenced or cited in the original case. By definition, a cited case is one that was issued earlier in time than the original case.

Citing case—a case decided later in time that cites or references the original case. Also known as a treatment case.

Depth of treatment—how much attention a citing case gives to a case it cites (e.g., can vary between a mere cite with no discussion to a detailed discussion of the earlier case).

History—what happens on appeal in the same litigation. Depending upon which case you are reading, there may be prior history (what happened in this case before the opinion you are reading) and subsequent history (what happened on appeal after the case you are reading was issued).

Modify—something a higher court can do to a lower court opinion on appeal; the higher court changes a part of the lower court's opinion if they modify. This is a part of the history of a case.

Original case—the case you are reading and Shepardizing. When Shepardizing a case, it helps to keep clear who is citing whom by using the phrase "original case" to reference the case that is being Shepardized. Those cases which the original case relied upon and cited are called "cited cases" (see Table of Authorities below) and those that were decided after the original case and that cite to the original case are called "citing cases."

Overrule—the same court that issued the original opinion or a higher court within the same jurisdiction may completely change the rule of law applied in an earlier case. This is part of the treatment of a case.

Prior history—see History.

Reverse—something a higher court does on appeal to a lower court opinion. A reversal renders the lower court opinion void. This is a part of the history of a case.

Status indicator—see case status indicator above.

Subsequent history—see History.

Superseding jurisdiction—in subjects where the federal government and states share authority to regulate, the federal government can assert its authority and supersede state law.

Table of Authorities—a table that lists those cases cited (relied upon) by the original case. These cases all precede the original case.

Treatment case—see Citing case.

Treatment indicator—used by the citators to indicate, in their judgment, how each citing case has treated the original case.

Summary

1. Once you locate a case within your jurisdiction that is on point, you must determine whether the rule of law it applied remains good law or has been modified or changed in some way.

2. Besides helping you find additional cases on a subject, citators can also be used to help you determine whether the rule of law you are working with remains valid.

3. The possible ways in which a rule of law can change include:

   A. Reversed or otherwise modified on appeal. (This is part of the case history.)

      1. Citators thoroughly cover prior and subsequent history of a case involving the same litigants.

2. Sometimes the higher court remands a decision to the lower court which may then issue a different ruling so you must pay attention to all subsequent history, not just those decisions from higher courts.

B. Overruled, modified, or otherwise adversely impacted by later decisions on the same subject. (This is treatment of the case.)

1. If the rule of law in the opinion you started with is overruled by a higher court that cites your original opinion, the citator will alert you to this fact.

2. If the rule of law in the opinion was overruled by a higher court that does not cite your original opinion, the citator will not alert you to this fact. To be sure you don't miss such occurrences, you need to Shepardize all cases that are on point.

a. Ravel View on Lexis can assist in identifying other cases and the ones that are considered the most important.

b. Ravel View is limited, however, so do not completely rely upon it.

3. Sometimes a case your original case relied upon is overruled or altered. If the case that overruled the earlier rule doesn't cite your original case, Shepardizing will not alert you to this fact. Using the Table of Authorities (TOA) to check on the status of cited cases will help alert you to this possibility.

a. Westlaw may alert you when this has happened by associating the "Overruling Risk" warning with cases.

b. Again, you must always check this yourself to verify if this event has happened.

4. Sometimes, rules from cases never receive much attention and courts just move on as if the earlier case didn't apply. This is referred to as an implicit overruling. This is the most difficult situation to identify because it usually doesn't receive explicit discussion. You can only identify this by reading all cases on point within your jurisdiction and/or reading secondary sources that discuss the law.

C. The legislature in the same (or superseding) jurisdiction enacts legislation that alters the common law rule used by the court.

1. Statutes take priority over common law; if the legislature enacts legislation that conflicts with the common law rule, the statute governs.

2. Citators will alert you to this when the following conditions are true.

a. A later case references the new statute and states that it supersedes the common law rule,

b. The same case cites to your original case, and

c. The discussion of the statutory change explicitly mentions the original case.

3. Since you cannot rely on the citators to provide notification of every instance of this type, you must be sure to also check statutes for any superseding legislation.

4. An instance of superseding jurisdiction references situations where the federal government enacts legislation that conflicts with and therefore supersedes state law.

D. An administrative agency in the same (or superseding) jurisdiction enacts an administrative rule that alters the common law rule used by the court. This situation is nearly identical to the legislative option above.

4. Features of citators.

A. When you view a case online, a status indicator will be associated with the case. This symbol indicates the status of one or more rules of law in a case based upon all the history and treatment cases identified by the citator. This is called a status indicator.

B. When you view the listing of citing (treatment) cases, there will be a treatment indicator associated with each citing case. This symbol indicates how this citing case treated the original case.

C. With each citing case, the citator will also provide a link to the case, indicate how much the citing case discusses the cited case, and indicate the subject matter from the original case which the citing case discusses.

D. The citator display can be customized to limit the list to help eliminate irrelevant cases for your research.

5. Lexis and Westlaw provide a Table of Authorities (TOA) which makes it easy to identify the cases upon which the original case relied.

6. When citing a case, Rules B10.1.6, 10.7.1, and Table 8 in *The Bluebook* specify how and when to include prior and subsequent history and treatment information.

Assignment 7

The following questions are based on material covered in section XII of the reading.

In this assignment you will use the ideas discussed in the reading and apply them to specific scenarios. Question 1 of this assignment involves the following issue; whether an at-will employee can successfully bring a legal action for wrongful termination when he was discharged from his job for refusing to perform work-related functions that violated a state statute or public policy.

Assume the following for purposes of this assignment.

1. Wisconsin state law applies to this issue; federal law is not involved.
2. You are bringing this case in a Wisconsin trial court.
3. The Wisconsin Court of Appeals is a single court and any decision issued by the Wisconsin Court of Appeals is mandatory authority for all trial courts in the state.

A partner in the law firm for which you work just gave you a copy of *Bushko v. Miller Brewing Co.*, a decision issued by the Wisconsin Court of Appeals. She indicates the case is relevant to the client's case and you should incorporate it into your research. This is an unreported, a.k.a. unpublished, case that is available on Lexis and Westlaw but not in the printed reporters. Many unreported state court cases are listed in a table in the West reporter with no opinion; the table only indicates the final action taken by the court, including but not limited to reversed or affirmed. This case (*Bushko*) appears in a table at 373 N.W.2d 88.

Sign-on to Westlaw and retrieve this case using the above citation. Because this case appears in a table, along with many other cases on the same page, you get a list of all the cases named on that page of the reporter. *Bushko* is the twenty-fifth case listed. Scroll down and click on the name of the case. Because the text of the opinion is available on Westlaw, you will now see the opinion, along with a prominent notice at the top indicating this is an unpublished opinion and that Wisconsin court rules limit the citation of this case. When you see a notice like this in the practice of law, you must consult the local court rules to determine when you may cite this case and what weight it will be given by the court. For this assignment, assume that Wisconsin court rules permit use of this case and that it carries the same weight as any other decision issued by the Wisconsin Court of

Appeals. (I know that the rule that appears at the top of the screen says it does not have precedential value, but I beg your indulgence in this matter!)

Look at the beginning of the opinion; is anything different from the usual? Specifically, is something missing from this case compared to the usual case on Westlaw? I'm sure I didn't even need to ask an ace legal researcher like yourself; you instantly noticed that there are no headnotes with assigned topics and key numbers. Some "unpublished" cases have headnotes but this one does not. You would have to read the opinion to understand this case. That is not a problem for you because you would have read the case anyway rather than rely upon the headnotes to accurately understand the case, right? Right!

So that you don't have to spend time reading this case, let me summarize. Mr. Bushko, an at-will employee (no written contract of employment), was fired by his employer. Mr. Bushko said he was fired because he complained about a company policy that violated the law. The company said he was fired because Mr. Bushko was a lazy bum who left his job twenty minutes early one day and left the workers unsupervised. The trial court granted the company's motion for summary judgment. This means the trial court judge, based only on the pleadings in the case, did not think the facts supported the plaintiff's claim of wrongful discharge even if you gave the plaintiff the benefit of the doubt and interpreted the facts alleged in the complaint in a manner most favorable to the plaintiff. The plaintiff appealed this ruling to the Wisconsin Court of Appeals, which disagreed with the trial court. In the opinion you now have on the screen, the Court of Appeals reversed the trial court on this ruling saying that the facts alleged by the plaintiff could be understood in such a way that the plaintiff would win and therefore the trial court should have allowed the case to proceed to trial instead of granting the motion for summary judgment. This doesn't mean that the Court of Appeals thinks the plaintiff will ultimately win, just that it is possible and should be tried by the trial court.

1. Let's use this case to learn more about using KeyCite and Shepard's. To reduce confusion, let me map out the decisions we are talking about in A through E below. We know there was a trial court decision, but it is not available in a reporter. The opinion you retrieve from 373 N.W.2d 88 is the opinion issued by the Court of Appeals of Wisconsin; questions A and B relate to this case. This case has a status indicator caused by a later decision; this later decision is related to questions C and D below. This later decision has its own status indicator caused by an even later case; question E relates to this latest case.

   A. Using Westlaw and looking at the Court of Appeals of Wisconsin decision in *Bushko* that is found at 373 N.W.2d 88, what does the status indicator located at the top of the screen say happened to the Court of Appeals decision?

   B. Is the status indicator assigned to *Bushko* the result of the case's history or treatment?

   C. A case that refers negatively to your original case does not necessarily mean the case is useless for your purposes. A case could be overruled or reversed on an issue completely different than the one that is relevant for your purposes. Identify and retrieve the text of the decision that is responsible for the status indicator assigned to the court of appeals decision in *Bushko*; does the action taken by this court relate to the issue we are concerned with or to different issue?

   D. Which court issued the opinion that treated the court of appeals decision negatively? Concentrating on this opinion, not the court of appeals opinion, look at the status indicator assigned to it. Is the status indicator assigned to this case based upon the history or treatment of this case? Explain.

   E. How much weight does the case that caused this status indicator have in determining Wisconsin state law?

2. So far, we have used KeyCite to determine the status of a rule of law by following up on one case. In real life, as the reading emphasized, you can't get away with just KeyCiting the one case. The first example was straightforward. Let's get more realistic and throw a more difficult situation your way. In the mid-20th century, Illinois courts applied a doctrine called "contributory negligence." This doctrine basically said that a plaintiff, who was injured because of the negligence of another, was barred from recovering any damages if the plaintiff had in any way contributed to the injury. This doctrine came under attack by the 1960's and in 1967 the Appellate Court of Illinois changed the doctrine to one known as "comparative negligence" in a case reported at 229 N.E.2d 284. Comparative negligence does not totally bar recovery by a plaintiff who was partly to blame but instead apportions the damages according to how much each party was at fault. Assume that you must determine whether this rule of comparative negligence is still valid law in Illinois.

A. The first step is to KeyCite the case at 229 N.E.2d 284. Based only upon the information found when KeyCiting this case, is comparative negligence still the law in Illinois? Why or why not?

B. Now, does KeyCite indicate any negative history or treatment related to the decision of the Illinois Supreme Court in *Maki*? What does this suggest about the current status of the rule of law in Illinois related to contributory negligence?

C. With the Illinois Supreme Court decision in *Maki* on the screen, select the cases listed under the "citing references" tab. In the list of citing cases you will see one entitled *Alvis v. Ribar*. Retrieve *Alvis* and look at headnote 2. Immediately after *Alvis* was decided, was contributory negligence the law in Illinois?

D. Bet you didn't see this one coming. How could KeyCite miss the fact that *Alvis* totally changed the rule from the Illinois Supreme Court decision in *Maki*? Why wasn't a red flag assigned to *Maki*, given what *Alvis* did to it, especially since *Alvis* cites *Maki*? (Give the explanation your best shot.)

E. *Alvis* is **the** Illinois case that marked the transition to comparative negligence. Look at the KeyCite entry for *Alvis*; do you think the rule of law in *Alvis* still represents good law?

F. We have just seen where KeyCite references a superseding statute; does this mean that the editors involved with KeyCite are watching for statutes that affect previous cases? Explain.

3. **For this question, use Shepard's on Lexis.**

When citing to a case which has subsequent history or treatment, the *Bluebook* requires citation to that subsequent history (with a few exceptions spelled out in Rule 10.7). See Rule B10.1.6 and Rule 10.7 for details.

The *Bluebook* says **not to include any mention of cert. denied unless the decision is less than two years old; also, omit references to a remand (when a higher court sends the case back to the lower court)**. Abbreviations for the history and treatment indicators are listed in T.8 of the *Bluebook*. With the above information in mind, assume you are citing the case found at 351 N.E.2d 454. Please provide a complete cite to the case including subsequent history; no pinpoint cite is needed. Be sure to use Shepard's to check for any relevant subsequent history! Be sure to abbreviate any words that Table 6 says should be abbreviated.

CHAPTER 5

STATUTORY RESEARCH

XIII. STATUTES

A. OVERVIEW OF STATUTORY RESEARCH— PUBLIC LAWS AND THE CODE

We have spent a considerable amount of time discussing cases, the available tools that assist in locating them, and determining the validity of rules of law found in them. We are finally ready to proceed to another form of primary law, statutes. As you already know, statutes are enacted by legislators that are elected to serve in that capacity.

As an attorney who needs to conduct statutory research, you must take the following steps.

1. Locate the relevant statute(s),
2. Identify the latest changes to the statutory language (or the version of the statute that was in effect when the events occurred),
3. Identify interpreting cases related to the statute, and
4. Locate any secondary sources that can assist in understanding the statute.

To help you successfully accomplish this project, you need to understand a little about the legislative process and how bills become law.

1. Introduction to Statutes

Statutes exist in two forms: public laws (a.k.a. session laws) and sections in the United States Code. When a bill is enacted into law by Congress, it is known initially as a public law. A public law is assigned a number; this number is based upon the number of the Congress which enacted the law and a sequential number based upon how many laws have been passed during that Congress. For example, Public Law 111–2 was the second public law enacted by the 111th Congress.

Congresses have been numbered since the first Congress met in 1789. Each Congress lasts two years, beginning in odd numbered years immediately following the congressional election in November of even numbered years and ending when Congress adjourns at the end of the next even numbered year. In 2022 we are currently in the second year (a.k.a. term) of the 117th Congress.[22]

Statutes enacted by Congress are typically referenced in one of four ways: by a popular or common name (e.g., Lilly Ledbetter Fair Pay Act), by the public law number (e.g., Pub. L. 111–2), by the *Statutes at Large* cite (e.g., 123 Stat. 5), or by a cite to the United States Code (e.g., 29 U.S.C. § 626). *Statutes at Large* is the title of the print publication produced by the government that publishes the text of public laws. Public laws are available at https://www.govinfo.gov/app/collection/plaw and on Lexis/Westlaw. The United States Code is a subject arrangement of all public laws still in force. The Code is available at uscode.house.gov and on Lexis/Westlaw.

As previously mentioned, when Congress passes a bill into law, the new law is known as a "public law."[23] Public laws are not always easy to work with. They may contain material on a variety of

[22] If you are interested, https://www.congress.gov/help/field-values/congresses contains a table that shows the correspondence between Congress and years.

[23] There is a category of laws known as private laws, but they are few and not important for most statutory research.

subjects and the subjects often are not related to one another. In other words, a single public law may cover one, ten, twenty, or more subjects. In addition, when Congress wants to change a previous law, they must pass a new public law that makes the changes. Often, they only change one small part of the law and don't reprint the entire law that is being amended; they just indicate which words in the old law are deleted and which words replace them. This situation makes statutory research on a subject very difficult if using only public laws. For example, imagine you want to read the current law about copyright infringement. If public laws were the only source of statutes available, you would have to search decades of public laws to locate the various ones that, when pieced together, contain the language of the current law.

To make researching statutes easier, in the early 20th century, the government created what is known as the *United States Code.* The Code takes all public laws and arranges them by subject. It also eliminates any language that is deleted by later amendments. As a result, the language of the Code indicates the actual language of the statute as it reads on a specific date. For example, all statutory provisions from various public laws discussing copyright infringement are put together in Title 17 of the United States Code, Chapter 5. Language from seven different public laws make up the language of this chapter in the Code. It should be apparent that the Code makes the job of finding current and relevant statutes much easier than if public laws were the only available source for statutory language.

The Code is divided into 54 titles, each title covering a broad subject area.[24] A list of titles and the corresponding subjects is available at a web page maintained by the government.[25] We will discuss this in greater detail later but let's continue our discussion of statutes by looking at how they are referenced.

2. Recognizing References to a Public Law

Public laws may be referenced three different ways: by popular name, public law number, and *Statutes at Large* cite. To illustrate this, let's look at a public law Congress passed in 2009. Its popular name is "Lilly Ledbetter Fair Pay Act of 2009" and you can retrieve a copy at https://www.congress.gov/111/plaws/publ2/PLAW-111publ2.pdf. This name is referenced in section 1 of the act itself.

Popular names are derived from various sources; in this example, the popular name derives from the name of a plaintiff in a case that was ultimately decided by the U.S. Supreme Court. Congress did not like way the Court interpreted a statutory provision and passed this law to change the outcome for future cases. Sometimes popular names derive from the names of the members of Congress who sponsored the legislation; a good example of this is found in the law known as Sarbanes-Oxley. The sponsors of the bill that became the law were Sen. Paul Sarbanes and Representative Michael Oxley. Other popular names simply describe the subject matter; the Americans with Disabilities Act is an example of this type. Another version of a popular name isn't really the popular name although it is used like one. For example, you will frequently hear people refer to Title IX. This is a way of referencing a public law that sounds much like a popular name but it is actually referencing a numbered part of a public law. (Public laws are sometimes organized into titles; see the section on the organization of public laws later in this reading for further explanation.) Title IX is frequently used to reference Title IX of the Education Amendments Act of 1972, which contains provisions that prohibit discrimination between men and women in activities like sports at institutions of higher education. If you Google the phrase "Title IX" you will see references to this

[24] Technically, the Code consists of 53 titles because Title 53 contains no information. Supposedly, title 53 will soon be populated with statutes currently found in Title 15 that are related to small businesses.

[25] Uscode.house.gov.

public law. Everyone who uses this phrase knows which law is involved. In this situation, Google is your friend!

The Lilly Ledbetter Fair Pay Act of 2009 is also known as Public Law 111–2; this information appears at the top of the first page of the law. The number preceding the dash indicates the number of the Congress that passed the law; in this case it was the 111th Congress. The number following the dash indicates how many laws the current Congress has passed. Here, this law was the second public law passed by the 111th Congress.

Finally, this law is also referred to by the volume and beginning page where it may be found in the *Statutes at Large*, which is the official source for publication of federal statutes. This law is published in volume 123 of the *Statutes at Large*, beginning on page 5. The cite looks like this: 123 Stat. 5. This information appears in the top right portion of the first page of the law.

I mention these three methods because you should be able to locate and identify public laws using any one of these three methods. We will discuss the tools available for locating public laws shortly.

3. Subjects Included in a Public Law

As previously mentioned, each public law may contain material on a wide variety of topics; at the federal level, there is no limit on the number of topics a public law may cover. The Lilly Ledbetter Fair Pay Act, which is divided into six sections, is relatively simple as public laws go. Look at Section 3 of the law, the heading of which reads "Discrimination in compensation because of race, color, religion, sex, or national origin." The first sentence of this section indicates that the language of this section will be codified in 42 U.S.C. § 2000e–5(e).[26] Title 42 of the Code includes most of the civil rights statutes. Look at the public law again and scroll down to Section 4 of the Lilly Ledbetter Fair Pay Act. The public law says that this section amends language located in 29 U.S.C. § 626(d). Title 29 of the Code contains the text of most laws that apply to labor. So, this relatively simple law, only five pages in length, impacts two different titles in the United States Code. Imagine how many different parts of the Code could be altered by a public law that is hundreds, or even thousands, of pages in length!

4. Making Changes to Statutes

If Congress later wants to change the text of a public law, they must amend it by passing a new public law that repeals and/or changes language in the original law. To illustrate this point, look once more at Section 3 of the Lilly Ledbetter Fair Pay Act. The first sentence of Section 3 refers to the Civil Rights Act of 1964. This is the law that first created the language that was codified in § 2000e–5. Section 3 of the Lilly Ledbetter Fair Pay Act amends, or changes, the original language passed into law by the Civil Rights Act of 1964.

Something similar happened in Section 4 of the Lilly Ledbetter Fair pay Act; the section of the Code amended by Section 4 of the Lilly Ledbetter Fair Pay Act was originally created by the Age Discrimination in Employment Act of 1967. Section 4 of the Lilly Ledbetter Act changed some language that was a part of the original Act passed in 1967.

You can see a complete history of which public laws created and amended a specific Code section by looking at the history information, which always follows the text of the Code section in the United States Code. Let's look at the history of § 2000e–5 in Title 42 of the United States Code. Retrieve this Code section using the uscode.house.gov website. Simply insert 42 in the box labeled "Title" and

---

[26] The text of this Code section is available by going to uscode.house.gov. You will see a "Jump To" heading followed by a box under Title and Section. Enter 42 in the box under Title and 2000e–5 in the box under Section. The numbering of this section is rather odd. Normally there are just numbers with no letters and dashes. This is an example of what happens when Congress enacts many laws in a particular subject and runs out of numbers that can be used because of prior numbering in subsequent sections. In this case they had to resort to letters and then additional numbers.

2000e–5 in the box labeled "Section." Once the Code section appears, scroll down to the end of the Code section language; just above a section labeled "References in Text" you will see a parenthetical that lists public laws that have been included in § 2000e–5. The following information is shown for each public law: public law number, title number, section number, date passed, and *Statutes at Large* cite. The first public law listed, which created this section in the Code, was passed in 1964 (this is the Civil Rights Act of 1964 that was mentioned above). The last public law that amended this Code section is the Lilly Ledbetter Act, also referenced above. So, by looking up this one Code section, you can see information from all the public laws that have added language to this section.

Based on the information above, you should have a basic understanding of what makes the Code such a great tool for statutory research. Determining what statutory law says on any given subject at a specific point in time would be very difficult if the Code didn't exist and you had to conduct your research using only public laws; you would have to look at every public law passed since the first one that covered the subject you are researching to determine the state of the current law. The United States Code takes all the various public laws on point and combines them into one text. The Code also deletes any language that originally appeared in the statute but was deleted by a subsequent public law. This one source provides the current language of the statute and indicates all the various public laws from which this language is derived.

5. Why Public Laws Are Important

So, why bother learning about public laws since we have the Code? (I know you were thinking it!) Well, there are several reasons why a legal researcher should be aware of public laws. The first reason is that attorneys, and others, often refer to a public law by using the popular name of the law and you must have a basic awareness of this practice and what it references. As a result of this practice, there will be times when you must locate public laws.

Another reason is because the Code is only current as of a certain date and you must use public laws passed since that date to determine whether any changes were made to your statute that are not yet reflected in the Code. We will discuss this in more depth later.

There are addition reasons public laws are important but they are beyond the scope of this book.

6. Organization of Public Laws

Public laws vary in their organization. Every public law is organized into sections; many of the shorter ones are only organized into sections and subsections. The Lilly Ledbetter Fair Pay Act is an example of this.

Longer, more complicated, public laws are usually organized into titles, with each title further subdivided into sections and subsections. The Civil Rights Act of 1964 (https://www.congress.gov/88/statute/STATUTE-78/STATUTE-78-Pg241.pdf) is an example of this type of law. Typically, the sections of a public law organized into titles follow the numbering scheme of the title. For example, the first section in Title VII (title numbers use roman numerals) is numbered 701. The first number in the section number corresponds to the title in which the section is located. There are exceptions to this but it is generally true.

The numbers assigned to titles and sections in a public law are solely for organizational purposes within that public law. There is no scheme by which you can determine, using the number of a title and/or section in a public law alone, where a specific section of a public law is codified in the United States Code. You must use references in the text of the public law, in marginal notes in the public law, or a table to translate from public law section to Code section. This will be discussed in greater detail shortly.

7. Using Public Laws to Get to the United States Code

Most of the time your ultimate goal will be to find current statutory law on a particular subject. The best source for this job is the United States Code or one of the commercial alternatives: United States Code Service (U.S.C.S.) on Lexis or United States Code Annotated (U.S.C.A.) on Westlaw. For brevity and unless otherwise explicitly noted, any time I mention U.S.C., you can also use either U.S.C.A. or U.S.C.S.; they are all organized the same, by title and section. If you are searching for statutes purely by subject, it is best to search the United States Code or one of its commercial versions instead of Statutes at Large. There really is no general subject index for public laws themselves and you don't really need a public law if you are only looking for the current language of a statute.

The most common situation in which you may need to locate a public law is when you have a source that references a public law either by popular name, public law number, or *Statutes at Large* cite. In this situation, you need to use that information to get to the Code. So, which tools should you use?

If you know the popular name of an act, you have several options. The most obvious, and often most helpful, option is to simply Google the popular name. When you Google a popular name, you will usually see many sites that contain the text of the law, either in its public law form or Code form. How do you decide which sites to use? Sites that have a ".gov" extension are a good bet since they are generally more reliable than others. Sites that law firms or law schools have posted can also be very useful. You will, of course, almost always see a Wikipedia option. These can be good if the author knows what he/she is talking about. At a minimum, this source should at least provide a reference to the public law. Try googling the Lilly Ledbetter Act and see what you find.

What if Google doesn't help? For those situations, a popular names table can assist; it is available at uscode.house.gov/popularnames/popularnames.htm. With each popular name listed in the table there is an indication of the public law number of the act, where it is found in *Statutes at Large*, and where it is codified in the United States Code generally. To get more specific and determine where a single section of a public law is codified, use Table III, which is available at uscode.house.gov/table3/table3years.htm. To use this table, first select the year in which the public law was enacted and then select the public law number; you now should see a list of all sections in the public law and where each is located in the U.S.C. (where it is codified). Try using the table to locate the Lilly Ledbetter Act, which was passed in 2009 and is public law number 111–2.

If you already know the public law number or the Statutes at Large cite, you can skip the Popular Name Tool and use Table III to go directly to the relevant title and section(s) in the Code.

B. ORGANIZATION OF THE UNITED STATES CODE

As I just mentioned, the United States Code (U.S.C.) (or the commercial versions on Lexis (U.S.C.S.) or Westlaw (U.S.C.A.)) is the usual source used to find current statutes. It combines statutes on the same subject and deletes old, superseded language, making it easier to read the current law. The U.S.C. is organized into titles that are numbered, as discussed above.

Each title of the U.S.C. is further subdivided into various units. While every title varies slightly in its organization, they are usually subdivided into Parts, Chapters, Sections, and Subsections. As an example, view the organization of 29 U.S.C. Chapter 28. To access this, go to uscode.house.gov and scroll down to Title 29; now select the + symbol in front of the title. This view of the U.S.C. is known as the Table of Contents (TOC) since it shows you the organization of Title 29 and lists the headings associated with the various subunits; these headings provide an overview of the content of this part of the Code. From the TOC you can see that Chapter 28 of Title 29 contains the statutes related to the Family and Medical Leave Act. The chapter is further subdivided into subchapters and then sections. Viewing the TOC of the Code helps you to understand how the subject matter is organized and which sections are relevant to your research.

For example, if you were interested in the question of when an employee can take leave under the Family and Medical Leave Act, Subchapter 1 contains the relevant provisions. To see the subchapters in Title 29, select the + symbol in front of Chapter 28, and then select the plus in front of Subchapter 1. The first Section of this Subchapter, Section 2611, contains definitions. To view the text of the definitions, click anywhere on the line associated with Section 2611. The section should appear in a new window.

Notice that the beginning of Section 2611 states the definitions apply to "this subchapter." This is another reason that the TOC is important for statutory research. The definitions included in section 2611 only apply to those sections that are included in Subchapter I of Chapter 28, Title 29. To identify which sections are in Subchapter I, you must look at the TOC. Close the box that displays the text of this section and return to the TOC view. Which sections are included in Subchapter I? In other words, to which sections do these definitions apply? Sections 2612–2620. If one of the terms defined in sec. 2611 appears in sec. 2631, the definition does not apply because sec. 2631 is in Subchapter II.

Where can you find the U.S.C.? There are several options.

1. Lexis and Westlaw contain the U.S.C.

   A. Lexis: sign in and then select the Federal tab. Select the link labeled "USCS—United States Code Service." This is the commercial version of the U.S.C. available on Lexis. Once you select the U.S.C.A. link, you should see the TOC, which can be expanded by clicking on the + symbol located in front of a Title number.

   B. Westlaw: log in and select the Federal Materials tab. Select the link labeled "United States Code Annotated (USCA)". This is Westlaw's commercial version of the U.S.C. Once you select this link, you should now see the TOC of the Code, which can be expanded to show greater detail by clicking on the title link.

2. Numerous free versions of the Code are available on the web. The best one, in my judgment, is the one we have already used at uscode.house.gov. This site is operated by the Office of the Law Revision Counsel, which is the office charged with creating and maintaining the Code for the government.

C. STEP 1 OF STATUTORY RESEARCH—LOCATING RELEVANT STATUTES

So, what options are available for locating relevant sections of the U.S.C. when all you know is the subject matter? There are four options.

- Human created subject indexes on Lexis and Westlaw
- Browsing and/or searching the TOC of the Code
- Locating a secondary source that discusses relevant statutes
- Full text searching of the U.S.C.

You may (or should) notice that these options are very similar to searching for cases, except for the TOC approach which is not available for cases since cases are published in chronological order, not subject order.

1. Subject Index Approach to Locating Statutes

Let's use Lexis as an example. Log into Lexis and retrieve the main screen. In the search box, where you type the search query, begin typing United States Code. Several options beginning with these words will appear automatically. One of them is the USCS Index; select this option when it appears. Once selected, you should see letters of the alphabet preceded by the + symbol; clicking on the + allows one to view all subject headings under that letter. This will allow you to browse the main and subheadings included in the index. Alternatively, you can place a check mark in one or more boxes located between the + and the letter. Once you have selected all headings you think may be relevant, you can then enter search terms in the query box near the top of the screen. This will search for the word or phrase you entered in the entries you checked.

Let's look for statutes related to labor and employment by running a search. You do not have to check any boxes; if you just enter a search and run it, the search will look through all entries in the subject index. Enter the phrase "age discrimination" (including the quotes) in the search box and click on the red search button. The results should be a list of subject headings; select the one labeled "A-206 Age Discrimination." On the next screen, immediately below the heading, you will see references to 29 §§ 621 to 634. Select this link and § 621 will appear on your screen. This is the first section of the statute that deals with age discrimination in employment.

As you look at the screen, you will see the outline of the TOC for this title just above the section heading; the TOC outline looks like this:

United States Code Service

  TITLE 29. LABOR (Chs. 1–32)

    CHAPTER 14. AGE DISCRIMINATION IN EMPLOYMENT (§§ 621–634)

Click on the Chapter 14 heading and the full TOC will appear for Chapter 14 of Title 29. This is a good way to see how the material is arranged and to easily view the different sections that are relevant to this issue.

The subject index in Westlaw works much the same. Just like Lexis, you can begin typing "United States Code Annotated Index" in the search box and a link will appear for that source. Alternatively, you can select the "Federal materials" link on the main page after signing into Westlaw and selecting USCA. Once you see the USCA page, a link to the subject index will appear among various options on the right side of the screen under "Tools and Resources." Just like with Lexis, you can either browse the index or search for words that appear in the index.

2. Browsing the TOC of the Code

We have just seen how you can view the Code's TOC. Sometimes you can locate relevant sections this way, but not always. For example, if you are looking for sections of the Code that cover copyright infringement, you could look at the TOC. As you scan down the TOC, you will see that Title 17 covers copyrights. Expanding Title 17 and scanning through the TOC reveals that Chapter 5 contains provisions related to infringement and remedies. For this subject, a scan of the Code's TOC works very nicely. However, it isn't often this straightforward.

3. Locating a Secondary Source That Discusses the Statute

We previously discussed searching secondary sources, so we don't need to go over this again. When searching for discussion of statutory material in a secondary source, you can search using the popular name, public law number, U.S.C. cite, or just subject. You will only find something if an article or other secondary source has been written about it, of course, so this will not always result in relevant information. However, it can provide very valuable information, including cites to relevant statutes and background information.

4. Full Text Searching of the U.S.C.

You can also search the full text of the U.S.C., just like with cases, using the two commercial legal databases. Searching is a bit trickier mainly because it is much more difficult to anticipate the exact language that Congress used to discuss a particular problem. Cases are written in normal English, for the most part, but this isn't necessarily true for statutes. Also, many times the language of a statute is the result of compromise. This tends to result in ambiguous language which only makes searching that more difficult.

Let's run a search for Code sections related to fraud in the application for a passport. Just like with cases, you can use a natural language search or an advanced search using terms and connectors. Let's do a natural language search. Using Westlaw, get to the U.S.C.A. database and enter the following two words as your search: passport fraud. The first hit (or near the top of the list) should be title 18 U.S.C. § 1542, which deals with false statements in an application for and when using a passport.

Retrieve the full text of this Code section. If you want to see other sections in this same subject area, simply click on the "Chapter 75" link at the top of the screen and you will see the TOC for this part of the Code. In this example, we have hit home with the simple search. Trust me, it isn't usually this simple.

5. AI

The process of searching for statutes is similar to searching for cases. Questions about whether there is a statute on a specific subject are handled well. For example, you could ask if a statute exists that deals with false information on a passport application. However, because statutes are written using more precise language than court opinions, it can be more challenging to locate relevant statutes using AI. The point of not taking the result of an AI query as final is even more critical when searching for statutes. Again, using the various methods of searching for statutes is important.

Questions about interpretations of statutes are more complicated and often require additional research. For example, the following query, which is related to the discussion of whistleblowers from earlier in this chapter, received slightly different answers from Protégé and CoCounsel. I ran the following search: Does the provision of the Sarbanes-Oxley act related to a whisleblower require the whistleblower to report the infraction to the SEC? Protégé did not reference the decision by the U.S. Supreme Court in the *Digital Realty Trust* while CoCounsel did include a reference. This just illustrates the point I have made several times: AI is a tool for beginning to do research and can increase efficiency. However, it is only a place to begin. When looking for cases that have interpreted a statute, the annotated codes remain an important tool for the legal researcher.

Summary

1. Laws passed by Congress are called public laws.

2. A single public law can cover a multitude of subjects. There is no limit.

3. Public laws are published in *Statutes at Large*; as a result, they are also referenced by the number of the volume and first page where they appear in *Statutes at Large* (e.g. 81 Stat. 602).

4. Public laws are frequently known by a popular name (e.g. Americans with Disabilities Act (ADA)).

5. Public laws are also assigned a unique numerical identifier known as a public law number (e.g. Pub. L. 90–202; this is the 202nd public law passed by the 90th Congress).

6. To make statutory research easier, all provisions from public laws that are related to the same subject are reprinted together in the *United States Code* (U.S.C.) (e.g. 29 U.S.C. § 626). For example, most statutes related to labor law are found in Title 29 of the U.S.C.

7. Because of 2 and 6 above, a single public law may be split into and found in various titles of the U.S.C.

8. When Congress wants to change (amend) an existing law, they must pass another public law that makes changes to the earlier public law.

9. Most of the time, it is easiest to conduct statutory research using the U.S.C. This statement is true because:

   A. The U.S.C. contains all statutes (no matter when they were enacted into law) currently in force and organizes them by subject.

   B. Repealed language is removed from the U.S.C.

   C. When you read a Code section, all laws currently in force are combined into one place. (Note: this doesn't mean that other titles and sections of the U.S.C. are not relevant to your problem; you always need to check for other relevant statutes.)

   D. Statutory research without the U.S.C. would involve searching many decades of public laws for anything passed on a subject. For this reason, the U.S.C. greatly simplifies the process of statutory research.

10. If you know the popular name of a public law and need to locate where language from the public law is found in the U.S.C., you have several tools at your disposal.

   A. Google the popular name.

   B. Popular Name Tool located at uscode.house.gov (select "Popular Name Tool" located in the left column).

11. These tools will provide the public law number of the relevant statute. You can then examine the public law and look for references to the U.S.C. in either the text of the public law itself or in a marginal note.

12. If a reference to the U.S.C. is not found in either place, look up the public law number in "Table III—Statutes at Large," which is available at the uscode.house.gov website under the "Other Tables and Tools" link. (This step also works if you are beginning with a public law number and need to locate the relevant provisions in the U.S.C.)

13. A cite to the U.S.C. may be plugged directly into Westlaw, Lexis, or uscode.house.gov and it will retrieve the relevant section of the Code.

14. Structure of the U.S.C.

   A. The U.S.C. is organized into fifty-four numbered titles; each title represents a broad subject area (e.g., all provisions from public laws related to copyright are codified in Title 17 of the U.S.C. A list of the subject headings assigned to Code titles is available at uscode.house.gov).

   B. You must understand the Code hierarchy (a.k.a. the statutory scheme) to effectively work with statutes in the U.S.C. The Table of Contents (TOC) displays the statutory scheme.

Title

Part

Chapter

Section

Subsections

Paragraphs

Subparagraphs

Clauses

Subclauses

Items

C. All titles are not subdivided into the same subunits (e.g., not all titles are divided into parts) but the example above gives you an idea of how they are typically organized.

D. Why should you be familiar with the Code hierarchy?

1. Rarely is a single Code section the only one that applies; you must always consult the surrounding Code sections to be sure you have all relevant information.

2. You will frequently find definitions of significant terms in a section at the beginning of a part, chapter, or another unit of the Code. A section of the Code that contains definitions will specify the unit of the Code to which the definitions apply. To determine which sections are a part of the specified unit, you must consult the Table of Contents (TOC) for that part of the Code involved.

15. Several methods are available for locating relevant Code sections by subject.

A. Use the subject index on Westlaw of Lexis.

B. Manually search the TOC for relevant portions of the Code starting with the title and selecting the relevant titles, chapters, etc.

C. Conduct a full-text search. Keep in mind that full-text searching of statutes can be more challenging than cases because of the nature of the legislative process and the language in which statutes are written.

D. USING THE UNITED STATES CODE IN STATUTORY RESEARCH

1. Step 2 of Statutory Research—Locating the Version of the Code Needed in Your Research

Let's turn our attention to a few details about using the United States Code. On Westlaw, return to the Code section you just had on the screen, 18 U.S.C. § 1542. Recall the steps of statutory research we discussed earlier.

1. Locate the relevant statute(s),

2. Be sure you have the latest changes to the statutory language (or the version of the statute that was in effect when the events occurred),

3. Identify interpreting cases related to the statute, and

4. Locate any secondary sources that can assist in understanding the statute.

We have covered the basics of number 1 above, locating relevant statutes, so let's move on to number 2, how you can be sure you have the version of the Code you need. One of two scenarios will be true; you either need to have the most current, up-to-date, version of a statute or you need to know how the statute read on a specified date in the past. The latter scenario is involved when you need to know how a statute read when certain critical events took place.

a. Locating the Current Version of a Statute in the United States Code

Let's begin with the assumption that you need to know how a Code section reads today. With 18 U.S.C. § 1542 on the screen, you should see the cite to the Code, followed by the section heading, which reads "False statement in application and use of passport." Just below the heading is a link labeled "Currentness." Selecting this link will take you to a statement that indicates how up to date the database is. This information is located on Westlaw at the end of the Code section. This specific Code section is short enough that you can view the entire section on one screen. Towards the bottom of the screen, you should see the line that reads "Current through P.L. ###–###." If the section was large enough to take up more than one screen, selecting the "Currentness" link would take you immediately to the end of the document where the "Current through" statement is located. The "###" following the dash represents the numbers assigned to the latest public law that has been included in the database.[27]

The "current through" line indicates that all laws enacted by Congress through the number of the public law listed has been incorporated into the Code on Westlaw. Sometimes the "Current Through" line also indicates that a part of an earlier public law is not yet included. Just be sure to read this line closely.

If one or more public law(s) has been enacted after the last one incorporated into the database, how do you know if any of these later laws changed language found in the Code section you are researching, in this case 18 U.S.C. § 1542? Well, you can relax if using Westlaw because it continually checks these public laws and if one of them, that was enacted after the last update, made a change to the Code section you are looking at, a red flag would appear at the top of the Code section along with a link to the text of the public law that made the change.

Red flags caused by new public laws don't remain long because Westlaw updates the Code frequently. As a result, I can't show you one that currently has the red flag. A screen shot of a Code section with a red flag because of a recent amendment is shown in Exhibit XIII-A. You will see that it provides a link to the recently enacted legislation that amends the relevant Code section.

Let's now look at a nearby section in Title 18, § 1546 on Westlaw. You will see two yellow flags located near the top of the screen. One of them is present because of proposed bills that, if enacted into law, would amend the language of this section. Yellow and red flags are not limited to only these two situations; they are also used for other reasons that may impact the status of the statutory language. We will cover these shortly.

Like Westlaw, Lexis also indicates when the Code database was last updated. Lexis includes this information near the top of the Codes section; it simply reads "Current through PL ###–##, approved (date)." Unlike Westlaw, Lexis does not provide status indicators notifying you of a statute that was enacted after the database was updated which also made changes to the Code section you are viewing. However, there is an easy way to check this. It involves two steps:

1. Note the number of the public law listed in the "current through" statement in the database, the last public law incorporated into the Code.

[27] Please note that this only tells you that the Code database is current through the specified public law. This does not indicate that the specific section you are viewing was updated by the listed public law. The last public law to amend this specific Code section is shown in the credits or history section immediately following the language of the Code section.

2. Consult the table for the current year located at http://uscode.house.gov/classification/tables.shtml. Select the html format for the table that is sorted in U.S. Code order. As the name of the table suggests, it is organized by Code title and, within each title, by Code section. In our example involving § 1542, you look down the list of titles in the first column to locate title 18 and then look in the second column for 1542, the section number. This table lists all changes made during the current year. If there has been a change to the Code title and section you are updating any time during the current calendar year, it will be listed in this table. The entry will also indicate the number of the public law that amended it.

If a public law is listed in the table for the Code section you are working with, you need to compare the number of the public law listed in the table with the number of the last public law included in the Code database on Lexis. If the number of the amending law from the table is larger than the number from the database, you must locate and read the public law because it was enacted after the Lexis database was last updated. If the number of the amending law is less than the last one included in Lexis, the change has already been incorporated in the Code on Lexis and you need do nothing further.

For example, assume that Lexis tells you the database is current through Public Law 117–32. Next, assume that the update table at the uscode.house.gov website indicates that 18 U.S.C. § 1542 was amended by Public Law 117–35. In this case, since the amending public law number is higher than the last update to the database, the change made by this public law has not been incorporated into the Code language on Lexis. Therefore, you would need to read the public law to see what changes it made. On the other hand, if the amending law listed in the table was a lower number, say 117–31, you would not need to locate the public law because the change has already been incorporated into the database. You know this because the database says that the Code is current through Public Law 117–32 and the table indicated that the amendment was made by Public Law 117–31. You could also confirm that the changes made by the public law were already incorporated into the Code by checking to see if the number of the public law appears in the credits for that specific Code section. The credits for a Code section are listed immediately following the text of the Code section.

If the Code title and section you are updating are not listed in the table, that means no changes were made to that Code section during the current calendar year and you have the latest language in the database.

If you need to look up the text of a recent public law, you can do so at the congress.gov website. On the main page at congress.gov, just below and to the right of the main search box, is a heading labeled "Bill Searches and List." One of the options under this heading is "Public Laws." Selecting this option will open a list of public laws with links to the full text. Lexis and Westlaw also have the text of public laws.

b. Locating a Section in the United States Code as It Read in the Past

Enough about updating the Code; let's now look at the options for locating the language of a Code section as it read in the past. Return to 18 U.S.C. § 1542 on Westlaw. Looking further at § 1542, you will see a section labeled "CREDIT(S)" followed by dates and cites to public laws. As of the writing of this text, the credits appears like the paragraph below.

(June 25, 1948, c. 645, 62 Stat. 771; Pub.L. 103–322, Title XIII, § 130009(a)(2), Title XXXIII, § 330016(1)(I), Sept. 13, 1994, 108 Stat. 2030, 2147; Pub.L. 104–208, Div. C, Title II, § 211(a)(2), Sept. 30, 1996, 110 Stat. 3009–569; Pub.L. 107–273, Div. B, Title IV, § 4002(a)(3), Nov. 2, 2002, 116 Stat. 1806.)

This section identifies the history of the Code section. This section was created on June 25, 1948, by a public law that is found in vol. 62 of Statutes at Large, starting on page 771. Prior to the 1950's public laws were assigned chapter numbers, which is what the c. 645 references. It was amended by public laws enacted in 1994, 1996, and 2002. This information can be useful if you want to research what is known as the "legislative history" of this Code language. However, we won't discuss this now since it is beyond the scope of an introductory work on legal research.

On Westlaw, there is a tab near the top of the screen labeled "History (###)" that provides cites and links to various materials about the history. One of the links under this tab is labeled "Versions (#)." If you click on this, you will be given the option of seeing how the Code read in the past. This is the quickest way to see how this Code section read before amendments were made. In this case, for example, the last amendment was in 2002. So, if you needed to see how this Code section read before the change made in 2002, you could select the first link under the "Prior Versions" heading. If the events involved in your client's case happened in 2000, for example, this is the version you would need to use. This is especially true in this example because Title 18 of the U.S.C. contains criminal provisions. If your client is accused of violating a criminal law in 2000, the version that was in force at that time is the one that would apply. One cannot be criminally charged for a law that didn't exist when the events that constitute the crime took place.

Westlaw also allows you to quickly compare two versions so you can easily see the change made by an amendment. In this example, suppose you want to see the change made in 2002 to 18 U.S.C. § 1542; you simply select the "Add to compare" button under the latest version and the same button under the prior version that was in force until the change in 2002. Once you have selected both, click on the "Compare" link located on the right side. The screen will now display the changes, crossing out the language deleted and highlighting the added material. In this case, the 2002 amendment just made a change to a word that was used incorrectly.

Can you view earlier Codes on Lexis? Yes! Go back to Lexis and retrieve 18 U.S.C. § 1542. In the lower-right part of the screen, you will see a link labeled "Archived code versions(###)." Selecting this option will allow you to look at historical versions.

2. Step 3 of Statutory Research—Locating Relevant Cases That Interpret and Apply the Code Language

So much for being sure you have the correct version of the Code for the situation you are working with. Recall the steps of statutory research again.

1. Locate the relevant statute(s),
2. Be sure you have the latest changes to the statutory language (or the version of the statute that was in effect when the events occurred),
3. Identify interpreting cases related to the statute, and
4. Locate any secondary sources that can assist in understanding the statute.

Now, on to step three of research using statutory Codes, reading court cases that interpret and apply the statutory language. Why are cases important? Because it is in court where actual controversies are decided and the court must interpret and apply the statute to specific facts. It is imperative that you understand how decisions that are mandatory for the court you will be in, when representing your client, will apply a specific statute. This option may also help in determining the meaning of a word or phrase that is not defined in the statute.

Let's illustrate this. Assume you are representing a client that reported information to his employer about a fraud committed by his supervisor that constitutes a violation of the federal securities laws. Your client is concerned that the company may retaliate against him for revealing this information. Society wants to encourage individuals who are aware of illegal actions to come forward and reveal what they know about the crime. These individuals are known as "Whistleblowers" and anyone who qualifies as a whistleblower receives protection from retaliation by their employer. Part of the issue is whether your client is a "whistleblower" as defined by the relevant statute and is thus entitled to the protections offered by the statute. The relevant statute is found at 15 U.S.C. § 78u–6(h)(1)(A)(iii),[28] which reads as follows.

(h) Protection of whistleblowers

(1) Prohibition against retaliation

(A) In general

No employer may discharge, demote, suspend, threaten, harass, directly or indirectly, or in any other manner discriminate against, a whistleblower in the terms and conditions of employment because of any lawful act done by the whistleblower—

(i) in providing information to the Commission in accordance with this section;

(ii) in initiating, testifying in, or assisting in any investigation or judicial or administrative action of the Commission based upon or related to such information; or

(iii) in making disclosures that are required or protected under the Sarbanes-Oxley Act of 2002 (15 U.S.C. 7201 et seq.), this chapter, including section 78j–1(m) of this title, section 1513(e) of Title 18, and any other law, rule, or regulation subject to the jurisdiction of the Commission.

The controversy comes in interpreting clause (iii). Whistleblower is defined in this statute as someone who discloses information about a violation of the securities laws to the Securities and Exchange Commission (SEC), referred to as "the Commission" in clauses (i) and (ii). Clause (iii) was added later in time and includes a reference to another statute, the Sarbanes-Oxley Act. The Sarbanes-Oxley Act does not require disclosure to the SEC as part of the definition of a whistleblower. So, the question is whether Congress intended to broaden the definition of whistleblower in this statute when it incorporated this reference to the Sarbanes-Oxley Act and protect even those who did not directly report to the SEC. This impacts your client since he reported the issue to his employer instead of the SEC.

Various federal circuit courts were split on the answer to this question. The Fifth Circuit in *Asadi v. G.E. Energy (USA), L.L.C.*, 720 F.3d 620 (5th Cir. 2013) held that a person had to disclose the information to the SEC to qualify as a whistleblower and receive the protections offered by this statute. On the other hand, the Second (*Berman v. Neo@Ogilvy L.L.C.*, 801 F.3d 145 (2d Cir. 2015)) and Ninth Circuits (*Somers v. Digital Realty Trust Inc.*, 850 F.3d 1045 (9th Cir. 2017)) held that a person who disclosed information to his employer, but not to the SEC, still qualified as a whistleblower and therefore was eligible for protection afforded by this statute.

If you face a similar question in a case before a federal district court, the district court will have to follow the rule established by the circuit in which the district court is located. This will determine which interpretation is mandatory.

Question: What would resolve this issue and make all circuits uniform? Well, Congress could amend the existing Code language by adding a provision that would resolve the issue or the U.S. Supreme Court could rule on this issue. The latter occurred in *Digital Realty Trust, Inc. v. Somers*, 138 S. Ct.

---

[28] As we have seen, the U.S.C. is organized into titles, chapters, subchapters, parts, subparts, and sections. As we noted earlier, not all titles are divided into these same units but this is the basic layout. In this example, § 78u–6(h)(1)(A)(iii), the section is further subdivided. The number assigned to this section is "78u–6"; "(h)" designates the subsection, "(1)" designates the paragraph, "(A)" designates the subparagraph, and "(iii)" designates the clause.

767 (2018).[29] The Ninth Circuit case was appealed to the U.S. Supreme Court and the Court reversed, agreeing with the position taken by the Fifth Circuit. This U.S. Supreme Court decision has now resolved the issue for all courts across the country and only Congress can now change the outcome by enacting appropriate legislation. Of course, the Supreme Court could overrule its decision, but this is unlikely to happen soon, if at all. The point is, you must be sure how mandatory decisions issued by higher courts in your jurisdiction have interpreted and applied the statute.

You have a couple options for locating these cases using Westlaw and Lexis. Westlaw offers two options for locating cases that have discussed a particular statute. The first option is a list of cases selected by editors. Using Westlaw, return to 15 U.S.C. § 78u–6. Look once more at the tabs along the top of the screen. The second from the left is labeled "Notes of Decisions." Select this option. The West editors have selected cases they think are important and listed them here. The parenthetical indicates there are 67 cases in the list (the actual number will likely be higher when you view it). Once you are viewing the list of cases, on the left is an outline of the main topics used to organize the cases. Selecting a heading will display the cases related to that subject.

The second option for viewing cases related to a statute is based upon KeyCite. If you wish to see all cases that have discussed this Code provision, you can select the "Citing References" tab, which is located two tabs to the right of the "Notes of Decisions" tab. Mouseover the citing references tab. As you mouseover, but before you click on it, it will list the types of citing documents. Cases is the first option and what you want here. Select this option.

Westlaw indicates there are approximately 286 cases (maybe more by the time you look at this list) that have cited to this Code section. So, you can see that many more cases cite to this statute than Westlaw included in their notes of decisions. Most of these cases that were not included in the Notes of Decisions simply make passing reference to the statute with no discussion. The list you are viewing here is generated by KeyCite and is based solely on citation of the statute by the case. As you see, you can narrow the results by additional terms, jurisdiction, and dates if you desire by selecting the "Filter" option on the right side of the screen.

The same two options we saw on Westlaw are available on Lexis. View the current version of 15 U.S.C. § 78u–6 on Lexis. Scroll down past the text of the statute and the history and you will see a section labeled "Notes to Decisions." This is where editors that work for Lexis provide a selective list of cites to cases that discuss this statute, much like Westlaw's "Notes of Decisions." As a rule, Lexis is even more selective than Westlaw, so you will generally see references to fewer cases here than on Westlaw. Lexis, like Westlaw, has organized the case references by subject matter to make it easier to locate relevant cases on a specific aspect of the statute involved.

Lexis also has Shepard's, which will provide a complete list of all citing cases. When viewing a Code section, in the upper right part of the Code display, you will see the link labeled "Shepardize document." Lexis also has a tab labeled "Citing Decisions" at the top of the statutory text. Selection of either option will display a complete list of citing cases. Again, you will notice on the left side of the Shepard's screen the various options for limiting the list of cites to help focus on relevant cases.

E. USE OF RED WARNING SYMBOLS WHEN CASES HAVE TREATED THE STATUTE NEGATIVELY

As mentioned earlier, Westlaw uses the red flag symbol with Code sections to indicate that a recent amendment to the statutory language was enacted that has not been incorporated into the version of the Code you are reading. Westlaw also uses the red flag to indicate that a case has held some part of the statutory language unconstitutional or otherwise invalid. Lexis also indicates cases that

[29] You may notice that this cite references S. Ct. (the West published reporter covering the U.S. Supreme Court) instead of U.S., which is the reporter *The Bluebook* indicates you should cite. Why? Well, the official reporter (U.S.) is several years behind so it is not possible to cite a case decided in 2018 to U.S. The rule in T1.1 says "[c]ite to U.S. if therein; otherwise, cite to S. Ct. . . . ."

have found part of the statute unconstitutional; it appears in the upper right corner next to the "Shepardize this document." On Lexis, the symbol is a red circle with an exclamation mark inside the circle. Exhibits XIII-B and C shows an example of this on Westlaw and Lexis.

Yellow symbols related to statutes are generally used to indicate the existence of proposed bills that, if enacted, would amend the language of the Code section. You will also see yellow symbols when some part of an earlier version of a statute was declared to be unconstitutional. This indicates the current version may be good, unless the courts haven't yet decided whether the changes made to the statutory language were sufficient to remedy the problem.

F. STEP 4 OF STATUTORY RESEARCH—SECONDARY SOURCES

As with court opinions, you can use articles and books to locate relevant statutes. The information about secondary sources discussed earlier covers everything you need to know about this, so we won't repeat it here.

G. CITING TO STATUTES IN THE U.S.C.

Finally, we need to examine how you should cite to statutes. Below are the rules from *The Bluebook* about citing to statutes. Once again, *The Bluebook* prefers citation to the print version of U.S.C. Rules B12.1.1 and R12.1–.3 cover how to cite to the print version of the official U.S.C. and the unofficial U.S.C.A. and U.S.C.S. However, we will only cover how to cite to the online version since almost everyone will use a database and, frankly, the rules about citing to the print version quickly become complicated. To simplify, you will find examples below:

1. Consult Rule R12.5 in *The Bluebook*.

   Examples:

   18 U.S.C.A. § 1030 (West, Westlaw through Pub. L. No. 11#–###).

   18 U.S.C.S. § 1030 (LexisNexis, LEXIS through Pub. L. No. 11#–###).

2. If citing a specific subsection of the statute at 18 U.S.C. § 1030, the cite looks like this:

   18 U.S.C.S. § 1030(a) (LexisNexis, LEXIS through Pub. L. No. 11#–###).

Summary

1. Having identified relevant Code sections, you must be sure the language you are viewing is current (i.e., the statutory language has not been amended since the database was last updated).

   A. When viewing a Code section, Lexis and Westlaw indicate when the database was last updated. Currency is shown by specifying that the database is up to date through a specified public law and the date that public law was enacted (approved). **This statement about how current the Code is does not mean the Code section you are reading was amended by the listed public law; it just means that all changes through that public law are included in the database.**

   B. Westlaw alerts the reader about very recent changes using flags. A red flag will appear with a Code section if: 1) the Code section was amended by a recent public law and 2) the change is not yet included in the text of the Code. When a Code section is assigned a red flag for this reason, you will need to read the relevant provisions in the public law to see what changes were made by the statute. Westlaw provides a link to the public law.

   C. Lexis will not alert you to a very recent update, so you must perform an extra step to accomplish this goal. The best tool to use is the "Classification Tables" at uscode.house.gov.

      1. You only need to consult the table that covers the current year.

2. Choose the table that is "Sorted in U.S.Code order."

3. This table is ordered by Code title and, within each title, numerically by section number.

4. Simply look up your Code title and section. If any public laws have amended your Code section, they will be shown. If a change is indicated, the table identifies the public law number and section of that public law that amended your Code section.

5. You only need to be concerned with any public law enacted after the last public law included in the database. In other words, you are only concerned with public laws that are higher in number than the last one included in the database. Put another way, if the public law number of the amending law is a lower number than the last one included in the database, the change has already been reflected in the Code.

6. For example, if Lexis indicates it is up to date through Public Law 117–30. When you check the Classification Table, only public laws higher than 30 would be of interest. All others are already included in the database.

2. Lexis and Westlaw both provide access to earlier versions of the U.S.C., making it easy to see how the Code read at a specific date in the past.

3. After taking the steps to be sure you have the Code language needed, your next concern involves how court decisions have interpreted and applied the Code language, especially those cases that would be mandatory for the court in which your lawsuit is being heard.

A. Westlaw and Lexis provide references to selected cases that cite to the Code section.

1. Westlaw displays this list under the "Notes of Decisions" tab.

2. Lexis displays this list following the text of the Code section; just scroll down to view.

B. Lexis and Westlaw provide a complete list of citing cases through links to their citators (Shepard's on Lexis, KeyCite on Westlaw).

C. Westlaw and Lexis also provide extensive references to secondary sources that discuss the Code section.

D. When viewing the list of citing cases, you can limit the citing cases by:

1. Jurisdiction.

2. Date.

3. Language within results.

4. Westlaw uses "status indicators" like those used with cases.

These are used to warn the reader of:

- Recent amendments not yet included in the Code language (red) (basically, Westlaw does the work of updating the Code language described above for you).
- Proposed legislation (yellow).
- Court cases that found some provision unconstitutional (red).
- Court cases that found an earlier version of the Code unconstitutional (yellow).

As with cases, these status indicators are only aids intended as general guidelines. You must determine whether the Code section is still good law for your purposes by reading the relevant cases.

5. Lexis also indicates if any pending bills would change the Code language if enacted. This is shown above the Shepard's heading on the right side of the screen. Lexis also offers a red symbol associated with Code sections that have been declared unconstitutional.

Assignment 8
Statutes (Part 1)

The following questions are based on material covered in section XIII of the reading.

1. Assume you need to locate the public law known as the Sarbanes-Oxley Act. Use this public law to answer the following questions.

A. Examine the entry for this statute in the Popular Name Tool available at uscode.house.gov. What is the public law number assigned to this statute?

B. Click on the number assigned to this public law that appears in the Popular Name Tool. This will display information about this public law found in "Table III—Statutes at Large." Scan the third column of this table, which indicates the titles in the U.S.C. into which this public law is codified. In which titles of the United States Code are the various sections of this public law codified?

C. Now, we need to retrieve the text of this public law. Near the top of the screen in Table III is the public law number in large, bold type. Immediately to the right of this number are the letters pdf in parentheses. Click on this pdf link. A new window should open and display the text of the public law. (If this doesn't work for some reason, you can also retrieve this public law by going to congress.gov, selecting the "Public Laws" link in the upper-right part of the screen, selecting the appropriate Congress in the pull-down window, and clicking on the public law number in the list.)

In which year was this statute enacted?

D. At the top of the public law, following public law number and date, you see the following information: 116 Stat. 745. What does this mean (or tell you)?

E. Examine the Table of Contents found in Section 1(b) of the law. Which section of the public law contains definitions?

F. Some public laws indicate in the text where each section is codified in the United States Code (U.S.C.) Other public laws include this information in marginal notes. If this information is not displayed in a public law, Table III will provide this information. Does this public law indicate where each section is located in the U.S.C. and, if so, where do you find this information?

G. Where is the main definitions section of this public law located in the U.S.C.?

H. Locate section 201 of this public law, which is found on page 771. § 201(a) indicates that it is amending a Code section. Which title and section does it amend?

I. Retrieve the Code section you identified in H above, using any database (Westlaw, Lexis, or the version at uscode.house.gov) listed in the reading. Scroll down to the end of the statutory language in this Code section to the credits or history information. This should list every public law that has contributed to the language found in this section. The first statute listed is the one that created this Code section. How many public laws are identified as contributing to this section? (Hint: Public laws enacted prior to the mid 1950's were assigned chapter numbers (abbreviated ch.) instead of public law numbers.)

2. Let's take a closer look at the U.S.C. and how statutes are arranged in it. Retrieve Title 21 of the U.S.C. on Westlaw.

A. Examine the table of contents (TOC) for this Title of the U.S.C. What subject matter does this title cover generally?

B. Which Chapter of this Title contains provisions from the Federal Food, Drug, and Cosmetic Act?

C. Does the Code define the word "label" for purposes of this Chapter? If so, where?

D. To which sections of the U.S.C. does this definition apply? How did you determine the answer to this question?

3. Let's try a couple different methods of searching for statutes: full-text and subject index.

A. Use the full-text, natural language, search method to locate relevant Code sections about the use of polygraph tests for employees.

1. Which title and section of the U.S.C. cover this subject?

2. What penalty is allowed for violation of the statute? Where is this found in the U.S.C.?

B. Now, give the subject index on Westlaw a try. You have most likely heard about Somali pirates holding tankers for ransom. If the pirates were arrested and brought to the U.S., what crime could they be charged with? I'll leave this one totally up to you to locate but please use the U.S.C. subject index on Westlaw. Indicate the heading in the index that worked and list the title and section of the U.S.C. that applies.

Assignment 9
Statutes (Part 2)

The following questions are based on material covered in section XIII of the reading.

1. Assume that you are dealing with the exact same question discussed in the reading in section XIII.D.2 and you are arguing prior to the 2018 decision by the U.S. Supreme Court that resolved the issue. You are in an Ohio state trial court. The court must decide whether an individual, who reported to his employer an act by a supervisor that violated the federal securities laws, qualifies as a whistleblower and receives the protection afforded by 15 U.S.C. § 78u–6. Given the state of the law on this topic prior to 2018, which laws would be mandatory and which would be persuasive? Explain the steps you took to answer this question. (This question is challenging but give it your best shot!)

2. Use Lexis for the following questions. You are working with 18 U.S.C. § 2334, which relates to jurisdiction and venue in civil cases related to acts of terrorism brought under § 2333 of this title.

A. The phrase "international terrorism" appears in § 2334(e)(1). You must determine what constitutes international terrorism; in other words, how is this phrase defined? Is it defined for purposes of this Code section? If so, where?

B Assume for the moment that the statute does not define it. In this situation, how might you determine if it has ever been defined? Explain.

C. When was § 2334 last amended? How did you answer this question?

D. When was the U.S.C.S. database last updated?

E. How would you determine if a public law had amended this Code section since the database was last updated? Take the steps necessary and describe what you find?

3. Still using Lexis, examine 18 U.S.C. § 3583.

A. A red Circle with an exclamation mark (status indicator) is assigned to this Code section. This is located under the Shepard's label on the right side. Why is this status indicator displayed?

B. How many cases does Lexis indicate are associated with the status indicator for this Code section?

C. Look up this same Code section on Westlaw; does it assign a similar status indicator for the same reason? How many cases does Westlaw say are responsible for this status indicator?

4. You are now working with the Age Discrimination in Employment Act of 1967 (A.D.E.A.).

A In which section of the public law do you find the definitions?

B. According to the public law version of the A.D.E.A., how many employees must a person have, after June 30, 1968, to fit the statutory definition of employer?

C. Where does this definition section appear in the U.S.C.?

D. In the current version of the U.S.C., how many employees must a person have, after June 30, 1968?

E. Subsequent amendments to the definition section of the A.D.E.A. have added two additional entities that qualify as employers. The current definition is found in the U.S.C. What additional entities can now be "employers" under this statute?

F. The question has arisen whether the minimum number of employees required in the original A.D.E.A. also apply to the two additional entities added by later public laws. You have been told that a 2017 decision by the 9th Circuit addresses this issue. Locate the case. How did you do this?

G. Do different circuits provide different answers to this question?

H. Provide a cite to the exact unit in the Code where the definition of employer is found on Westlaw; follow the relevant rules in *The Bluebook*.

I. Cite the 9th Circuit case on point, following rules in *The Bluebook*.

CHAPTER 6

ADMINISTRATIVE REGULATIONS RESEARCH

XIV. ADMINISTRATIVE REGULATIONS

Administrative agencies, and the laws they produce, constitute an important component of our federal government. The number and authority of administrative agencies increased dramatically from the 1930's through the 1970's and administrative law continues to play a major role in many areas of the law today.

Congress can grant agencies a variety of powers. A partial list of these powers includes issuing licenses, conducting "trials" through an administrative tribunal which can punish those who violate the law, and issuing regulations that have the force of law much like a statute. Many agencies are given the power to create administrative rules (a.k.a. regulations) and in this reading we will concentrate on administrative agency rules, how to locate them, and the basics of working with them.

To address issues regarding access to regulations, Congress enacted the Federal Register Act of 1935 (codified in 44 U.S.C. §§ 1501–1511). This statute mandates the publication of the *Federal Register* (Fed. Reg.) and the *Code of Federal Regulations* (C.F.R.), two publications we will examine shortly. The publication of administrative agency regulations follows a pattern much like the publication of statutes. Rules are initially published in the Fed. Reg. All final rules adopted through time and that remain in force today are organized by subject into a Code, which is known as the C.F.R.

Additionally, there were concerns about the accountability of agencies to the public, since individuals who work for the agencies are not elected. This concern led to passage of the Administrative Procedure Act in 1946 (codified at 5 U.S.C. §§ 551–559, 701–706), which specifies the process that agencies must use when creating new regulations. This statute specifies a couple different methods that an agency may follow when preparing to issue a regulation. The most used method, known as informal rulemaking, requires the agency to publish the regulation as a proposed rule and allow the public the opportunity to provide input by submitting comments about the rule before it can be made final.

When the informal method is used, administrative rules appear at least twice in the Fed. Reg., once as a proposed rule and a second time as a final rule.[30] When published as a proposed rule, the agency will specify a period of time during which interested parties may submit comments about the proposed rule and the methods available for submitting comments. When the rule is published as a final rule (not all proposed rules get to the final stage), the agency will publish the comments received and respond to them, along with the text of the final rule, in the Fed. Reg. The text of all final rules, and only final rules, are combined with the text of previously enacted regulations on the same subject and published in a codified version known as the C.F.R. Let's begin our exploration of administrative law by looking at regulations as they are published in the Fed. Reg. and C.F.R. and how you can use these sources to locate relevant regulations and helpful information about them.

---

[30] Occasionally, a proposed rule may appear several times as a proposed rule if major changes are made after each publication.

A. FEDERAL REGISTER

The Federal Register (Fed. Reg.) is available in many different sources. The government has a website dedicated to it at www.federalregister.gov. You can also access the Fed. Reg. on any of the commercial databases. We will concentrate mostly on using the government website in this section.

When you first go to the website listed above, you will see information about the Fed. Reg. and you should see a link to the current issue. (F.Y.I., the Fed. Reg. is published every day the government does business, so every day except for Saturday, Sunday, and federal holidays.) Select the link for the current issue. On the right side you will see a calendar that shows the current month. This website provides access to the Fed. Reg. going back to January 1994. Use the calendar to select Thursday, July 12, 2018. After selecting this date, select the link located just above the calendar labeled "Download Issue PDF."

This will download and display a pdf of the issue of the Fed. Reg. for that day. On the cover page you will see the page numbers included in that issue; this issue contains pages 32191–32562. As you can see, the pages are numbered consecutively throughout the calendar year. Let's look at a proposed rule that begins on page 32252.

On page 32252, toward the bottom of the second column, you will see the heading "Department of Health and Human Services." This is the agency that is issuing the rule. A few lines farther down this page you will see a line labeled "**Action**: Proposed Rule." This indicates that this is a new rule being proposed by the agency. Under the heading **Dates**, which is found toward the top of column three, you will see the deadline for submitting comments about this proposed change, which is followed by an explanation of the different options one has for submitting comments. This information is followed by background information on why the agency believes the rule is needed.

On page 32255 you will find the actual text of the proposed rule. At the bottom of the first column, you will see the following:

> "For the reasons set forth in the preamble, the Centers for Medicare & Medicaid Services proposes to amend 42 CFR chapter IV as set forth below."

This is followed by the language of the proposed rule with information about which sections in the C.F.R. are being amended or added. This regulation, if made final, would go in title 42 of the C.F.R., Part 447. More about the organization and content of the C.F.R. a little later.

After it is published and the comment period has ended, the agency proposing the regulation must decide, considering the comments received, whether to proceed to make the rule final, radically change it and resubmit as a new proposed rule, or abandon it altogether. If they decide to make it a final rule, they must make any changes they think are necessary and republish it as a final rule in the Federal Register. When it is published as a final rule, they must print the comments received and respond to them.

For an example, let's look at a final rule on page 60170 in the August 31, 2016 issue of the Federal Register. You can do this by going back to the calendar and retrieving the pdf of that day's issue. Locate page 60170 and note that under the action heading it states that it is a final rule. This is followed by a summary of the provisions, discussion of and response to the comments received starting on page 60176, and the text of the final rule itself starting on page 60212.

B. CODE OF FEDERAL REGULATIONS

The final rule we just looked at in the Fed. Reg., like all other final rules, are codified in the Code of Federal Regulations (C.F.R.). Let's look at it in the C.F.R. The final rule in the Fed. Reg. states that this is codified in various parts of Title 21 in the C.F.R. Let's look at 21 C.F.R. Part 207. Retrieve this Part by going to www.govinfo.gov, select the A to Z tab, select the letter C, and scroll down to the entry labeled "Code of Federal Regulations (CFR), 1997 to Present. Select the + symbol in front of the latest year and then scroll down to the correct title and part numbers.

On page 137 of the C.F.R. you will see the beginning of Part 207. (The page number may vary with later years of the C.F.R.). It shows the table of contents (TOC) of the regulations, much like the TOC of statute Code titles in the U.S.C. Each Part consists of multiple sections. After the TOC (on page 136) you see a heading labeled "Source." This indicates where in the Fed. Reg. the sections in the Part were published originally as a final rule. Here, it indicates the source is 81 FR 60212, Aug. 31, 2016.[31] This references the pages in the Fed. Reg. where this final rule was published, which we just examined. Here, in the C.F.R., you are only reading the text of the regulation without all the history and background information we saw in the Fed. Reg.

At the top of the next page you will see a date in parentheses. Each title in the official C.F.R. is updated once a year. Title 21 is always updated as of April 1 each year. (The government is currently behind in publishing the C.F.R. so a version for the current year may not be available.)

All regulations on this subject are compiled here into this title of the C.F.R. When you want to locate the current version of a regulation, the C.F.R. is the source to use. If you need background information about a final regulation, the Fed. Reg. is the source to use.

The C.F.R. is available in Lexis and Westlaw; it can be searched the same as statutes. It is also available on various government websites. The official version of the C.F.R. is available at www.govinfo.gov, the site we just used. The easiest to use and most current version is found at another government website at ecfr.gov. Let's look at this site.

After going to ecfr.gov, you will notice that next to each title is a line that indicates when that title was last amended. Updating is done frequently and this source is usually as current as the commercial databases.

Now, retrieve the same part we were looking at before: 21 C.F.R. Part 207. You can retrieve this provision by entering the cite, 21 CFR 207, in the search box located above the list of titles. You can also select the relevant title and the table of contents for that title will appear.

In the TOC of Part 207 you should see a list of subunits. Select the link that contains part 207. Once you have a section on the screen, you will see, near the top of the screen, the path that indicates where you are in this source. In this situation, it indicates that you are viewing Title 21, Chapter I, Subchapter C, Part 207. Subpart A includes sections 207.1–207.13.

As you look at the TOC, you will notice that all sections in part 207 begin with 207. In other words, the numbers located to the left of the decimal point in a section number indicates the Part number. The entire number, including numbers to the left and to the right of the decimal point, constitutes the section number. Also notice that the numbers to the right of the decimal point are not treated like true decimals, where the number indicates a fraction of a whole. For example, if the numbers were treated as true decimals, 207.13 would follow 207.1 but precede 207.9. However, since the C.F.R. treats the numbers to the right of the decimal point as whole numbers, 207.1 is followed by 207.9 which is followed by 207.13.

Now, select and look more closely at section 207.1; it specifies that definitions included in sections 201 and 510 of the Federal Food, Drug, and Cosmetic Act (a statute) apply to those terms included in Part 207 of Title 21 of the C.F.R., unless otherwise defined in section 207.1 of Title 21 of the C.F.R. It also contains a list of additional definitions for this part. As we learned when we discussed

---

31 Following the reference to the source in the C.F.R., you see the words "unless otherwise noted." This indicates that if any additional final rules have amended a specific section in this Part of the C.F.R., this will be indicated in a separate source note located at the end of the relevant section.

statutes, you must be aware of definitions that are provided and to which sections the definitions apply.

Now, for comparison, retrieve this same section of the C.F.R. on Lexis by entering 21 CFR 207.1 in the search box after you sign into Lexis. When the section appears on the screen, you will see that the TOC is shown at the top of the screen. Just above that is a statement of how current the CFR database is on Lexis. It indicates that everything published in the Federal Register through a specific date has been included in the C.F.R.[32] Now, scroll down to the end of the section. In the history section you will see all the entries from the Federal Register that have gone into the language you are now reading. This works the same as the U.S.C.; the history, or credits as they are sometimes referenced, indicate all the various provisions that are included in a section of the Code. In this example, a final rule that was published in volume 45 of the Federal Register, page 38043 (June 6, 1980) created this Code section.

When you need to locate an agency regulation as it reads today or how it read at some point in the past, the C.F.R. is the best and easiest source to consult. If you know the date when a final rule was published, the Federal Register is the best and easiest source to start. Obviously, if you are looking for a proposed rule and/or background information related to a regulation, the Fed. Reg. is the best source.

Enough of an introduction to the Fed. Reg. and the C.F.R. How do you use them to do research in administrative law?

C. ADMINISTRATIVE LAW RESEARCH

Here is an outline of what we will cover in the next several pages:

1. Methods available for searching administrative rules in the C.F.R.
    - A. Known cite to the CFR
    - B. Known statute
    - C. Table of Contents (TOC) (a.k.a. a topic approach)
    - D. Human created subject search
    - E. Full-text searching
2. Locating the version of the rule you need
    - A. Earlier versions
    - B. Updating the C.F.R. for the latest
3. Identifying and reading court opinions that have interpreted and applied language of the rule
4. Locating information about administrative agencies
5. Relationship between regulations, statutes, and cases
6. Citing rules found in the C.F.R.

The first thing you should notice is that this process is nearly identical to working with statutes; only the names of publications have changed. Steps 4, 5, and 6 are different because of the nature of administrative agency rules.

[32] As with statutes, this indicates that all sections of the C.F.R. are current through the specified date. It does not indicate that this specific section (207.1) was amended by something in that day's issue of the Fed. Reg.

1. Searching for Relevant Administrative Rules

a. *Known Cite to C.F.R.*

If you know of a cite to an administrative regulation in the C.F.R., it is very simple to retrieve the text of the regulation. In the commercial databases, simply enter the cite (number of the title, C.F.R., section number (e.g. 21 C.F.R. 207.1)). We already did this earlier with cases and statutes, so it should be no problem. On the government's website, ecfr.gov, you simply browse using the list of titles that we used earlier.

b. *Known Statute*

If you have a statute in the U.S.C. and want to see if there are any related administrative regulations, you have several options.

Lexis—With the relevant statute on the screen, scroll down to the section labeled "Research References & Practice Aids." As an example, retrieve 5 U.S.C. § 504 on Lexis. Now, select the link labeled "Research References & Practice Aids" located on the left side of the screen. If there are any administrative rules related to this Code section, they should be listed. In this example, there are several.

Westlaw—Retrieve the same statutory Code section on Westlaw. Once the section of the U.S.C. is visible on the screen, select the tab near the top labeled "Context & Analysis." Look for a section labeled "Code of Federal Regulations." Again, there are several references with cites to the relevant sections in the C.F.R.

Govinfo.gov—Here you will see a link labeled "Parallel Table of Authorities and Rules." After selecting the link to the most recent table, the subject index to the C.F.R. will open. The table is located near the end of the subject index. This table is organized by U.S.C. title and section. Look down the table for 5 U.S.C. Under Title 5, locate the Code section, 504. You will see references to various titles and parts in the C.F.R. The typical entry looks like this: 5 Parts 2430, 2610. This indicates that Title 5 of the C.F.R., parts 2430 and 2610, are related to this statute.

A couple of points of clarification are in order here:

- not every section in the U.S.C. will have a related regulation. So, don't be surprised if you don't see any references to the C.F.R. in these sources.
- these lists and tables are not exhaustive. If you don't see a listing for parts of the C.F.R., it doesn't mean there is nothing. You must use other options, such as subject index or full text searching of the C.F.R., to verify whether there are any related regulations.
- even though statutes in the U.S.C. and administrative regulations in C.F.R. are both organized by numbered titles, the title numbers do not necessarily correspond. In other words, the regulations related to a section in 5 U.S.C. do not all appear in title 5 of the C.F.R. If you look at that parallel table we just consulted, you will see that related regulations appear in various titles.

c. *Table of Contents (TOC)*

Another option for searching for relevant regulations is the table of contents (TOC) approach; this works just like it does when using the TOC to locate statutes in the U.S.C. You can simply browse the headings assigned to a Title, chapter, etc. and attempt to find related regulations. Just as with statutes, this approach works sometimes and doesn't other times.

The TOC for the C.F.R. is available when working with the C.F.R. on all the commercial databases and at the ecfr.gov website. Return to the initial page of the ecfr.gov site which lists the titles. If you are looking for regulations related to banks and banking, browsing the title headings shows that Title 12 is likely the title to investigate. Select title 12.

The TOC for Title 12 will appear. You can see the headings associated with Parts. If you know that you need regulations related to the Federal Reserve System, Parts 200–299 are likely the ones on which you want to concentrate.

d. Human Created Subject Index

If the TOC doesn't work, and many times it won't, there is a human created subject index you can use (just like looking for statutes in the U.S.C.). In both Lexis and Westlaw, all you need to do is type Code of Federal Regulations Index in the search box and the link will appear for your selection. This index works the same as the subject index for the United States Code; it can be browsed by main subject headings or searched.

Another government website also has a subject index; go to govinfo.gov and click on the "A to Z" section. Now, select the letter C; this should display all items beginning with the letter C. There is a listing labeled "CFR Index and Finding Aids." Select this link and the most recent year; you will see the option to open a pdf of the government prepared subject index to the C.F.R. This index is not as detailed as the commercial versions on Lexis and Westlaw but, hey, it's free!

e. Full-Text Searching

Last, but not least, is the full-text searching function. Again, we have discussed this for both cases and statutes; this works much the same. The only thing to keep in mind is the challenge of guessing which words an administrative agency used to discuss the topic in which you are interested. Just as before, this method of searching is not recommended if you are not familiar with the subject area and don't really know the terminology being used. This is where a good book or law review article on the subject, or the subject indexes, will be of great help.

The ecfr.gov website also allows for full-text searching. Enter the search terms in the same box at the top of the page where you entered a cite to the CFR earlier.

f. AI

Searching for regulations is much like statutory research. I checked to see if AI would assist in locating materials in the C.F.R. based on a statutory cite, which is discussed in Chapter 6.XIV.C.1.b. in the text but it does not seem to answer this question directly. It does search cases that mention this but it is not a reliable source on this question. The tools discussed in the book are still the most efficient way to go from statute to regulation.

Searching for the existence of regulations on a specific subject and interpretation of regulations is much like statutory research and tends to work well. Just like using AI to search for statutes, the terminology you use in your query seems to have more impact than when searching for cases because of the more technical language compared to the more common English language of court cases. Being precise as possible will help retrieve more relevant information.

2. Locating the Version of the C.F.R. You Need

As with statutes, you must be aware of the version of a regulation that applies to the situation your client faces. In other words, do you need a version of the regulation as it read at some time in the past when the events involved took place or do you need to know how the regulation reads today? Only the facts of your case can determine the answer to this question.

On Westlaw, the C.F.R. is available back to 1984. In the search box on Westlaw, just type Code of Federal Regulations and the historical view will be one of the options. Simply select the year you want. You can also see historical versions of a specific C.F.R. section; when viewing the relevant section, select the "History" tab and then "Versions." This is identical to the process we used with statutes.

On Lexis, you must first retrieve the section of the C.F.R. you are working with and then you should see the link to "Archived code versions." Lexis currently goes back to 1981 in the C.F.R.

At the ecfr.gov website, you can search and browse back to 2017. To access historical versions, retrieve a title of the C.F.R. On the left side of the screen is a link labeled "Go to Date." Selecting this option permits one to select a date of an earlier version. The C.F.R. at govinfo.gov goes back to 1996.

If you need to locate the latest version of an administrative regulation in the C.F.R., the process is very similar to updating a statutory Code section.

> **Westlaw**—Westlaw uses the red flag status indicator to warn you about a recent administrative regulation that has been amended or otherwise changed since the database was last updated.
>
> **Lexis**—Lexis indicates recent updates not yet incorporated into the text on the screen in the "Pending & Adopted" link located at the top of the screen when viewing a section of the C.F.R.
>
> With both Lexis and Westlaw you may also want to consult the ecfr site to be sure to catch all recent amendments.

3. Reading Cases That Have Interpreted and Applied Language from the C.F.R.

Just like statutes, you must know how the courts have interpreted and applied the administrative regulations. Once more, this process is nearly identical to locating cases related to statutory Code sections.

Westlaw provides links to selected cases under the "Notes of Decisions" tab and a complete list, based on KeyCite, under the "Citing References" tab. Lexis provides links to cases under the "Annotations" portion and has a link to the complete list of citing cases under the "Shepardize document" link or the "citing decisions" tab. As discussed earlier, you **must** be aware of how courts that are mandatory for your situation have interpreted and applied the rules.

4. Locating Information About Administrative Agencies

If the research in which you are engaged involves administrative research, you should be aware that most agencies have valuable websites with substantial amounts of information beyond just the regulations. We don't have time to cover this subject in detail here, but agencies produce many types of documents that are never published in either the Fed. Reg. or the C.F.R. because they are not technically "rules."

Agencies will have links from their page to their administrative rules, but they will also contain links to a lot more. As an example, look at the website for the Consumer Financial Protection Bureau (cfpb.gov). Look at the tab labeled "Data & Research" which is located along the top of the page. Select the "Research & Reports" option. Here you will find many materials the agency has produced, which include information they have collected and positions the agency takes on various legal issues.

5. Relationship Between Regulations, Statutes, and Cases

Statutes are often left vague and/or brief on the details when an administrative agency is charged with filling the gaps by issuing regulations. If a legal issue involves an area of the law that is within the jurisdiction of an administrative agency, an interplay between statutes, regulations, and court interpretations of those regulations will frequently be involved. For example, the statute may prescribe a certain outcome but leave it to an agency to provide the details of how this outcome is to be achieved. Once the agency generates regulations on the subject, the obvious question will be whether the agency fulfilled its statutory obligation with the regulations. The courts may consider the issue, resulting in circuit splits that result in differences across the country. The agency can then go back and amend its regulations in an attempt to fulfill and clarify its position. Another option is for the U.S. Supreme Court to decide the issue. Additionally, Congress could amend the statute to provide details the agency isn't providing or to direct the agency to regulate in a specific way.

As you can see, it can become complicated very quickly. Additionally, all three forms of law mentioned, statutes, regulations, and court decisions, are subject to the standards and requirements imposed by the U.S. Constitution. You will need to remain aware of this as you conduct legal research involving regulations.

In addition to the federal agencies, states also have governmental agencies. Most states have a system like the federal government for the proposal and publication of agency rules. State agencies will also have websites with additional information beyond regulations.

6. Citing to the Rules Found in the C.F.R.

The Bluebook covers citing to sections in the C.F.R. in Rule B14. The cite looks like the example below.

46 C.F.R. § 166.01 (2009).

You should recognize that 46 is the title number and the section number follows the abbreviation for the C.F.R. The date in the parenthetical is the year on the printed version of the C.F.R. *The Bluebook* assumes you are using the printed version, which is available on the govinfo.gov website. Rule B14 in *The Bluebook* covers this.

What if you are citing to the C.F.R. using a database? You might think (and it would make sense) that it would follow the same basic format we saw with statutes. Think again! Rule R14.5 shows a different form that looks like the example below.

16 C.F.R. § 444.1 (2000), WL 16 CFR § 444.1.[33]

I have no idea where this comes from; it still assumes you know the date on the print version and just repeats the title and section number. In my judgment, a much better option would look like this (assuming you are citing to the C.F.R. found on Lexis).

16 C.F.R. § 444.1 (LEXIS through Aug. 1, 20##).

Keep in mind, however, this example is not approved by *The Bluebook*, so when citing this in a memo written in your Legal Writing class, be sure you know what your instructor wants you to use. Once again, you can cite to the print version by looking at the pdf version of the C.F.R. at govinfo.gov. Simply go to govinfo.gov, select the letter C at the top of the page, and locate the link labeled "Code of Federal Regulations (CFR), 1996 to Present." You then simply select the year and retrieve the

[33] The title assigned to the rule shown in the example in *The Bluebook* is optional; only the title, C.F.R., section number, and date are required.

title and section. This looks exactly like the print version and provides you with all the information you need to cite it according to Rule B14.

One more thing you must understand if citing to the print version. All 50 titles of the C.F.R. are not published at the same time each year. Titles 1–16 are published early in the calendar year and are current through January 1 of that year. Titles 17–27 are current through April 1, Titles 28–41 are current through July 1, and Titles 42–50 are current through October 1. So, if is September and you are citing to a regulation found in Title 45, you will not find that title in the volumes published in the current year. In this instance, you will have to cite to the prior year's version. If the section you are citing has been amended since October of the prior year, you will have to also cite to the Fed. Reg. where the final rule amending your C.F.R. section is found. Rules for citing the Fed. Reg. are found in Rule 14.2(b).

How would you know if the section in Title 45 (or any other title for that matter) had been amended after October of the prior year? Use any of the commercial databases or the governments electronic version at ecfr.gov. These are all very current and the credits associated with the section will indicate if it has been amended since October of the prior year.

Lexis and Westlaw will always show the credits at the end of each section so you can easily see the final rules that comprise the language found in the section. However, when using the official CFR at govinfo.gov or the version found at ecfr.gov, the credits do not appear at the end of each section. The credits are listed under the "Source" heading, which is located at the beginning of the Part in which the section is located. This is beyond the scope of this book so don't worry about understanding it; I just wanted to let you know about this, so you are not surprised when you don't see credits (or history) at the end of a section of the C.F.R. on the government websites.

Summary

1. The informal method of rulemaking (a.k.a. notice and comment) requires publication of a rule in the Fed. Reg. as a proposed rule with the opportunity for the public to respond to the rule.

2. Before a rule can have the force of law, it must be published a second time as a final rule in the Fed. Reg.

3. The Fed. Reg. contains historical information about a rule that can help in understanding and interpreting the regulation.

4. The Fed. Reg. is available online from the government (www.federalregister.gov) or in the major legal databases.

5. All final rules are published, along with all other regulations on the same subject, in the C.F.R. The C.F.R. is a Code that does for regulations what the U.S.C. does for statutes.

6. The C.F.R.:

   A. Is a subject compilation of final regulations.

   B. Is organized into titles and sections, with chapters, parts, and other units between title and section, much like the U.S.C. organizes statutes.

   C. Identifies where all the final rules, of which the text is composed, are published in the various issues of the Fed. Reg.

   D. Is updated annually, with about one quarter of the titles updated as of Jan. 1, the second quarter as of April 1, etc.

7. Relevant regulations can be found by:

   A. A known statute, by using the governments "Parallel Table of Authorities" or the commercial legal databases.

   B. Browsing or searching the TOC in the commercial legal databases.

   C. Using the subject indexes available on Lexis and Westlaw or the government subject index at govinfo.gov.

   D. Full-text searching.

8. If you need to see how a regulation read on a specific date in the past, Lexis, Westlaw, or the official government version provide historical versions of the C.F.R.

9. If needed, you can update the version of a rule in the C.F.R. by using the C.F.R. Parts Affected table.

   A. Make a note of the last time the version of the C.F.R. you are using was updated.

   B. Consult the most recent Parts Affected table in today's issue, or the latest issue, of the Fed. Reg.

   C. This table appears in the daily issue of the Fed. Reg.; these tables cover all changes made during the current month only.

   D. If the C.F.R. you consulted was updated through a date in the current month, the Parts Affected table will cover any later changes.

   E. If the C.F.R. you consulted was last updated in the previous month, you need to consult the Parts Affected table for the last issue in the previous month and the one in today's Fed. Reg.

   F. Westlaw will display a red flag if you are looking at a section of the C.F.R. that has been amended since the database was last updated.

10. The commercial databases will provide cites to cases interpreting and applying the sections of the C.F.R., just like they do for statutes.

   A. You must pay attention to court treatment, especially those that will be mandatory for the court in which your litigation is filed.

   B. The same principles related to statutes on this issue apply to regulations.

11. Administrative agencies have very helpful websites if you need additional information about an agency. A Google search using the name of the agency should direct you to the website.

12. Agencies frequently use regulations to provide additional detail and enforcement of related statutes.

13. *The Bluebook* requires that you cite to the printed version of the C.F.R., which is available through the govinfo.gov website.

Assignment 10

This assignment is based on section XIV of the reading.

1. Assume that the date today is Oct. 20, 2019 for the following question. A partner in the firm for which you work wants to see amendments made by the Office of the Comptroller of the Currency (OCC) to regulations related to stress testing of banks. She believes the changes were made sometime during the last few weeks.

A. She wants to see only the changes made by this recent change. Based upon what you have learned about the Federal Register and the Code of Federal Regulations, which source would be best for locating this information?

B. The source you just located identifies when this final rule takes effect; what is the date?

C. If the partner wanted complete background information, where could you locate this rule when it was proposed? Provide a cite to the source (cite does not need to comply with *The Bluebook*).

D. Is this regulation adding something completely new to the rules or amending already existing rules?

E. According to the background information reprinted with the publication of the final rule, why is this regulation being added/amended?

F. If the partner wants to see the complete rules as they read after the recent changes, where could these be located?

2. You are working with 47 U.S.C. § 227 and need to identify any regulations related to the subject matter.

A. Name two sources, one of which is free to use, that assist in performing this task.

B. Using one of these sources, where can you find related regulations?

C. The sources we have discussed that lead from a statute to regulations are very general and will not lead you to every section in the C.F.R. that is relevant. Once you have a general idea of where relevant regulations are found, which tools (that we have discussed in the reading) could you use to locate specific provisions?

D. Use one of these tools to locate the specific section in the regulations that covers the transmission of inaccurate or misleading caller identification?

E. Which agency issued this regulation?

F. When was this specific regulation published in the Federal Register and has it been amended since it was originally published?

3. You have a client living in Dallas, Texas, who applied for social security benefits because of a disability. The Administrative Law Judge (ALJ), within the Social Security Administration, denied benefits. The client then sought review by the Appeals Council, also a part of the Social Security Administration. He attempted to present new medical information about his disability to the Appeals Council, but they denied the appeal. He now wants to appeal that decision to a federal district court and is seeking your assistance.

One issue you are facing relates to a regulation found at 20 C.F.R. § 404.981. On appeal to the federal district court in Texas, you want the court to consider the new information the client attempted to present to the Appeals Council. Whether you can get the district court to consider this new information depends upon what is considered a "final decision." Only final decisions are reviewable by a federal district court. If the denial of benefits by the ALJ is considered the final decision, then you cannot bring up the new evidence on appeal to the court because the new evidence was not a part of the final decision. However, if the denial by the Appeals Council is a part of the final decision, then you can raise the new information on appeal to the court.

A. Using Westlaw, what law would clarify this issue for you in the federal district court in Texas? Provide a cite to that authority.

B. What steps did you take to identify this authority?

C. Does the authority you located in A. above appear to still be valid law? Why or why not? (A quick check is sufficient for purposes of this assignment; don't spend too much time on it.)

D. Would the outcome be the same if your client resided in Illinois and the appeal was in a federal district court in Illinois? Cite the appropriate authority. (Note: this question is especially challenging so don't spend too much time on it but give it a try. You will need to use various methods of locating relevant cases we have discussed throughout this book. This example is a good illustration of how challenging legal research can be, so don't feel incompetent if you don't find it; you are still new to legal research. This example will provide the opportunity to review and discuss the various options for locating relevant cases and why each one does or doesn't work.)

CHAPTER 7

PRACTICAL RESEARCH TIPS

XV. PRACTICAL RESEARCH TIPS

Knowing how to use and becoming comfortable using the primary and secondary materials discussed here is essential for conducting legal research. The readings have covered:

- The nature of the primary sources so you understand the part they play in our legal system and the information you get from each.
- The tools that can be used to locate and work with these primary sources.
- Use of AI in beginning legal research
- How to locate the latest version (update) or locating historical versions of statutes and regulations. For case law research, we discussed updating a rule of law found in a case to determine whether it remains good law.
- The alternatives available for locating relevant materials so you have options if your first or second choice don't work.
- The use of secondary sources to better understand the law and for cites to relevant primary sources.

Additionally, an efficient searcher must also consider other factors that influence the decision about beginning and proceeding with your research. This is often a difficult part of doing legal research because there are so many variations; it can be difficult to wrap your mind around all the details. Let's look at some additional items you must consider when beginning and working through the process of legal research.

A. Be sure you take the time to fully analyze the facts so that you have a good idea of the possible legally significant facts and relationships involved. Don't rush into searching without careful consideration of the facts and relationships involved.

B. Always take advantage and make full use of all the information you know when starting. As discussed, AI can assist in learning the basics about a legal issue. If you have any known authority of any type, take time to understand it and start with that information. It is amazing how often this guideline is ignored. Any known case, statute, regulation, or secondary source should be incorporated into your search. Use the tools we have discussed in this book when working with the different types of authorities. For example, if you have a case, use the subject index approach and the citators to locate additional cases. Also, use the case to learn the relevant terminology that will help if you need to develop a full-text search. Additionally, use the cases cited by your case as another way to pursue your research. Don't begin searching by subject when you have a known authority. You may ultimately have to do some searching by subject, depending on how your research goes, but be sure to take full advantage of the information you know when you begin and use the tools and methods discussed to locate related information.

C. The key to efficient and effective research is knowing the terminology used in the subject area. If you are not familiar with the subject matter, spend time exploring with AI and locating a good secondary source. This will save you so much time in the long run, even though it doesn't feel like it when you first begin. When practicing in a law office setting, be sure to determine if there are in-house documents that attorneys have created about the subject that will assist. You can also locate some of these general types of materials using a docket if you know of a case that covers the same subject matter. Complaints, memos, and briefs filed in a case can be good sources for background and relevant primary sources.

D. Be careful about relying on older cases as the law may have changed; be sure to update your research.

E. AI is always a good place to begin. The ultimate result that comes from your research is your responsibility; do not rely exclusively on what AI tells you or someone else has written about the topic. You must work with the sources we have discussed to determine the law on an issue.

F. Remember the relationship between the various types of primary sources and follow the steps outlined in this reading while working with each source. One of the biggest wastes of time happens when you see a list of primary sources that look relevant and you rush off to read them all. You quickly begin to skip steps and jump around within the resources without keeping track of what steps you have taken to update the resources. Working fast and skipping steps is very tempting as you begin your research because you are in a rush to get things done. However, doing this will likely mean that you must spend time locating some of the materials a second time to get more information and finish collecting all the data. This is not an efficient use of your time. Get organized and have a systematic method of working with the primary sources as you locate them.

G. Keep in mind that often there will be both federal and state laws that can be used and that states often provide greater protection to plaintiffs than federal law. Don't forget to look for laws from both jurisdictions when researching an issue. Sometimes state constitutions can be useful; we haven't really looked at them but keep them in mind.

H. Never assume that one or two online searches will locate all the relevant information. Try various approaches to the subject.

I. Each of the methods for locating information (AI, subject index, full text, etc.) has its advantages and disadvantages. In any given situation, when you are new to the subject, you do not know which method will work best. Again, always consider a good secondary source in this situation and make an educated guess from the information learned about how to proceed.

J. How do you know when you have all that is available? This is the million-dollar question; besides knowing the terminology used, this is the next major problem. The general rule of thumb is that when you begin to see the same sources cited repeatedly and stop finding new sources, it is time to stop looking for new resources. This works well unless you are completely missing something. Reading secondary sources are often a good way to be sure you aren't missing a crucial aspect of an issue.

K. Keep accurate notes of which sources you have consulted and what information you found in each. While this feels time-consuming when conducting research, it will greatly speed up the process of writing when you get to that stage and help avoid the frustration of having to look up sources a second time to verify something. It is easy when you first begin research to think that you will remember what you found in a specific source but as time goes on and you consult additional sources, memory of what each source contributed to your knowledge begins to blur and frustration quickly sets in as a result.

L. When the first approach to a subject doesn't seem to be working, drop it and use an alternative approach. While you need to give your method a chance, don't stick with it if it isn't working.

M. Don't assume that every issue you research will provide the answer you want or need. If you have tried all options and found little, you will need to become creative and develop new ideas that draw upon existing law but also go beyond it.

N. There are many tools which the commercial databases are incorporating in their products to assist in locating relevant law. We have only touched on a few of them; there are many more that we haven't specifically discussed. AI is being incorporated into general searches on Lexis and Westlaw and this development will certainly continue. Attend sessions offered by the representatives of the databases and do online tutorials they offer through their websites. Additional features are covered in Advanced Legal Research classes which you can take in your second and third years of law school.

O. You may also have access to other commercial databases, either in law school or the workplace. If you understand the terminology and methods used by Westlaw and Lexis, learning how to use the others will be straightforward.

Becoming good at legal research involves lots of practice and continual learning about the laws and tools available to access them. It also, of course, involves learning the substantive content of the law and using that in service to your clients and the good of society. I wish you the best in your endeavors.

APPENDIX

EXHIBITS

Trial Court Docket

Exhibit IV-A

U.S. District Court
District of Columbia (Washington, DC)
CIVIL DOCKET FOR CASE #: 1:93-cv-01791-HHK

YESUDIAN, et al v. HOWARD UNIVERSITY, et al
Assigned to: Judge Henry H. Kennedy
Demand: $0
Cause: 28:1331 Fed. Question: Breach of Contract

Date Filed: 08/26/1993
Jury Demand: Both
Nature of Suit: 790 Labor: Other
Jurisdiction: Federal Question

Plaintiff

DANIEL YESUDIAN
United States of America ex rel.

represented by **James L. Kestell**
KESTELL & ASSOCIATES
1012 14th Street, NW
Suite 630
Washington, DC 20005
(202) 347-3889
Fax: (202) 347-4481
Email: jlkestell@cox.net
LEAD ATTORNEY
ATTORNEY TO BE NOTICED

V.

Defendant

HOWARD UNIVERSITY

represented by **Charles Samuel Fax**
SHAPIRO SHER GUINOT & SANDLER

Exhibit IV-B

Date Filed	#	Docket Text
08/26/1993	1	COMPLAINT filed by plaintiff USA/YESUDIAN; jury demand; attachment (dcn) (Entered: 11/14/1995)
08/26/1993		SUMMONS issued for defendant HOWARD UNIVERSITY, defendant GEORGE K. VARGHESE, defendant JOSEPH B. PARKER, defendant JAMES A. FLETCHER II (dcn) (Entered: 11/14/1995)
05/27/1994	2	ORDER by Judge Harold H. Greene : unsealing the complaint and directing that service shall be made upon defendants; directing that all remaining documents shall remain under seal, not be made public, or served upon defendants;, directing plaintiffs to serve copies of all pleadings filed in this action upon the Department of Justice (N) (dcn) (Entered: 11/14/1995)
07/19/1994		SUMMONS reissued for defendant HOWARD UNIVERSITY (dcn) (Entered: 11/14/1995)
07/28/1994	3	MOTION filed by defendant HOWARD UNIVERSITY to extend time to 8/23/94 to answer complaint [1-1] (dcn) (Entered: 11/14/1995)
08/24/1994	4	ATTORNEY APPEARANCE for defendant HOWARD UNIVERSITY by Jeffrey M. Ford (dcn) (Entered: 11/14/1995)
08/24/1994	5	ANSWER TO COMPLAINT [1-1] by defendant HOWARD UNIVERSITY .; jury demand (dcn) (Entered: 11/14/1995)
09/01/1994	6	ORDER by Judge Harold H. Greene : granting motion to extend time to 8/23/94 to answer complaint [1-1] [3-1] by HOWARD UNIVERSITY (N) (dcn) (Entered: 11/14/1995)

Exhibit IV-C

10/03/1994	7	NOTICE TO TAKE DEPOSITION of Daniel Yesudian by defendant HOWARD UNIVERSITY . (dcn) (Entered: 11/14/1995)
10/03/1994	8	FIRST SET OF INTERROGATORIES filed by defendant HOWARD UNIVERSITY to plaintiff USA/YESUDIAN (dcn) (Entered: 11/14/1995)

10/05/1994	9	RESPONSE by defendant HOWARD UNIVERSITY to first request for production of documents (dcn) (Entered: 11/14/1995)
11/04/1994		STATUS HEARING before Judge Harold H. Greene : discovery closes 2/28/95 ; dispositive motions due 3/30/95 ; Reporter: Laura Beasley (dcn) (Entered: 11/14/1995)
11/04/1994	11	ATTORNEY APPEARANCE for defendant HOWARD UNIVERSITY by James Lester Kestell (dcn) (Entered: 11/14/1995)
11/14/1994	10	ORDER by Judge Harold H. Greene : Case assigned to the Standard track (track two). , discovery closes 2/28/95 ; dispositive motions due 3/30/95 ; , Referred to Magistrate Judge for discovery and pretrial (N) (dcn) (Entered: 11/14/1995)
08/01/1995		SCHEDULING NOTICE: status hearing set for 10:00 8/21/95 ; before Judge Harold H. Greene . (dcn) (Entered: 11/14/1995)

Exhibit IV-D

11/21/1995		JURY TRIAL before Judge Harold H. Greene same jury of 7 resumed and concluded reporter: Laura Beasley (dcn) (Entered: 11/22/1995)
11/21/1995		JURY VERDICT for plaintiff USA/YESUDIAN against defendant HOWARD UNIVERSITY, defendant JOSEPH B. PARKER for Daniel Yesudian in the amount of $180,000.00 and to have termination stricken from the record and plaintiff shall be allowed to retire as of 5/1/92, before Judge Harold H. Greene , jury discharged reporter: Laura Beasley (dcn) Modified on 12/07/1995 (Entered: 11/22/1995)
11/21/1995	28	JURY NOTES filed (4) (dcn) (Entered: 11/22/1995)
11/21/1995	29	VERDICT FORM (dcn) (Entered: 11/22/1995)
12/01/1995	30	MOTION filed by plaintiff USA/YESUDIAN for post-verdict equitable relief for reinstatement and credit for back benefits, double pay, front pay, pre and post judgment interest on the backpay, litigation costs and attorney fees' (JMF) (Entered: 12/04/1995)
12/12/1995	31	JUDGMENT by Judge Harold H. Greene in favor of plaintiff USA/YESUDIAN against defendant HOWARD UNIVERSITY, defendant JOSEPH B. PARKER in the amount of $180,000.00 and other damages (dcn) (Entered: 12/13/1995)
12/15/1995	32	MOTION filed by defendant to extend time to 12/22/95 to respond to plaintiff's motion for post-verdict equtable relief (ted) (Entered: 12/18/1995)
12/22/1995	33	ORDER by Judge Harold H. Greene : granting motion to extend time to 12/27/95 to respond to plaintiff's motion for post-verdict equtable relief [32-1] by JAMES A.

Exhibit IV-E

09/06/1996	46	MEMORANDUM AND ORDER by Judge Harold H. Greene : granting motion of defendant Parker's for a directed verdict as to plaintiffs False Claims Act retaliation claim; denying motion of Howard University's motion for directed verdict as to plaintiffs contract claim; denying motion of defendants for a new trial [35-1], entering judgment in favor of defendant Parker on plaintiffs retaliation claim; entering judgment, consistent with the jury's verdict, in favor of plaintiff in the amount of $180,000.00 on plaintiffs contract claim against Howard University; striking the jury's recommendation that plaintiff be awarded the option to have the termination stricken from his record and be allowed to retire as of May 1, 1992 in accordance with the rules in effect at Howard University at that time; denying motion for post-verdict equitable for reinstatement and credit for back benefits, double pay, front pay, pre and post judgment interest on the backpay, litigation costs and attorney fees' [30-1] by USA/YESUDIAN (dcn) (Entered: 09/09/1996)
09/20/1996	47	MOTION filed by plaintiff DANIEL YESUDIAN for reconsideration of order [46-1], order [46-2], order [46-3] (lkn) (Entered: 09/24/1996)
10/07/1996	48	NOTICE OF APPEAL by plaintiff DANIEL YESUDIAN from order [46-1], order [46-2], order [46-3] , entered on: 09/09/96; $5.00 filing fee and $100.00 docketing fee paid. Copies mailed to Timothy F. McCormack, Esq. (lkn) (Entered: 10/07/1996)

Exhibit IV-F

10/07/1996	49	NOTICE OF APPEAL by defendant HOWARD UNIVERSITY from order [46-1], order [46-2], order [46-3], entered on September 9, 1996, and order [19-1] entered on December 13, 1995. $5.00 filing fee and $100.00 docketing fee paid. Copies to James L. Kestell, Esq. (lkn) (Entered: 10/08/1996)
10/08/1996		TRANSMITTED PRELIMINARY RECORD on appeal [49-1] by HOWARD UNIVERSITY to U.S. Court of Appeals (lkn) (Entered: 10/08/1996)
10/08/1996	50	MEMORANDUM by defendant HOWARD UNIVERSITY in opposition to motion for reconsideration of order [46-1], order [46-2], order [46-3] [47-1] by DANIEL YESUDIAN (lkn) (Entered: 10/09/1996)
10/18/1996		USCA # 96-7225 assigned for appeal [48-1] by DANIEL YESUDIAN (lkn) (Entered: 10/21/1996)
10/18/1996		USCA # 96-7226 assigned for appeal [49-1] by HOWARD UNIVERSITY (lkn) (Entered: 10/21/1996)
12/17/1996	51	TRANSCRIPT filed for date(s) of November 14, 1996. Reporter: Laura M. Beasley (Volume 1). (lkn) (Entered: 12/18/1996)
12/17/1996	52	TRANSCRIPT filed for date(s) of November 15, 1996. Reporter: Laura M. Beasley (Volume 2). (lkn) (Entered: 12/18/1996)
12/17/1996	53	TRANSCRIPT filed for date(s) of November 16, 1996. Reporter: Laura M. Beasley (Volume 3). (lkn) (Entered: 12/18/1996)
12/17/1996	54	TRANSCRIPT filed for date(s) of November 17, 1996. Reporter: Laura M. Beasley (Volume 4). (lkn) (Entered: 12/18/1996)

Trial Court Opinion

Exhibit IV-G

YESUDIAN v. HOWARD UNIVERSITY 31
Cite as 946 F.Supp. 31 (D.D.C. 1996)

UNITED STATES ex rel. Daniel R. YESUDIAN, Plaintiff,

v.

HOWARD UNIVERSITY, et al., Defendants.

Civil Action No. 93-1791 (HHG).

United States District Court, District of Columbia.

Sept. 6, 1996.

University employee who repeatedly complained to upper level officers at university about his supervisor and about various alleged improprieties in the purchasing department and who was subsequently terminated brought action against university and supervisor, alleging violations of the False Claims Act (FCA) and breach of contract. After jury returned verdict in favor of employee on his claim against supervisor for unlawful retaliation and on his claim against university for breach of contract, supervisor and university moved for judgment as a matter of law or, in the alternative, for new trial. The District Court, Harold H. Greene, J., held that: (1) employee did not establish claim of retaliatory discharge in violation of whistleblower provision of the FCA, and (2) under District of Columbia law, employee

2. Federal Civil Procedure ⚷2608.1

When presented with defendant's motion for judgment as a matter of law, the question is whether there is sufficient evidence upon which jury could properly base verdict for plaintiff. Fed.Rules Civ.Proc.Rule 50, 28 U.S.C.A.

3. Master and Servant ⚷30(6.35)

To find for employee on his claim of retaliatory discharge in violation of whistleblower provision of False Claims Act (FCA), jury had to find that employee engaged in conduct protected under the Act, supervisor was aware of employee's actions, and employee was terminated in retaliation for his conduct. 31 U.S.C.A. § 3730(h).

4. Colleges and Universities ⚷8.1(3)

University employee's complaints to upper level officers at university about his supervisor and about various alleged improprieties in the purchasing department were those of a disgruntled worker and not those of a worker concerned that his employer was defrauding the federal government and as such, employee did not establish claim of retaliatory discharge under whistleblower provision of False Claims Act (FCA); employee had never initiated government investigation or a private qui tam suit. 31 U.S.C.A. § 3730(h).

5. Master and Servant ⚷30(6.35)

To prove second element of his claim of retaliatory discharge in violation of whistle-

Appeals Court Document

Exhibit IV-H

General Docket
US Court of Appeals for the DC Circuit

```
                D.C. Circuit Court of Appeals

Court of Appeals Docket #: 96-7225                          Filed: 10/17/96
Nsuit: 3790  Labor: Other
USA/Daniel Yesudian v. Howard Univ, et al
Appeal from: U.S. District Court

- - - - - - - - - - - - - - - - - - - - - - - - - - - - - - - - - - -
Lower court information:

     District: 0090-1 : 93cv01791            lead: 93cv01791
     Court Reporter: Laura Beasley, Court Reporter
     Trial Judge: Harold H. Greene, US District Judge
     Date Filed: 8/26/93
     Date order/judgment: 9/6/96
     Date NOA filed: 10/7/96
- - - - - - - - - - - - - - - - - - - - - - - - - - - - - - - - - - -
Fee status: paid

- - - - - - - - - - - - - - - - - - - - - - - - - - - - - - - - - - -
Prior cases:
   None
Current cases:
                  Lead         Member       Start        End
   Cross-appeal:
                  96- 7225     96- 7226     10/17/96

Docket as of August 25, 2000 0:39 am                    Page 1


96-7225  USA/Daniel Yesudian v. Howard Univ, et al
```

Exhibit IV-I

96-7225 USA/Daniel Yesudian v. Howard Univ, et al

6/23/97	BRIEF filed by Appellant/Cross-Appellee USA in 96-7225, 96-7226 [280762-1] . Copies: 15 . Certificate of service date 6/23/97 . [96-7225, 96-7226] (wmw) [96-7225 96-7226]
6/25/97	JOINT APPENDIX filed by Appellant USA, Appellee's Howard Univ, et al., in 96-7225, 96-7226 [281226-1]. Copies: 10. Certificate of service date 6/23/97. [96-7225, 96-7226] (wmw) [96-7225 96-7226]
7/9/97	Letter sent advising the parties that the panel to hear argument in these cases on 10/6/97 will be Judges PMW, DBS, KLH. [283262-1] [96-7225, 96-7226] (cwc) [96-7225 96-7226]
7/15/97	Letter sent changing panel for oral argument. [284465-1] Case now scheduled before Judge Initials: PMW KLH MBG 10/6/97. [96-7225, 96-7226] (cwc) [96-7225 96-7226]
7/23/97	BRIEF filed by Appellee/Cross-Appellant's Howard Univ, et al., in 96-7225 [286316-1]. Copies: 15. Certificate of service date 7/23/97. [96-7225, 96-7226] (wmw) [96-7225 96-7226]
7/23/97	APPENDIX filed by Appellees/Cross-Appellants in 96-7225, 96-7226 [286329-1]. Copies: 15. Certificate of service date 7/23/97. [96-7225, 96-7226] (wmw) [96-7225 96-7226]
8/22/97	REPLY BRIEF filed by Appellant/Cross-Appellee USA ex rel.

Exhibit IV-J

9/25/97	FORM 72 filed by Attorney James L. Kestell in 96-7225, 96-7226 [299812-1] on behalf of appellant Daniel R. Yesudian [299812-2] . [96-7225, 96-7226] (sgh) [96-7225 96-7226]
10/6/97	ORAL ARGUMENT HELD before Wald, Henderson, Garland. [96-7225, 96-7226] (edb) [96-7225 96-7226]
9/1/98	JUDGMENT for the reasons in the accompanying opinion reversing the grant of judgment as a matter of law on the retaliation claim [378782-1] and affirming the denial of judgment as a matter of law on the contract claim [378782-2]. Before Judges Wald, Henderson, Garland. [96-7225, 96-7226] (edb) [96-7225 96-7226]
9/1/98	OPINION (31 pgs) for the Court filed by Judge Garland, DISSENTING IN PART OPINION (1 pgs) filed by Judge Henderson. [96-7225, 96-7226] (edb) [96-7225 96-7226]
9/1/98	CLERK'S ORDER filed that the Clerk is directed to withhold issuance of the mandate pending disposition of any timely petition for rehearing. [96-7225, 96-7226] (edb) [96-7225 96-7226]
11/4/98	MANDATE ISSUED to Clerk, District Court [393879-1] Awaiting rehearing petition cancelled. in 96-7225 & 96-7226. [96-7225, 96-7226] (edb) [96-7225 96-7226]

Appeals Court Opinion

Exhibit IV-K

U.S. EX REL. YESUDIAN v. HOWARD UNIVERSITY 731
Cite as 153 F.3d 731 (D.C. Cir. 1998)

UNITED STATES of America, ex rel. Daniel YESUDIAN, Appellant/Cross-Appellee,

v.

HOWARD UNIVERSITY, et al., Appellees/Cross-Appellants.

Nos. 96-7225, 96-7226.

United States Court of Appeals, District of Columbia Circuit.

Argued Oct. 6, 1997.

Decided Sept. 1, 1998.

Former employee of university purchasing department brought action against university and supervisor, alleging submission of false claims in violation of False Claims Act (FCA), retaliation for reporting alleged false claims, and breach of contract. After jury returned verdicts for former employee on certain claims, the United States District Court for the District of Columbia, Harold H. Greene, J., 946 F.Supp. 31, granted supervisor's motion for judgment as matter of law on retaliation claim, but denied university's motion for judgment as matter of law on contract claim. Parties appealed. The Court of Appeals, Garland, Circuit Judge, held that: (1) employee's failure to initiate private qui tam suit did not defeat FCA retaliation claim

reach verdict rendered in the case. Fed. Rules Civ.Proc.Rule 50, 28 U.S.C.A.

3. Federal Civil Procedure ⇐2142.1, 2148.1, 2609

In determining whether to grant judgment as matter of law, court may not assess credibility of witnesses or weigh the evidence. Fed.Rules Civ.Proc.Rule 50, 28 U.S.C.A.

4. Federal Civil Procedure ⇐2111, 2601

Because judgment as matter of law intrudes upon rightful province of the jury, it is highly disfavored. Fed.Rules Civ.Proc.Rule 50, 28 U.S.C.A.

5. Master and Servant ⇐30(6.35)

To make out claim of retaliation under False Claims Act (FCA) whistleblower provision, employee must demonstrate that: (1) he engaged in protected activity, that is, acts done in furtherance of an action under FCA; and (2) he was discriminated against "because of" that activity. 31 U.S.C.A. § 3730(h).

6. Master and Servant ⇐30(6.35)

For employee to establish that he or she was discriminated against "because of" protected activity under False Claims Act (FCA), for purposes of whistleblower claim, employee must show that (a) employer had

Exhibit IV-L

276 Wash. 748 PACIFIC REPORTER, 2d SERIES

prosecutor's judgment, they are not warranted. The criteria used to determine that only a single charge should be brought, may indicate that the election of one particular act for conviction is impractical.

Petrich, 572, 683 P.2d 178. Therefore, we conclude that under the facts of this case, the trial court was not required to run appellant's sentences concurrently.

⊥The remainder of this opinion has no precedential value. Therefore, it will be filed for public record in accordance with the rules governing unpublished opinions.

PEKELIS and SHUMACHER, JJ., Pro Tem., concur.

50 Wash.App. 405

⊥STATE of Washington, Respondent,

v.

Donald Fredric BROWN, Appellant.

No. 18640-0-I.

Court of Appeals of Washington, Division 1.

Jan. 20, 1988.

Defendant was convicted in Superior Court, King County, David Hunter, J., of threats to bomb or injure property, and defendant appealed. The Court of Appeals, Scholfield, C.J., held that statute that defendant was convicted under was neither vague nor overbroad.

Affirmed.

1. Constitutional Law ⇔251.4

When a claim is made that statute is void for vagueness on its face, test is whether statute satisfies due process requirements of adequate notice and adequate standards to prevent arbitrary enforcement. U.S.C.A. Const.Amends. 5, 14.

2. Criminal Law ⇔13.1(1)

Statute gives adequate notice when it describes proscribed conduct sufficiently that persons of ordinary intelligence are not required to guess at its meaning. U.S.C.A. Const.Amends. 5, 14.

3. Criminal Law ⇔13.1(1)

Statute has adequate standards for adjudication if there is sufficient specificity so that police, judges, and jury are not free to decide what is or is not prohibited depending on facts in each case, and standards must be sufficiently definite that one can evaluate the lawfulness of particular conduct. U.S.C.A. Const.Amends. 5, 14.

4. Constitutional Law ⇔48(3)

Statute is presumed constitutional, and challenging party must prove unconstitutionality beyond reasonable doubt.

5. Constitutional Law ⇔42.2(1)

Defendant had standing to challenge statute on vagueness grounds where defendant asserted that statute under which he was charged was in its entirety unconstitutionally vague on its face. U.S.C.A. Const.Amends. 5, 14.

6. Extortion and Threats ⇔25

Statute which makes it unlawful to threaten to bomb premises used for human occupancy adequately describes offense and gives adequate notice of what conduct is proscribed. West's RCWA 9.61.160.

7. Statutes ⇔188

Where term used in statute is not defined therein, it should be given its ordinary meaning and where term is defined by legislature, that definition will be applied by courts construing term.

8. Extortion and Threats ⇔25

From plain meaning and legislative definition of "threaten" in statute making it unlawful to threaten to bomb premises used for human occupancy it is implicit that "threaten to bomb" means expressing intent to cause injury or damage. West's RCWA 9A.04.110(25).

See publication Words and Phrases for other judicial constructions and definitions.

Exhibit IV-L Continued

9. Extortion and Threats ⚬=25

Words "threaten" and "bomb" in statute making it unlawful to threaten to bomb certain property are terms readily understood by persons of ordinary intelligence; overwhelming likelihood that threat to bomb will cause fear, alarm or worse makes it unnecessary to expressly add additional elements to statute to give adequate notice of conduct proscribed. West's RCWA 9.61.160; U.S.C.A. Const.Amends. 5, 14.

10. Extortion and Threats ⚬=25

Words "or otherwise injure" found in statute making it unlawful for any person to threaten to bomb or otherwise injure certain property was not vague where State was not attempting to enforce that provision against defendant. West's RCWA 9.61.160; U.S.C.A. Const.Amends. 5, 14.

11. Extortion and Threats ⚬=25

Statute making it unlawful for any person to threaten to bomb or otherwise injure certain property set forth adequate enforceable standards. West's RCWA 9.61.160; U.S.C.A. Const.Amends. 5, 14.

12. Constitutional Law ⚬=82(4)

Statute is overly broad where it is susceptible of application to protected speech, and if reach of statute can reasonably be construed to apply only to unprotected speech, then its validity can be sustained.

13. Constitutional Law ⚬=90.1(1)

Threats of harm to others do not fall within realm of protected speech.

14. Constitutional Law ⚬=90.1(1)
Extortion and Threats ⚬=25

Statute making it unlawful for any person to threaten to bomb or otherwise injure certain property was not overbroad because it was readily susceptible to narrow construction consistent with statutory definition of "threaten," which limited its application to unprotected speech. West's RCWA 9.61.160.

Christine Marie Hassenstab, Washington Appellate Defender, Seattle, for appellant.

Lloyd Corgan, King County Deputy Prosecuting, Seattle, for respondent State.

₁₉₅SCHOLFIELD, Chief Judge.

Donald Fredric Brown appeals his conviction for threats to bomb or injure property pursuant to RCW 9.61.160, a gross misdemeanor. We affirm.

FACTS

On the evening of October 3, 1985, Brown, a regular customer at the Scarlet Tree, came into the restaurant three ₁₉₆times, after walking back and forth in front of the building. McDonell, the bartender and manager of the Scarlet Tree, testified that Brown had a habit of walking up and down the street in front of the restaurant, standing in front of the windows, peering in, and making signs which he concluded Brown expected to cast some kind of a spell against the Scarlet Tree.

Brown first entered the restaurant around 11:30 p.m. He looked around, made eye contact with McDonell, and left. At that time, Brown had been told by the management to stay out of the restaurant. Just after Brown left, he came in a second time, and McDonell explained to him that he could not stay. Moments later, Brown walked in the front door for the third time, looked into the dining room and said, " 'You're going to burn in hell, you're all sinners. I have just planted dynamite here and it's going to blow.' " Brown then turned and ran out the door.

The Scarlet Tree was approximately 50 percent occupied that night. Brown had spoken loudly enough for the people in the front part of the lounge to hear him and for everyone in the dining room to hear him. Some people looked frightened, and others looked amused. Approximately 12 customers left the restaurant.

McDonell followed Brown as he ran out of the bar, crossed the street, and ducked behind a mailbox, and said to McDonell, " 'You don't have to believe it, but it's going to blow.' " McDonell returned to the restaurant and called the police.

Exhibit IV-M

McDonell originally was quite concerned, but decided he did not believe Brown had planted dynamite inside the building because he had seen him three times and he was not carrying anything and did not appear to have had time to plant a bomb.

Officer William S. Leonard and his partner, Officer Donald Skaar, responded to the reported bomb threat. When they arrived, they spoke with McDonell. There were roughly 25 or 30 patrons in the restaurant and cocktail lounge. Leonard checked the restaurant and restroom for ⊥some type of explosive device, while Officer Skaar developed details from McDonell. No explosive device was found.

Brown was known to frequent a nearby convenience store, so the officers went to the store, where they observed Brown, who matched the description given them. They arrested him, advised him of his rights and took him into custody. Brown entered a plea of not guilty and testified at his trial that he did not go into the Scarlet Tree and that he did not tell anyone that he had planted dynamite. A jury found Brown guilty of threats to bomb a public place. Brown appeals on the ground that RCW 9.61.160 is unconstitutionally overbroad and vague on its face.

RCW 9.61.160 reads:

> It shall be unlawful for any person to threaten to bomb or otherwise injure any public or private school building, any place of worship or public assembly, any governmental property, or any other building, common carrier, or structure, or any place used for human occupancy; or to communicate or repeat any information concerning such a threatened bombing or injury, knowing such information to be false and with intent to alarm the person or persons to whom the information is communicated or repeated.

VAGUENESS

[1–4] When the claim is made that a statute is void for vagueness on its face, the test is whether the statute satisfies the due process requirements of adequate notice and adequate standards to prevent arbitrary enforcement. *State v. Maciolek,* 101 Wash.2d 259, 676 P.2d 996 (1984). Adequate notice requiresdescribing the proscribed conduct sufficiently that persons of ordinary intelligence are not required to guess at its meaning. Adequate standards for adjudication require sufficient specificity so that police, judges and juries are not free to decide what is or is not prohibited depending on the facts in each case. *Maciolek,* at 264 676 P.2d 996 (quoting *State v. Carter,* 89 Wash.2d 236, 239–40, 570 ⊥P.2d 1218 (1977)). The standards must be sufficiently definite that one can evaluate the lawfulness of particular conduct. A statute is presumed constitutional, and the challenging party must prove unconstitutionality beyond a reasonable doubt. *Maciolek,* 101 Wash.2d at 263, 676 P.2d 996.

[5] The State contends initially that Brown does not have standing to challenge the statute for vagueness. However, when the challenge asserts that the statute under which the defendant is charged is in its entirety unconstitutionally vague on its face, the challenger has standing. *State v. Zuanich,* 92 Wash.2d 61, 63, 593 P.2d 1314 (1979).

[6] Brown argues that RCW 9.61.160 lacks adequate notice. He was prosecuted under the first portion of the statute which does not require proof of an intention to alarm or that persons threatened were alarmed. From that fact, Brown argues that the statute does not give adequate notice of what conduct is proscribed by the statute. We find this argument unconvincing. "[T]o threaten to bomb" premises used for human occupancy adequately describes the offense. While requiring additional elements would narrow the definition of the offense, the additional elements are not necessary to enable persons of ordinary intelligence to know what is meant by a threat to bomb a building.

[7] Where a term used in a statute is not defined therein, it should be given its ordinary meaning. *State ex rel. Graham v. Northshore School Dist. 417,* 99 Wash. 2d 232, 662 P.2d 38 (1983). To threaten is to express an intention to inflict evil, injury or damage on another. *Webster's Third New Internat'l Dictionary* 2382 (1969). The rules of statutory construction state

Exhibit IV-M Continued

that where a term is defined by the Legislature, that definition will be applied by the courts construing the term. *Seattle v. Shepherd*, 93 Wash.2d 861, 866, 613 P.2d 1158 (1980). "Threaten" is defined in the definitional section of the criminal code as communicating, directly or indirectly, the intent to cause bodily injury or physical damage to property of another. RCW 9A.04.110(26).

[8, 9] From both the plain meaning and the legislative definition of "threaten", it is implicit that "threaten to bomb" means expressing an intent to cause injury or damage. The words "threaten" and "bomb" are terms readily understood by persons of ordinary intelligence. The overwhelming likelihood that a threat to bomb will cause fear, alarm or worse makes it unnecessary to expressly add additional elements to give adequate notice of the conduct proscribed by the statute.

[10] Brown argues that the words "or otherwise injure" found in the first portion of the statute are potentially vague. However, the State is not attempting to enforce that provision against Brown. The possibility that a vagueness problem could arise when the State is forced to rely upon the phrase "or otherwise injure" is not relevant to a decision here where Brown's conduct falls squarely within the constitutional core of the statute. In this situation, the statute is not vague. *State v. Zuanich*, *supra* 92 Wash.2d at 68, 593 P.2d 1314.

[11] For the reasons expressed above, we are also satisfied that the statute sets forth adequate enforceable standards. The words "threaten" and "bomb" have a sufficiently specific meaning to remove the danger that persons responsible for enforcing the statute would have an impermissible discretion to expand or contract the meaning for purposes of a particular case.

OVERBREADTH

Brown contends RCW 9.61.160 is overly broad because it does not require an intent to alarm or actual alarm and contains no definition of "or otherwise injure".

[12] A statute is overly broad where it is susceptible of application to protected speech. *State v. Reyes*, 104 Wash.2d 35, 41, 700 P.2d 1155 (1985). If the reach of the statute can reasonably be construed to apply only to unprotected speech, then its validity can be sustained. *Reyes*, at 41–42, 700 P.2d 1155 (citing *New York v. Ferber*, 458 U.S. 747, 769 n. 24, 102 S.Ct. 3348, 3361 n. 24, 73 L.Ed.2d 1113 (1982)).

The thrust of Brown's argument is that since the part of the statute under which he was prosecuted does not require intent to alarm or actual alarm as elements of the offense, there is no compelling state need justifying the restriction.

[13] Threats of harm to others do not fall within the realm of protected speech. *Chaplinsky v. New Hampshire*, 315 U.S. 568, 62 S.Ct. 766, 86 L.Ed. 1031 (1942); *Phillips v. Purpear*, 403 F.Supp. 80, 88 (W.D.Va.1975); *Lanthrip v. State*, 235 Ga. 10, 218 S.E.2d 771 (1975).

> Statutes prohibiting terroristic threats, extortion, blackmail, and the like, though often applied to conduct involving "pure speech," have been consistently enforced and upheld. As an illustration, the federal statute that prohibits threatening death or bodily harm upon the President of the United States, 18 U.S.C. § 871(a), has been upheld by the Supreme Court of the United States against a first amendment challenge that it prohibits "pure speech." *Watts v. United States*, 394 U.S. 705, 89 S.Ct. 1399, 22 L.Ed.2d 664 (1969).

Carlsen v. Morris, 556 F.Supp. 320, 322 (D.Utah 1982).

[14] The statute challenged here is not overbroad because it is readily susceptible to a narrow construction consistent with the statutory definition of "threaten", which limits its application to unprotected speech. *Gooding v. Wilson*, 405 U.S. 518, 522, 92 S.Ct. 1103, 1106, 31 L.Ed.2d 408 (1972).

The judgment is affirmed.

COLEMAN and WILLIAMS, JJ., concur.

Exhibit IV-N

276 748 Pacific Reporter, 2d Series

Parallel Cite — **50 Wash. App. 405**

Names of parties

STATE of Washington, Respondent,

v.

Donald Fredric BROWN, Appellant

Docket number — **No. 18640-0-I.**

Court — Court of Appeals of Washington Division 1.

Date of Decision — Jan. 20, 1988

Exhibit IV-O

Synopsis (Syllabus)

Defendant was convicted in Superior Court, King County, David Hunter, J., of threats to bomb or injure property, and defendant appealed. The Court of Appeals, Scholfield, C.J., held that statute that defendant was convicted under was neither vague nor overbroad.

Disposition

Affirmed.

Exhibit IV-P

West Topic & key numbers

1. Constitutional Law 251.4
When a claim is made that statute is void for vagueness on its face, test is whether statute satisfies due process requirements of adequate notice and adequate standards to prevent arbitrary enforcement.

Headnote Number

West headnotes

2. Criminal Law 13.1(1)
Statute gives adequate notice when it describes proscribed conduct sufficiently that persons of ordinary intelligence are not required to guess at its meaning. U.S.C.A. Const. Amends. 5, 14.

. . . .

Exhibit IV-Q

Use headnotes to jump to the relevant portion of the opinion

Headnote is found on page 276 of the case

5. Constitutional Law 42.2(1)
Defendant had standing to challenge statute on vagueness grounds where defendant asserted that statute under which he was charged was in its entirety unconstitutionally vague on its face. U.S.C.A. Const. Amends. 5, 14.

Headnote 5 is based upon information found on p. 278 of the case

[5] The State contends initially that Brown does not have standing to challenge the statute for vagueness. However, when the challenge asserts that the statute under which the defendant is charged is in its entirety unconstitutionally vague on its face, the challenger has standing.

Exhibit IV-R

Names of counsel

Christine Marie Hassenstab, Washington Appellate Defender, Seattle, for appellant.

Lloyd Corgan, King County Deputy Prosecuting, Seattle, for respondent State.

Exhibit IV-S

Majority opinion

⊥406 SCHOLFIELD, Chief Judge.

Donald Fredric Brown appeals his conviction for threats to bomb or injure property pursuant to RCW 9.61.160, a gross misdemeanor. We affirm.

FACTS

On the evening of October 3, 1985, Brown, a regular customer at the Scarlet Tree, came into the restaurant three⊥407 times, after walking back and forth in front of the building.

. . .

Star pagination

Exhibit IV-T

. . .

The judgment is affirmed.

Coleman and Williams JJ. concur.

Lukoski v. Sandia Indiana Management Co., Supreme Court of New Mexico

Opinion

Ransom, Justice

. . .

IT IS SO ORDERED.

SCARBOROUGH, C.J., SOSA, Senior **Justice**, and WALTERS, J., concur.

STOWERS, J., **dissents**.
STOWERS, Justice, dissenting.
I respectfully **dissent** from the majority's holding that SIMCO did not abide with the termination procedures.

Citing Court Opinions Step-by-Step

Exhibit X-A

276 Wash. 748 PACIFIC REPORTER, 2d SERIES

prosecutor's judgment, they are not warranted. The criteria used to determine that only a single charge should be brought, may indicate that the election of one particular act for conviction is impractical.

Petrich, 572, 683 P.2d 173. Therefore, we conclude that under the facts of this case, the trial court was not required to run appellant's sentences concurrently.

⊥390The remainder of this opinion has no precedential value. Therefore, it will be filed for public record in accordance with the rules governing unpublished opinions.

PEKELIS and SHUMACHER, JJ., Pro Tem., concur.

50 Wash.App. 405

⊥405STATE of Washington, Respondent,

v.

Donald Fredric BROWN, Appellant.

No. 18640-0-I.

Court of Appeals of Washington, Division 1.

Jan. 20, 1988.

Defendant was convicted in Superior Court, King County, David Hunter, J., of threats to bomb or injure property, and defendant appealed. The Court of Ap-

2. Criminal Law 🔑13.1(1)

Statute gives adequate notice when it describes proscribed conduct sufficiently that persons of ordinary intelligence are not required to guess at its meaning. U.S.C.A. Const.Amends. 5, 14.

3. Criminal Law 🔑13.1(1)

Statute has adequate standards for adjudication if there is sufficient specificity so that police, judges, and jury are not free to decide what is or is not prohibited depending on facts in each case, and standards must be sufficiently definite that one can evaluate the lawfulness of particular conduct. U.S.C.A. Const.Amends. 5, 14.

4. Constitutional Law 🔑48(3)

Statute is presumed constitutional, and challenging party must prove unconstitutionality beyond reasonable doubt.

5. Constitutional Law 🔑42.2(1)

Defendant had standing to challenge statute on vagueness grounds where defendant asserted that statute under which he was charged was in its entirety unconstitutionally vague on its face. U.S.C.A. Const.Amends. 5, 14.

6. Extortion and Threats 🔑25

Statute which makes it unlawful to threaten to bomb premises used for human occupancy adequately describes offense and gives adequate notice of what conduct is proscribed. West's RCWA 9.61.160.

7. Statutes 🔑188

Where term used in statute is not defined therein, it should be given its ordinary meaning and where term is defined by legislature, that definition will be applied

Exhibit XI-A

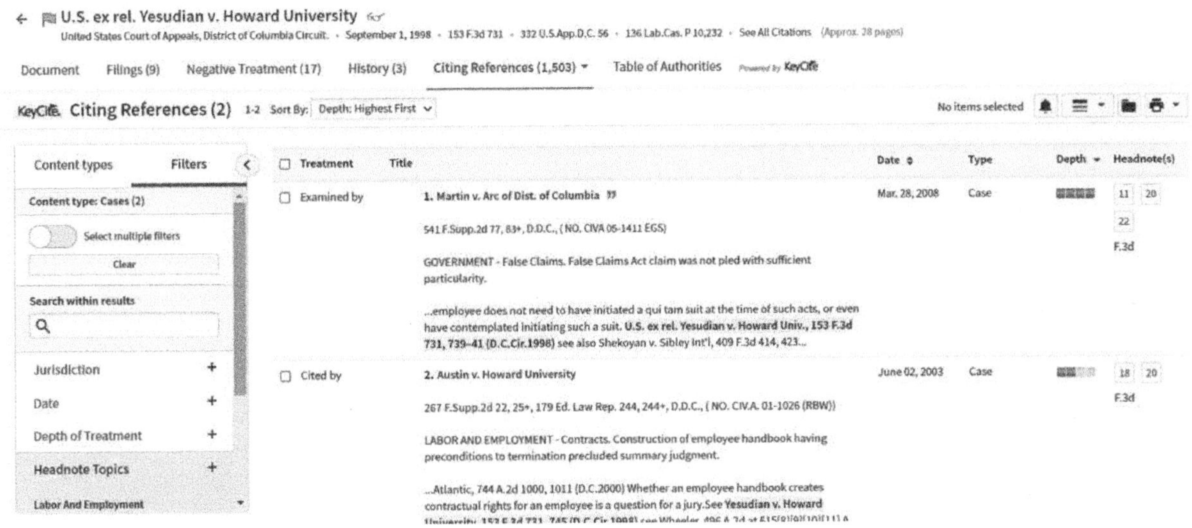
← U.S. ex rel. Yesudian v. Howard University

United States Court of Appeals, District of Columbia Circuit. · September 1, 1998 · 153 F.3d 731 · 332 U.S.App.D.C. 56 · 136 Lab.Cas. P 10,232 · See All Citations (Approx. 28 pages)

Document | Filings (9) | Negative Treatment (17) | History (3) | Citing References (1,503) | Table of Authorities | Powered by KeyCite

KeyCite. Citing References (2) 1-2 Sort By: Depth: Highest First

No items selected

Content types | Filters

Content type: Cases (2)

Select multiple filters

Clear

Search within results

Jurisdiction +

Date +

Depth of Treatment +

Headnote Topics +

Labor And Employment

Treatment	Title	Date	Type	Depth	Headnote(s)
Examined by	**1. Martin v. Arc of Dist. of Columbia** 541 F.Supp.2d 77, 83+, D.D.C., (NO. CIVA 05-1411 EGS) GOVERNMENT - False Claims. False Claims Act claim was not pled with sufficient particularity. ...employee does not need to have initiated a qui tam suit at the time of such acts, or even have contemplated initiating such a suit. **U.S. ex rel. Yesudian v. Howard Univ., 153 F.3d 731, 739–41 (D.C.Cir.1998)** see also Shekoyan v. Sibley Int'l, 409 F.3d 414, 423...	Mar. 28, 2008	Case		11 20 22 F.3d
Cited by	**2. Austin v. Howard University** 267 F.Supp.2d 22, 25+, 179 Ed. Law Rep. 244, 244+, D.D.C., (NO. CIV.A. 01-1026 (RBW)) LABOR AND EMPLOYMENT - Contracts. Construction of employee handbook having preconditions to termination precluded summary judgment. ...Atlantic, 744 A.2d 1000, 1011 (D.C.2000) Whether an employee handbook creates contractual rights for an employee is a question for a jury.See **Yesudian v. Howard**	June 02, 2003	Case		18 20 F.3d

Exhibit XI-B

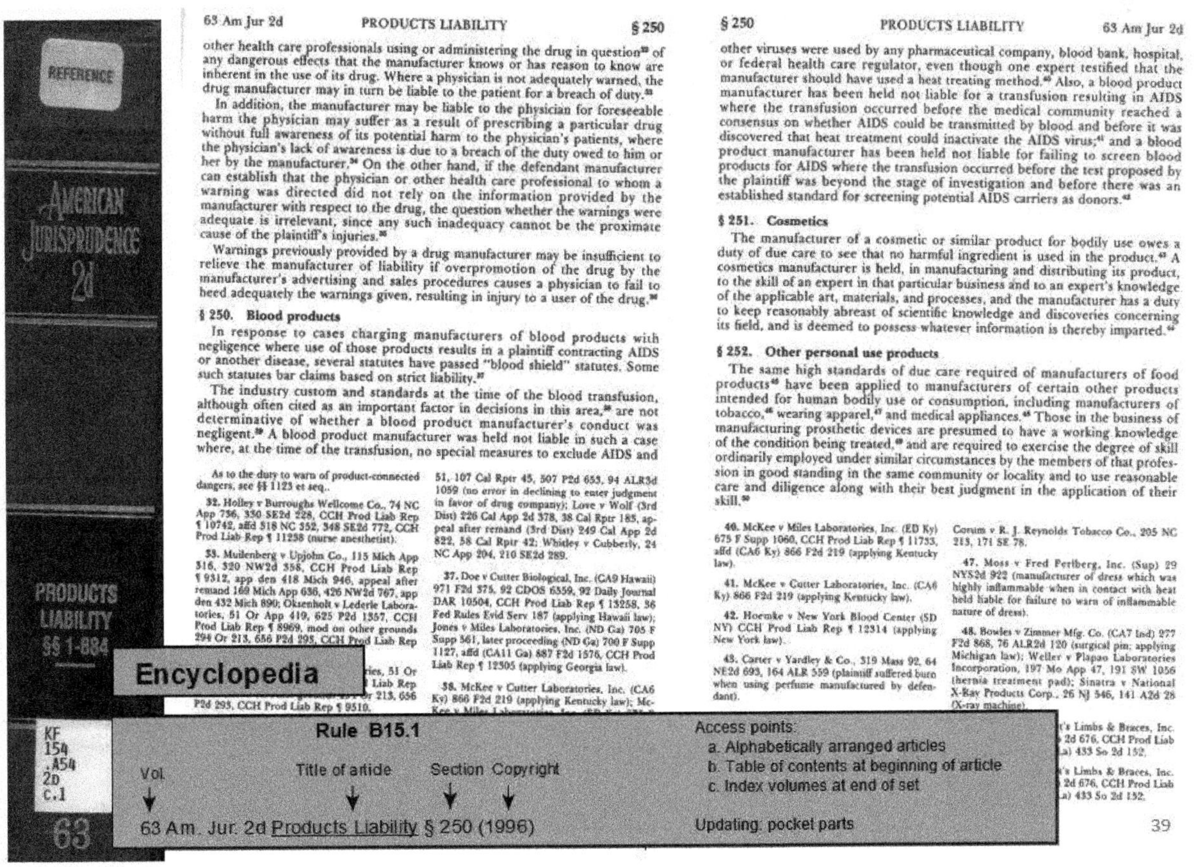
63 Am Jur 2d PRODUCTS LIABILITY § 250

other health care professionals using or administering the drug in question[32] of any dangerous effects that the manufacturer knows or has reason to know are inherent in the use of its drug. Where a physician is not adequately warned, the drug manufacturer may in turn be liable to the patient for a breach of duty.[33]

In addition, the manufacturer may be liable to the physician for foreseeable harm the physician may suffer as a result of prescribing a particular drug without full awareness of its potential harm to the physician's patients, where the physician's lack of awareness is due to a breach of the duty owed to him or her by the manufacturer.[34] On the other hand, if the defendant manufacturer can establish that the physician or other health care professional to whom a warning was directed did not rely on the information provided by the manufacturer with respect to the drug, the question whether the warnings were adequate is irrelevant, since any such inadequacy cannot be the proximate cause of the plaintiff's injuries.[35]

Warnings previously provided by a drug manufacturer may be insufficient to relieve the manufacturer of liability if overpromotion of the drug by the manufacturer's advertising and sales procedures causes a physician to fail to heed adequately the warnings given, resulting in injury to a user of the drug.[36]

§ 250. Blood products

In response to cases charging manufacturers of blood products with negligence where use of those products results in a plaintiff contracting AIDS or another disease, several statutes have passed "blood shield" statutes. Some such statutes bar claims based on strict liability.[37]

The industry custom and standards at the time of the blood transfusion, although often cited as an important factor in decisions in this area,[38] are not determinative of whether a blood product manufacturer's conduct was negligent.[39] A blood product manufacturer was held not liable in such a case where, at the time of the transfusion, no special measures to exclude AIDS and

As to the duty to warn of product-connected dangers, see §§ 1123 et seq..

32. Holley v Burroughs Wellcome Co., 74 NC App 736, 330 SE2d 228, CCH Prod Liab Rep ¶ 10742, affd 318 NC 352, 348 SE2d 772, CCH Prod Liab Rep ¶ 11258 (nurse anesthetist).

33. Muilenberg v Upjohn Co., 115 Mich App 316, 320 NW2d 358, CCH Prod Liab Rep ¶ 9312, app den 418 Mich 946, appeal after remand 169 Mich App 636, 426 NW2d 767, app den 432 Mich 890; Oksenholt v Lederle Laboratories, 51 Or App 419, 625 P2d 1357, CCH Prod Liab Rep ¶ 8969, mod on other grounds 294 Or 213, 656 P2d 293, CCH Prod Liab Rep

...ries, 51 Or ... Liab Rep ...r 213, 656 P2d 293, CCH Prod Liab Rep ¶ 9510.

51, 107 Cal Rptr 45, 507 P2d 653, 94 ALR3d 1059 (no error in declining to enter judgment in favor of drug company); Love v Wolf (3rd Dist) 226 Cal App 2d 378, 38 Cal Rptr 183, appeal after remand (3rd Dist) 249 Cal App 2d 822, 58 Cal Rptr 42; Whitley v Cubberly, 24 NC App 204, 210 SE2d 289.

37. Doe v Cutter Biological, Inc. (CA9 Hawaii) 971 F2d 375, 92 CDOS 6359, 92 Daily Journal DAR 10504, CCH Prod Liab Rep ¶ 13258, 36 Fed Rules Evid Serv 187 (applying Hawaii law); Jones v Miles Laboratories, Inc. (ND Ga) 705 F Supp 561, later proceeding (ND Ga) 700 F Supp 1127, affd (CA11 Ga) 887 F2d 1576, CCH Prod Liab Rep ¶ 12305 (applying Georgia law).

38. McKee v Cutter Laboratories, Inc. (CA6 Ky) 866 F2d 219 (applying Kentucky law); Mc-

§ 250 PRODUCTS LIABILITY 63 Am Jur 2d

other viruses were used by any pharmaceutical company, blood bank, hospital, or federal health care regulator, even though one expert testified that the manufacturer should have used a heat treating method.[40] Also, a blood product manufacturer has been held not liable for a transfusion resulting in AIDS where the transfusion occurred before the medical community reached a consensus on whether AIDS could be transmitted by blood and before it was discovered that heat treatment could inactivate the AIDS virus;[41] and a blood product manufacturer has been held not liable for failing to screen blood products for AIDS where the transfusion occurred before the test proposed by the plaintiff was beyond the stage of investigation and before there was an established standard for screening potential AIDS carriers as donors.[42]

§ 251. Cosmetics

The manufacturer of a cosmetic or similar product for bodily use owes a duty of due care to see that no harmful ingredient is used in the product.[43] A cosmetics manufacturer is held, in manufacturing and distributing its product, to the skill of an expert in that particular business and to an expert's knowledge of the applicable art, materials, and processes, and the manufacturer has a duty to keep reasonably abreast of scientific knowledge and discoveries concerning its field, and is deemed to possess whatever information is thereby imparted.[44]

§ 252. Other personal use products

The same high standards of due care required of manufacturers of food products[45] have been applied to manufacturers of certain other products intended for human bodily use or consumption, including manufacturers of tobacco,[46] wearing apparel,[47] and medical appliances.[48] Those in the business of manufacturing prosthetic devices are presumed to have a working knowledge of the condition being treated,[49] and are required to exercise the degree of skill ordinarily employed under similar circumstances by the members of that profession in good standing in the same community or locality and to use reasonable care and diligence along with their best judgment in the application of their skill.[50]

40. McKee v Miles Laboratories, Inc. (ED Ky) 675 F Supp 1060, CCH Prod Liab Rep ¶ 11753, affd (CA6 Ky) 866 F2d 219 (applying Kentucky law).

41. McKee v Cutter Laboratories, Inc. (CA6 Ky) 866 F2d 219 (applying Kentucky law).

42. Hoemke v New York Blood Center (SD NY) CCH Prod Liab Rep ¶ 12314 (applying New York law).

43. Carter v Yardley & Co., 319 Mass 92, 64 NE2d 693, 164 ALR 559 (plaintiff suffered burn when using perfume manufactured by defendant).

Corum v R. J. Reynolds Tobacco Co., 205 NC 213, 171 SE 78.

47. Moss v Fred Perlberg, Inc. (Sup) 29 NYS2d 922 (manufacturer of dress which was highly inflammable when in contact with heat held liable for failure to warn of inflammable nature of dress).

48. Bowles v Zimmer Mfg. Co. (CA7 Ind) 277 F2d 868, 76 ALR2d 120 (surgical pin; applying Michigan law); Weller v Plapao Laboratories Incorporation, 197 Mo App 47, 191 SW 1056 (hernia treatment pad); Sinatra v National X-Ray Products Corp., 26 NJ 546, 141 A2d 28 (X-ray machine).

...'s Limbs & Braces, Inc. ...2d 676, CCH Prod Liab ...a) 433 So 2d 152.

...'s Limbs & Braces, Inc. ...2d 676, CCH Prod Liab ...a) 433 So 2d 152.

39

Exhibit XI-C

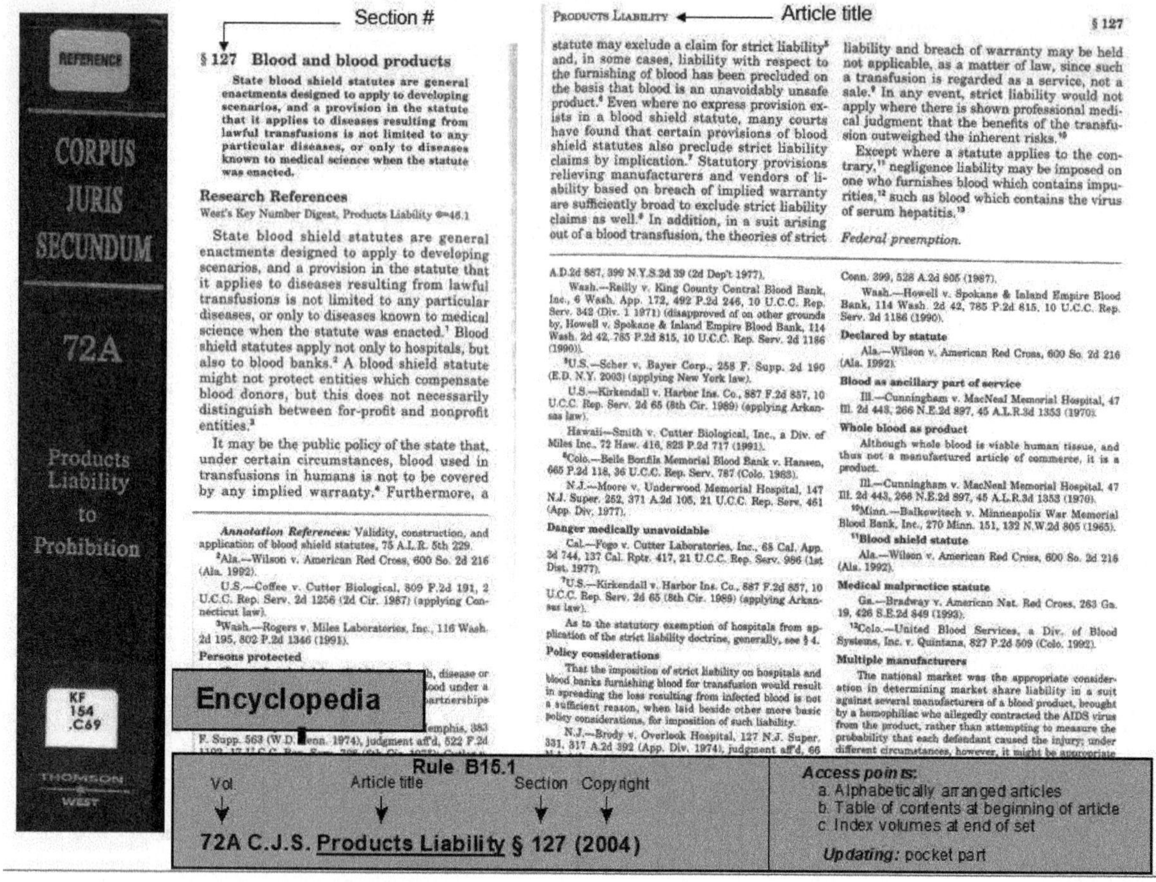

PRODUCTS LIABILITY § 127

§ 127 Blood and blood products

State blood shield statutes are general enactments designed to apply to developing scenarios, and a provision in the statute that it applies to diseases resulting from lawful transfusions is not limited to any particular diseases, or only to diseases known to medical science when the statute was enacted.

Research References

West's Key Number Digest, Products Liability ⚷46.1

State blood shield statutes are general enactments designed to apply to developing scenarios, and a provision in the statute that it applies to diseases resulting from lawful transfusions is not limited to any particular diseases, or only to diseases known to medical science when the statute was enacted.[1] Blood shield statutes apply not only to hospitals, but also to blood banks.[2] A blood shield statute might not protect entities which compensate blood donors, but this does not necessarily distinguish between for-profit and nonprofit entities.[3]

It may be the public policy of the state that, under certain circumstances, blood used in transfusions in humans is not to be covered by any implied warranty.[4] Furthermore, a statute may exclude a claim for strict liability[5] and, in some cases, liability with respect to the furnishing of blood has been precluded on the basis that blood is an unavoidably unsafe product.[6] Even where no express provision exists in a blood shield statute, many courts have found that certain provisions of blood shield statutes also preclude strict liability claims by implication.[7] Statutory provisions relieving manufacturers and vendors of liability based on breach of implied warranty are sufficiently broad to exclude strict liability claims as well.[8] In addition, in a suit arising out of a blood transfusion, the theories of strict liability and breach of warranty may be held not applicable, as a matter of law, since such a transfusion is regarded as a service, not a sale.[9] In any event, strict liability would not apply where there is shown professional medical judgment that the benefits of the transfusion outweighed the inherent risks.[10]

Except where a statute applies to the contrary,[11] negligence liability may be imposed on one who furnishes blood which contains impurities,[12] such as blood which contains the virus of serum hepatitis.[13]

Federal preemption.

Annotation References: Validity, construction, and application of blood shield statutes, 75 A.L.R. 5th 229.

[2]Ala.—Wilson v. American Red Cross, 600 So. 2d 216 (Ala. 1992).

U.S.—Coffee v. Cutter Biological, 809 F.2d 191, 2 U.C.C. Rep. Serv. 2d 1256 (2d Cir. 1987) (applying Connecticut law).

[3]Wash.—Rogers v. Miles Laboratories, Inc., 116 Wash. 2d 195, 802 P.2d 1346 (1991).

Persons protected

...h, disease or ...lood under a ...partnerships

...emphis, 383 F. Supp. 563 (W.D. Tenn. 1974), judgment aff'd, 522 F.2d ...

A.D.2d 887, 399 N.Y.S.2d 39 (2d Dep't 1977).

Wash.—Reilly v. King County Central Blood Bank, Inc., 6 Wash. App. 172, 492 P.2d 246, 10 U.C.C. Rep. Serv. 342 (Div. 1 1971) (disapproved of on other grounds by, Howell v. Spokane & Inland Empire Blood Bank, 114 Wash. 2d 42, 785 P.2d 815, 10 U.C.C. Rep. Serv. 2d 1186 (1990)).

[5]U.S.—Scher v. Bayer Corp., 258 F. Supp. 2d 190 (E.D. N.Y. 2003) (applying New York law).

U.S.—Kirkendall v. Harbor Ins. Co., 887 F.2d 857, 10 U.C.C. Rep. Serv. 2d 65 (8th Cir. 1989) (applying Arkansas law).

Hawaii—Smith v. Cutter Biological, Inc., a Div. of Miles Inc., 72 Haw. 416, 823 P.2d 717 (1991).

[6]Colo.—Belle Bonfils Memorial Blood Bank v. Hansen, 665 P.2d 118, 36 U.C.C. Rep. Serv. 787 (Colo. 1983).

N.J.—Moore v. Underwood Memorial Hospital, 147 N.J. Super. 252, 371 A.2d 105, 21 U.C.C. Rep. Serv. 461 (App. Div. 1977).

Danger medically unavoidable

Cal.—Fogo v. Cutter Laboratories, Inc., 68 Cal. App. 3d 744, 137 Cal. Rptr. 417, 21 U.C.C. Rep. Serv. 986 (1st Dist. 1977).

[7]U.S.—Kirkendall v. Harbor Ins. Co., 887 F.2d 857, 10 U.C.C. Rep. Serv. 2d 65 (8th Cir. 1989) (applying Arkansas law).

As to the statutory exemption of hospitals from application of the strict liability doctrine, generally, see § 4.

Policy considerations

That the imposition of strict liability on hospitals and blood banks furnishing blood for transfusion would result in spreading the loss resulting from infected blood is not a sufficient reason, when laid beside other more basic policy considerations, for imposition of such liability.

N.J.—Brody v. Overlook Hospital, 127 N.J. Super. 331, 317 A.2d 392 (App. Div. 1974), judgment aff'd, 66 ...

Conn. 399, 528 A.2d 805 (1987).

Wash.—Howell v. Spokane & Inland Empire Blood Bank, 114 Wash. 2d 42, 785 P.2d 815, 10 U.C.C. Rep. Serv. 2d 1186 (1990).

Declared by statute

Ala.—Wilson v. American Red Cross, 600 So. 2d 216 (Ala. 1992).

Blood as ancillary part of service

Ill.—Cunningham v. MacNeal Memorial Hospital, 47 Ill. 2d 443, 266 N.E.2d 897, 45 A.L.R.3d 1353 (1970).

Whole blood as product

Although whole blood is viable human tissue, and thus not a manufactured article of commerce, it is a product.

Ill.—Cunningham v. MacNeal Memorial Hospital, 47 Ill. 2d 443, 266 N.E.2d 897, 45 A.L.R.3d 1353 (1970).

[10]Minn.—Balkowitsch v. Minneapolis War Memorial Blood Bank, Inc., 270 Minn. 151, 132 N.W.2d 805 (1965).

[11]**Blood shield statute**

Ala.—Wilson v. American Red Cross, 600 So. 2d 216 (Ala. 1992).

Medical malpractice statute

Ga.—Bradway v. American Nat. Red Cross, 263 Ga. 19, 426 S.E.2d 849 (1993).

[12]Colo.—United Blood Services, a Div. of Blood Systems, Inc. v. Quintana, 827 P.2d 509 (Colo. 1992).

Multiple manufacturers

The national market was the appropriate consideration in determining market share liability in a suit against several manufacturers of a blood product, brought by a hemophiliac who allegedly contracted the AIDS virus from the product, rather than attempting to measure the probability that each defendant caused the injury; under different circumstances, however, it might be appropriate

Exhibit XI-D

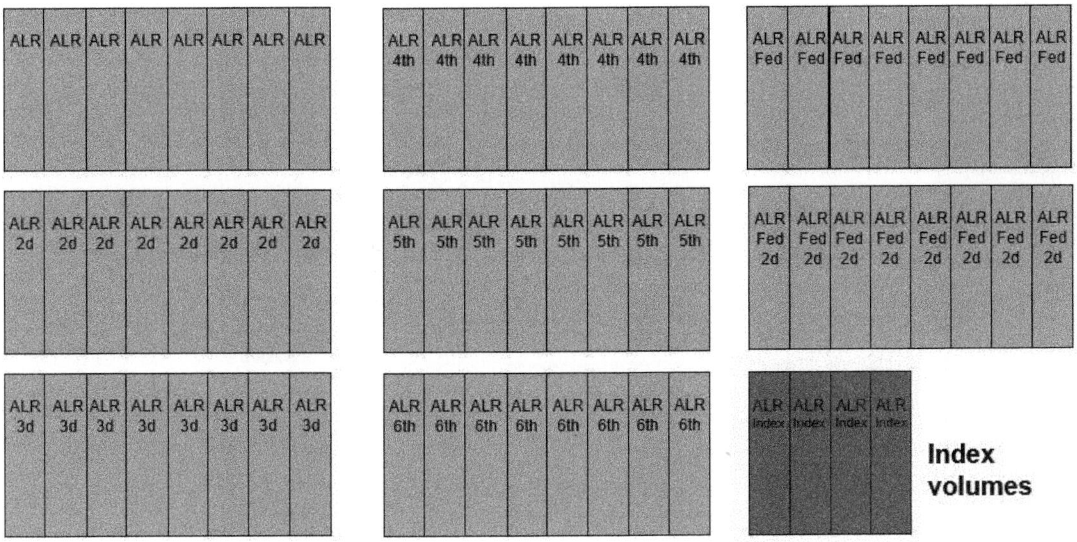

ALR

American Law Reports

– Random collection of articles (called "annotations") on narrow topics of law

– Each article analyzes cases from every jurisdiction that has taken a position on the topic

– References cases from both sides of an issue

– References statutes, digests, texts, treatises, law reviews, and legal encyclopedias

– Organized into different series (1st-6th and Fed/Fed 2d); articles in random order

– To access, use *Index* volumes at end of all ALR series

– Updated with pocket parts

Exhibit XI-E

75 ALR5th 229

VALIDITY, CONSTRUCTION, AND APPLICATION OF BLOOD SHIELD STATUTES

by
Patricia Kussman, J.D.

In recent times, many jurisdictions, concerned about the potential for ruinous litigation against hospitals, blood banks, physicians, and commercial suppliers of blood and blood products by persons injured by the introduction of tainted samples of these life-sustaining materials into medical patients, have enacted statutes that attempt to balance the need for protecting suppliers from unlimited liability and consequent withdrawal from the field with the public need for accountability in the medical professions and related fields by requiring that any such suits must allege negligence or another "fault" basis for recovery, thereby protecting those who deal in blood and blood products from "no-fault" liability on theories of strict tort liability or breach of implied warranty. One of these enactments, which have collectively become known as "blood shield" statutes, was at issue in Advincula v. United Blood Services, 176 Ill. 2d 1, 223 Ill. Dec. 1, 678 N.E.2d 1009, 75 A.L.R.5th 659 (1996), reh'g denied, (Apr. 24, 1997), in which the court held that the correct standard for determining negligence thereunder would be the care required of a professional in the field, and that under such a standard the defendant blood supplier could not be held liable because it had met the standard in its dealings with the tainted blood in question. The annotation that follows collects and discusses the cases in which the courts have addressed the validity, construction, or application of blood shield statutes.

Advincula v. United Blood Services is fully reported at page 659, infra.

BLOOD SHIELD STATUTES
75 ALR5th 229 — 75 ALR5th

TABLE OF CONTENTS

ARTICLE OUTLINE

ALR

Author — Annotation — Title (full title – not shortened form from header)

Patricia Kussman, Annotation, <u>Validity, Construction, and Application of Blood Shield Statutes</u>, 75 A.L.R.5th 229 (2000)

Vol. — Series — Page — Copyright

Rule 16.7.6

Exhibit XI-F

§ 13. Commercial entities

[a] Statute held applicable

Commercial or for-profit providers of blood are entitled to immunity under state blood shield statutes, the courts held in the following cases.

Because providing blood and blood products was statutorily defined as rendition of a service rather than a sale, a commercial manufacturer of a coagulant factor derived from blood plasma could not be found strictly liable for supplying a coagulating product containing hepatitis, the court held in Fogo v. Cutter Laboratories, Inc., 68 **Cal. App. 3d** 744, 137 Cal. Rptr. 417, 21 U.C.C. Rep. Serv. (CBC) 986 (1st Dist. 1977). A man suffering from mild hemophilia took an clotting plasma product before visiting his dentist for a tooth extraction. Although he stopped bleeding shortly after the extraction, he died from viral hepatitis two months later, having been infected by the plasma product. His children sued the manufacturer of the product, and the matter went to trial on the negligence claims. The children appealed the trial judge's refusal to instruct the jury on strict liability. The court first examined Cal. Health and Safety Code § 1606, which stated that the procurement, processing, distribution, or use of blood and blood products should be considered "for all purposes" to be the rendition of a service and not a sale. The rationale behind the statute, the court noted, was that a hospital was primarily devoted to the care of the sick, and supplying blood was subordinate to its paramount function of furnishing treatment. In addition, in normal commercial transactions contemplated in strict liability cases, the essence of the transaction relates to the article sold, and the seller is in the business of supplying the product, for which the seller is paid. While this case involved a private manufacturer of pharmaceuticals who put a product on the market to profit from its sale, the court reasoned, the blood shield statute clearly stated that providing a blood product was to be construed as rendering a service, rather than a sale. Moreover, despite every effort to screen donors, it was impossible to completely obviate the possibility of hepatitis in the plasma used to manufacture the clotting agent, and to impose strict liability on manufacturers would increase costs and potentially deter them from producing the product. Finally, there was nothing to indicate that the product had not been an effective coagulant, the court concluded.

b] Statute held not applicable

The courts in the following cases took the position that, under the terms f the particular blood shield statutes construed, commercial providers of lood and blood products were not entitled to immunity from warranty or trict liability.

Had the legislature intended to insulate pharmaceutical companies from roduct liability claims, it would have expressly done so in the state's lood shield statute, the court reasoned in JKB, Sr. v. Armour Pharmaceuical Co., 660 N.E.2d 602, Prod. Liab. Rep. (CCH) ¶ 14476 (**Ind. Ct. App.** 1996), reh'g denied, (Apr. 1, 1996) and transfer denied, (July 18, 1996), nd the court allowed the survivors of a hemophiliac who contracted AIDS rom a commercially prepared clotting agent to pursue a products liability ction against the manufacturers. The trial court granted the pharmaceutial companies' motion for partial summary judgment as to the strict liability count, finding that the provision of the clotting agent was the rendiion of a service, rather than a sale, and thus could not give rise to a roducts liability action. On interlocutory appeal, the reviewing court letermined that the pharmaceutical companies were not insulated from liability by the state's blood shield act. The blood shield statute, the court oted, applied to blood and organ banks, storage facilities, and hospitals. [illegible] nd a court interpreting the statute should presume that the legislature is ware of the common law and does not intend to make any changes beond the statute's express terms or by unmistakable implication. Under a trict interpretation, the court reasoned, it could not be concluded that the gislature intended to include pharmaceutical companies, which comercially manufacture blood products for mass distribution, as an entity the same class as a hospital or a blood bank, simply because the anufacture or production of blood products incidentally included their orage. Manufacturing and distributing blood products by pharmaceutial companies is better characterized as the sale of a product than provid g a service, the court continued, and had the legislature intended to xtend the protection of the blood shield statute to these entities, it would ave done so expressly. The trial court's grant of summary judgment was error, concluded the court, and reversed the judgment.

ALR — continued

Exhibit XI-G

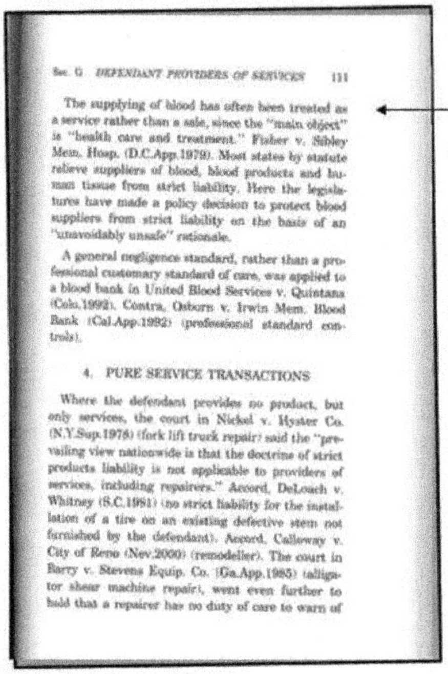

Sec. G DEFENDANT PROVIDERS OF SERVICES 111

The supplying of blood has often been treated as a service rather than a sale, since the "main object" is "health care and treatment." Fisher v. Sibley Mem. Hosp. (D.C.App.1979). Most states by statute relieve suppliers of blood, blood products and human tissue from strict liability. Here the legislatures have made a policy decision to protect blood suppliers from strict liability on the basis of an "unavoidably unsafe" rationale.

A general negligence standard, rather than a professional customary standard of care, was applied to a blood bank in United Blood Services v. Quintana (Colo.1992). Contra, Osborn v. Irwin Mem. Blood Bank (Cal.App.1992) (professional standard controls).

4. PURE SERVICE TRANSACTIONS

Where the defendant provides no product, but only services, the court in Nickel v. Hyster Co. (N.Y.Sup.1978) (fork lift truck repair) said the "prevailing view nationwide is that the doctrine of strict products liability is not applicable to providers of services, including repairers." Accord, DeLoach v. Whitney (S.C.1981) (no strict liability for the installation of a tire on an existing defective stem not furnished by the defendant). Accord, Calloway v. City of Reno (Nev.2000) (remodeller). The court in Barry v. Stevens Equip. Co. (Ga.App.1985) (alligator shear machine repair), went even further to hold that a repairer has no duty of care to warn of

Author — Title — Page # — Edition — Copyright

Jerry J. Phillips, <u>Products Liability in a Nutshell</u> 111 (6th ed. 2003)

Access points:
a. Index at end
b. Table of contents at beginning

Treatise
Rule B15.1 & 15

If sections are used, cite section numbers instead of page.

Exhibit XI-H

TOPIC 3. DEFINITIONS

§ 19. Definition of "Product"

For purposes of this Restatement:

(a) A product is tangible personal property distributed commercially for use or consumption. Other items, such as real property and electricity, are products when the context of their distribution and use is sufficiently analogous to the distribution and use of tangible personal property that it is appropriate to apply the rules stated in this Restatement.

(b) Services, even when provided commercially, are not products.

(c) Human blood and human tissue, even when provided commercially, are not subject to the rules of this Restatement.

— Black letter rule

Comment:

a. History. The question of whether something distributed in commerce is a product for purposes of tort liability is important in this Restatement, but relatively less so than it was in the period from the early 1960s to the early 1980s. Before 1960, American courts had not yet recognized strict liability in tort for harm caused by defective products, particularly if there was no privity of contract between

— Comments

c. Tangible personal property: human blood and human tissue. Although human blood and human tissue meet the formal requisites of Subsection (a), they are specifically excluded from the coverage of this Restatement. Almost all the litigation regarding such products has dealt with contamination of human blood and blood-related products by the hepatitis virus or the HIV virus. Absent a special rule dealing with human blood and tissue, such contamination presumably would be subject to the rules of §§ 1 and 2(a). Those Sections impose strict liability when a product departs from its intended design even though all possible care was exercised in the preparation and marketing of the product. However, legislation in almost all jurisdictions limits the liability of sellers of human blood and human tissue to the failure to

Annotations –
blurbs from
cases interpreting Restatement
provisions

Rule B12.1.3 & 12.9.4

Title — Section — Copyright (year published)

Restatement (Third) of Torts: Products Liability § 19 **(A.L.I. 1998).**

Exhibit XI-I

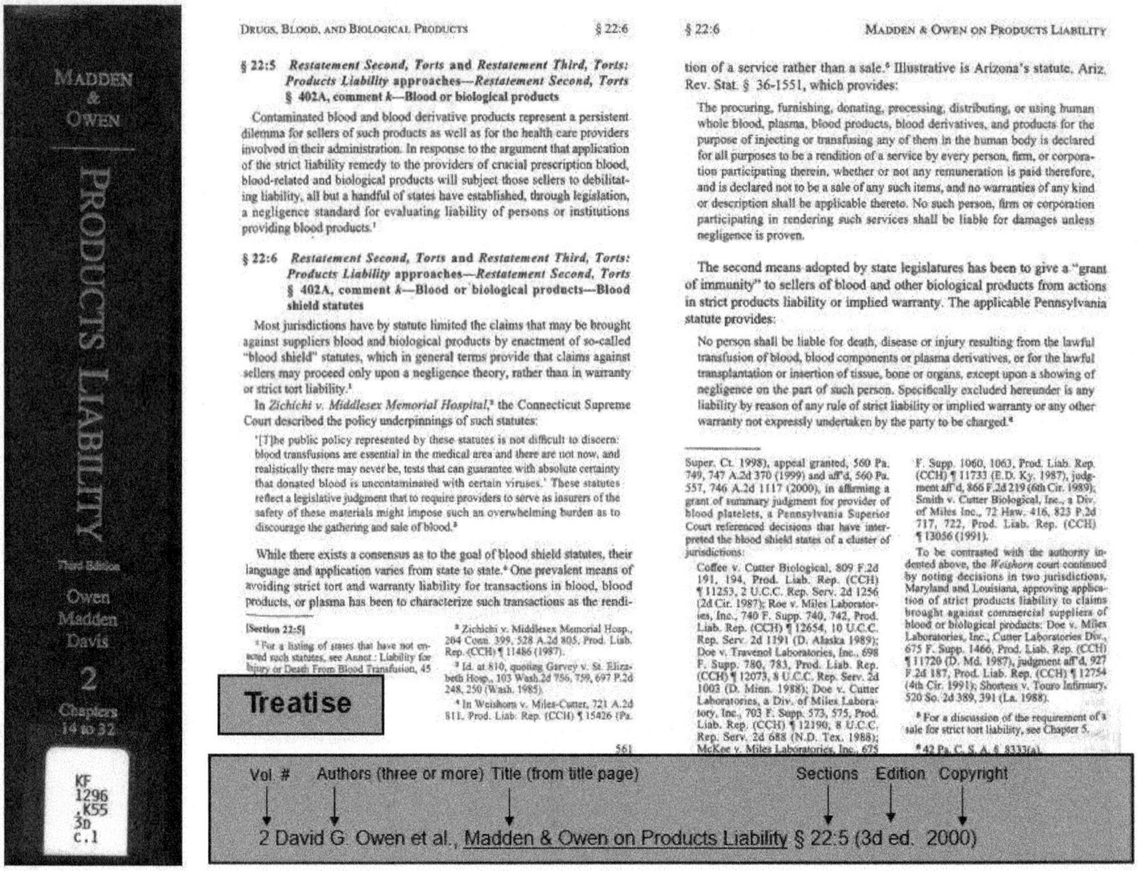

DRUGS, BLOOD, AND BIOLOGICAL PRODUCTS § 22:6

§ 22:5 *Restatement Second, Torts* and *Restatement Third, Torts: Products Liability* approaches—*Restatement Second, Torts* § 402A, comment *k*—Blood or biological products

Contaminated blood and blood derivative products represent a persistent dilemma for sellers of such products as well as for the health care providers involved in their administration. In response to the argument that application of the strict liability remedy to the providers of crucial prescription blood, blood-related and biological products will subject those sellers to debilitating liability, all but a handful of states have established, through legislation, a negligence standard for evaluating liability of persons or institutions providing blood products.[1]

§ 22:6 *Restatement Second, Torts* and *Restatement Third, Torts: Products Liability* approaches—*Restatement Second, Torts* § 402A, comment *k*—Blood or biological products—Blood shield statutes

Most jurisdictions have by statute limited the claims that may be brought against suppliers blood and biological products by enactment of so-called "blood shield" statutes, which in general terms provide that claims against sellers may proceed only upon a negligence theory, rather than in warranty or strict tort liability.[1]

In *Zichichi v. Middlesex Memorial Hospital,*[2] the Connecticut Supreme Court described the policy underpinnings of such statutes:

> '[T]he public policy represented by these statutes is not difficult to discern: blood transfusions are essential in the medical area and there are not now, and realistically there may never be, tests that can guarantee with absolute certainty that donated blood is uncontaminated with certain viruses.' These statutes reflect a legislative judgment that to require providers to serve as insurers of the safety of these materials might impose such an overwhelming burden as to discourage the gathering and sale of blood.[3]

While there exists a consensus as to the goal of blood shield statutes, their language and application varies from state to state.[4] One prevalent means of avoiding strict tort and warranty liability for transactions in blood, blood products, or plasma has been to characterize such transactions as the rendi-

[Section 22:5]

[1] For a listing of states that have not enacted such statutes, see Annot.: Liability for Injury or Death From Blood Transfusion, 45

[2] Zichichi v. Middlesex Memorial Hosp., 204 Conn. 399, 528 A.2d 805, Prod. Liab. Rep. (CCH) ¶ 11486 (1987).

[3] Id. at 810, quoting Garvey v. St. Elizabeth Hosp., 103 Wash.2d 756, 759, 697 P.2d 248, 250 (Wash. 1985).

[4] In Weishorn v. Miles-Cutter, 721 A.2d 811, Prod. Liab. Rep. (CCH) ¶ 15426 (Pa.

561

§ 22:6 MADDEN & OWEN ON PRODUCTS LIABILITY

tion of a service rather than a sale.[5] Illustrative is Arizona's statute, Ariz. Rev. Stat. § 36-1551, which provides:

> The procuring, furnishing, donating, processing, distributing, or using human whole blood, plasma, blood products, blood derivatives, and products for the purpose of injecting or transfusing any of them in the human body is declared for all purposes to be a rendition of a service by every person, firm, or corporation participating therein, whether or not any remuneration is paid therefore, and is declared not to be a sale of any such items, and no warranties of any kind or description shall be applicable thereto. No such person, firm or corporation participating in rendering such services shall be liable for damages unless negligence is proven.

The second means adopted by state legislatures has been to give a "grant of immunity" to sellers of blood and other biological products from actions in strict products liability or implied warranty. The applicable Pennsylvania statute provides:

> No person shall be liable for death, disease or injury resulting from the lawful transfusion of blood, blood components or plasma derivatives, or for the lawful transplantation or insertion of tissue, bone or organs, except upon a showing of negligence on the part of such person. Specifically excluded hereunder is any liability by reason of any rule of strict liability or implied warranty or any other warranty not expressly undertaken by the party to be charged.[6]

Super. Ct. 1998), appeal granted, 560 Pa. 749, 747 A.2d 370 (1999) and aff'd, 560 Pa. 557, 746 A.2d 1117 (2000), in affirming a grant of summary judgment for provider of blood platelets, a Pennsylvania Superior Court referenced decisions that have interpreted the blood shield states of a cluster of jurisdictions:

> Coffee v. Cutter Biological, 809 F.2d 191, 194, Prod. Liab. Rep. (CCH) ¶ 11253, 2 U.C.C. Rep. Serv. 2d 1256 (2d Cir. 1987); Roe v. Miles Laboratories, Inc., 740 F. Supp. 740, 742, Prod. Liab. Rep. (CCH) ¶ 12654, 10 U.C.C. Rep. Serv. 2d 1191 (D. Alaska 1989); Doe v. Travenol Laboratories, Inc., 698 F. Supp. 780, 783, Prod. Liab. Rep. (CCH) ¶ 12073, 8 U.C.C. Rep. Serv. 2d 1003 (D. Minn. 1988); Doe v. Cutter Laboratories, a Div. of Miles Laboratory, Inc., 703 F. Supp. 573, 575, Prod. Liab. Rep. (CCH) ¶ 12190, 8 U.C.C. Rep. Serv. 2d 688 (N.D. Tex. 1988); McKee v. Miles Laboratories, Inc., 675 F. Supp. 1060, 1063, Prod. Liab. Rep. (CCH) ¶ 11733 (E.D. Ky. 1987), judgment aff'd, 866 F.2d 219 (6th Cir. 1989); Smith v. Cutter Biological, Inc., a Div. of Miles Inc., 72 Haw. 416, 823 P.2d 717, 722, Prod. Liab. Rep. (CCH) ¶ 13056 (1991).

To be contrasted with the authority indented above, the *Weishorn* court continued by noting decisions in two jurisdictions, Maryland and Louisiana, approving application of strict products liability to claims brought against commercial suppliers of blood or biological products: Doe v. Miles Laboratories, Inc., Cutter Laboratories Div., 675 F. Supp. 1466, Prod. Liab. Rep. (CCH) ¶ 11720 (D. Md. 1987), judgment aff'd, 927 F.2d 187, Prod. Liab. Rep. (CCH) ¶ 12754 (4th Cir. 1991); Shortess v. Touro Infirmary, 520 So. 2d 389, 391 (La. 1988).

[5] For a discussion of the requirement of a sale for strict tort liability, see Chapter 5.

[6] 42 Pa. C. S. A. § 8333(a).

Exhibit XI-J

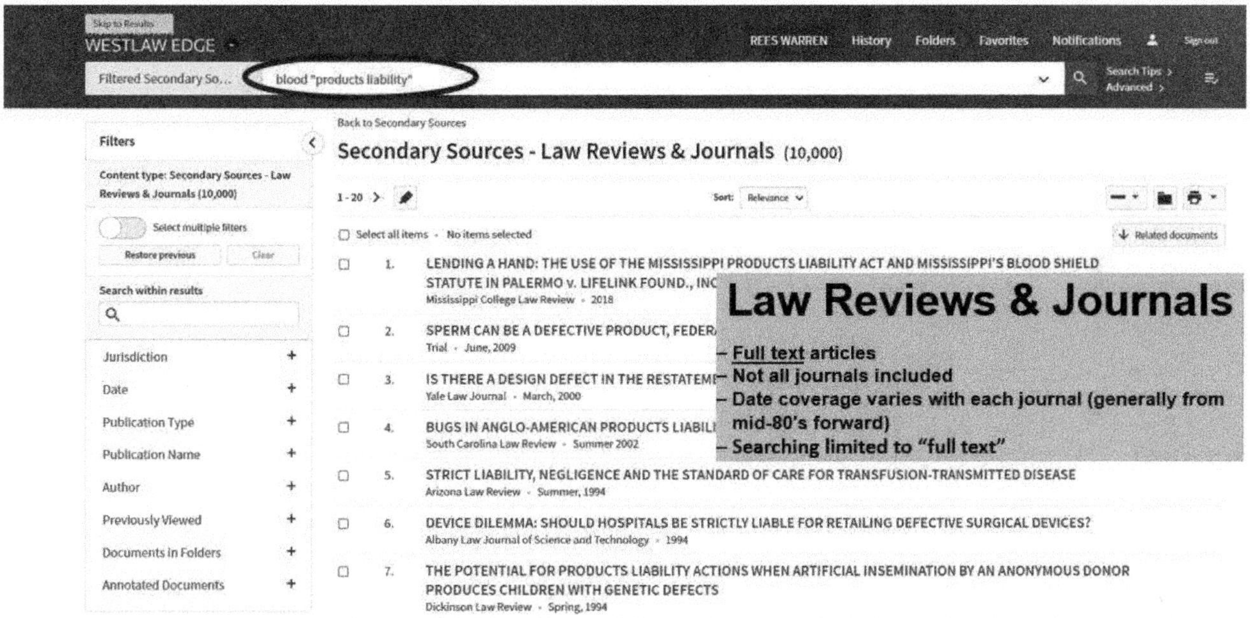
Skip to Results
WESTLAW EDGE
REES WARREN History Folders Favorites Notifications Sign out
Filtered Secondary So...
blood "products liability"
Search Tips
Advanced
Filters
Content type: Secondary Sources - Law Reviews & Journals (10,000)
Select multiple filters
Restore previous
Clear
Search within results
Jurisdiction
Date
Publication Type
Publication Name
Author
Previously Viewed
Documents in Folders
Annotated Documents
Back to Secondary Sources
Secondary Sources - Law Reviews & Journals (10,000)
1-20
Sort: Relevance
Select all items · No items selected
Related documents
1. LENDING A HAND: THE USE OF THE MISSISSIPPI PRODUCTS LIABILITY ACT AND MISSISSIPPI'S BLOOD SHIELD STATUTE IN PALERMO v. LIFELINK FOUND., INC
Mississippi College Law Review · 2018
2. SPERM CAN BE A DEFECTIVE PRODUCT, FEDER
Trial · June, 2009
3. IS THERE A DESIGN DEFECT IN THE RESTATEM
Yale Law Journal · March, 2000
4. BUGS IN ANGLO-AMERICAN PRODUCTS LIABIL
South Carolina Law Review · Summer 2002
5. STRICT LIABILITY, NEGLIGENCE AND THE STANDARD OF CARE FOR TRANSFUSION-TRANSMITTED DISEASE
Arizona Law Review · Summer, 1994
6. DEVICE DILEMMA: SHOULD HOSPITALS BE STRICTLY LIABLE FOR RETAILING DEFECTIVE SURGICAL DEVICES?
Albany Law Journal of Science and Technology · 1994
7. THE POTENTIAL FOR PRODUCTS LIABILITY ACTIONS WHEN ARTIFICIAL INSEMINATION BY AN ANONYMOUS DONOR PRODUCES CHILDREN WITH GENETIC DEFECTS
Dickinson Law Review · Spring, 1994
Law Reviews & Journals
– Full text articles
– Not all journals included
– Date coverage varies with each journal (generally from mid-80's forward)
– Searching limited to "full text"

Results of Full-Text Search in "Law Journal Library"

Exhibit XI-K

Hein Online

Exhibit XI-L

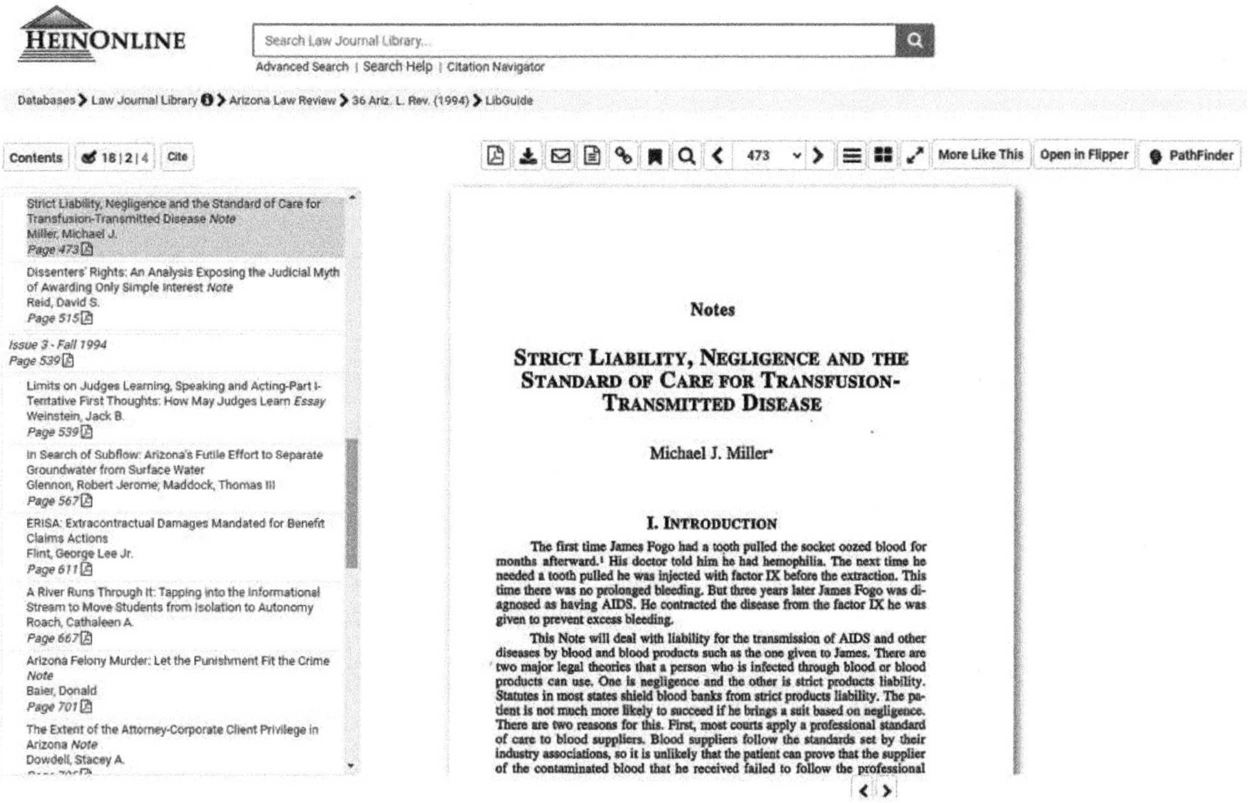
HEINONLINE

Search Law Journal Library...

Advanced Search | Search Help | Citation Navigator

Databases > Law Journal Library > Arizona Law Review > 36 Ariz. L. Rev. (1994) > LibGuide

Contents | 18 | 2 | 4 | Cite

473 | More Like This | Open in Flipper | PathFinder

Notes

STRICT LIABILITY, NEGLIGENCE AND THE STANDARD OF CARE FOR TRANSFUSION-TRANSMITTED DISEASE

Michael J. Miller*

I. INTRODUCTION

The first time James Fogo had a tooth pulled the socket oozed blood for months afterward.[1] His doctor told him he had hemophilia. The next time he needed a tooth pulled he was injected with factor IX before the extraction. This time there was no prolonged bleeding. But three years later James Fogo was diagnosed as having AIDS. He contracted the disease from the factor IX he was given to prevent excess bleeding.

This Note will deal with liability for the transmission of AIDS and other diseases by blood and blood products such as the one given to James. There are two major legal theories that a person who is infected through blood or blood products can use. One is negligence and the other is strict products liability. Statutes in most states shield blood banks from strict products liability. The patient is not much more likely to succeed if he brings a suit based on negligence. There are two reasons for this. First, most courts apply a professional standard of care to blood suppliers. Blood suppliers follow the standards set by their industry associations, so it is unlikely that the patient can prove that the supplier of the contaminated blood that he received failed to follow the professional

Exhibit XI-M

A Legislative Alternative to "No Cause" Liability in Blood Products Litigation

Andrew R. Klein†

The Yale Journal on Regulation Vol. 12:107, 1995

Introduction

Recently, tort law commentators have discovered truth in Justice Holmes' maxim that "hard cases make bad law."[1] In particular, commentators have criticized cases in which courts have relaxed the traditional rule of causation, permitting plaintiffs to recover damages without connecting their harm to a specific defendant.[2] A notable example has arisen in the context of litigation involving Factor VIII concentrate, a pharmaceutical product used by hemophiliacs to replace the clotting protein missing in their blood.[3]

Pharmaceutical companies have manufactured Factor VIII concentrate since the 1970s, processing the pooled blood plasma of thousands of individuals.[4] Initially, Factor VIII concentrate improved many hemophiliacs' quality of life.[5] In the early 1980s, however, portions of the nation's blood supply, including plasma collected to process Factor VIII concentrate, became

---

1. *See* Susan R. Poulter, *Science and Toxic Torts: Is There a Rational Solution to the Problem of Causation*, 7 HIGH TECH. L.J. 189, 197 (1992); Laura A. Abrams, Comment, *The DES Dilemma: A Study in How Hard Cases Make Bad Law*, 59 U. CIN. L. REV. 489 (1990); *see also* James A. Henderson, Jr. & Aaron D. Twerski, *Doctrinal Collapse in Products Liability: The Empty Shell of Failure to Warn*, 65 N.Y.U. L. REV. 265, 310 (1990). In a dissenting opinion in Northern Sec. Co. v. United States, Justice Holmes wrote:

> Great cases like hard cases make bad law. For great cases are called great, not by reason of their real importance in shaping the law of the future, but because of some accident of immediate overwhelming interest which appeals to the feelings and distorts the judgment. These immediate interests exercise a kind of hydraulic pressure which makes what previously was clear seem doubtful, and before which even well settled principles of law will bend.

193 U.S. 197, 400-01 (1904) (Holmes, J., dissenting).

2. *See supra* note 1 and articles cited therein; *see also* Andrew R. Klein, *Beyond DES: Rejecting the Application of Market Share Liability in Blood Products Litigation*, 68 TUL. L. REV. 883 (1994) (discussing litigation involving Factor VIII concentrate); David M. Schultz, *Market Share Liability in DES Cases: The Unwarranted Erosion of Causation in Fact*, 40 DEPAUL L. REV. 771 (1991) (discussing DES litigation); Nancy Lee Firak, *The Developing Policy Characteristics of Cause-in-Fact: Alternative Forms of Liability, Epidemiological Proof and Trans-Scientific Issues*, 63 TEMP. L.Q. 311 (1990) (discussing use of statistical probabilities to prove actual causation).

3. Doe v. Travenol Labs., Inc., 698 F. Supp. 780 (D. Minn. 1988); McKee v. Miles Labs., Inc., 675 F. Supp. 1060 (E.D. Ky. 1987), *aff'd*, 866 F.2d 219 (6th Cir. 1989). For a general discussion of the nature of Factor VIII concentrate and the plight of hemophiliacs, see Ron J. Perey, *Hemophiliacs, Transfusions, and AIDS*, 14 TRIAL DIPL. J. 137, 137-46 (1991).

4. Klein, *supra* note 2, at 907 & nn.126-28 (c... *also* Linda Bean, *No Class Action in Hemophilia-AID*... is "produced by a process that uses the blood plasma... Finn, *Hemophiliacs with AIDS Cry Murder; Firms B*... 1994, at 4 ("Each dose [of factor concentrate] is drawn from the pooled blood p...ma of up to 20,000 people.").

5. Hemophilia treatments prior to the advent of concentrates involved wh... blood transfusions.

Legal periodical

Rule B16

Author	Title of article	Vol.	Journal (T.13)	Page	Year
Andrew R. Klein,	A Legislative Alternative to "No Cause" Liability in Blood Products Litigation,	12	Yale J. on Reg.	107	(1995)

Exhibit XI-N

NOTES

A DUAL SYSTEM OF JUSTICE: FINANCIAL INSTITUTIONS AND WHITE-COLLAR CRIMINAL ENFORCEMENT

*Sebastian Bellm**

INTRODUCTION

In 2013, Deutsche Bank established a relationship with Jeffrey Epstein that was estimated to generate revenues of up to $4 million a year.[1] Seven years later, as a result of its dealings with Mr. Epstein, Deutsche Bank agreed to pay a fine of $150 million.[2] New York state regulators accused the bank of allowing "significant compliance failures" when processing hundreds of transactions for the late financier.[3] Throughout the relationship, regulators asserted that the bank had not properly addressed a plethora of red flags: Mr. Epstein's controversial past and criminal history of sexual misconduct, 120 wire transfers totaling $2.65 million to women with Eastern European surnames, suspicious payments to past coconspirators,[4] and suspiciously large cash withdrawals, including a cash withdrawal of $100,000 for "tips and

* Candidate for Juris Doctor, Notre Dame Law School, 2022; Bachelor of Business Administration in Accounting and Finance, St. Bonaventure University, 2016. I would like to thank Professor Jimmy Gurulé for his guidance, Maria Ianni for her feedback and never-ending support, and my friends on the *Notre Dame Law Review* for their diligent editing and unparalleled commitment to excellence. Finally, I would like to thank my parents, family, and friends for their boundless love and encouragement. All remaining errors are mine alone.

1 James B. Stewart, *These Are the Deutsche Bank Executives Responsible for Serving Jeffrey Epstein*, N.Y. TIMES (July 13, 2020), https://nyti.ms/3eroVqg.

2 *Deutsche Bank Faces $150m Fine for Jeffrey Epstein Ties*, BBC NEWS (July 7, 2020), https://www.bbc.com/news/business-53324888.

3 *Id.*

4 *Id.*; *see also* Matthew Goldstein, *Deutsche Bank Settles over Ignored Red Flags on Jeffrey Epstein*, N.Y. TIMES (July 7, 2020), https://nyti.ms/3cDwOdy. Outgoing payments were sent "to three people who had been named as co-conspirators in suits by Mr. Epstein's accusers that were related to his 2008 guilty plea to prostitution charges in Florida." *Id.*

2007

Legal periodical (student author)

Author	Student pub.	Title of article	Vol	Journal	Page	Year	
Sebastian Bellm,	Note,	A Dual System of Justice: Financial Institutions and White-Collar Criminal Enforcement,	96	Notre Dame L. Rev.	2007	(2021).	**Rule B16.1.3**

Exhibit XI-O

Current versions of Restatements

1. Restatement of Agency, Third (2006);
2. Restatement of Conflict of Laws, Second;
3. Restatement of Contracts, Second;
4. Restatement of Foreign Relations Law of the United States, Third;
5. Restatement of Judgements, Second;
6. Restatement of Law Governing Lawyers, Third;
7. Restatement of Property;
8. Restatement of Property, Landlord and Tenant, Second;
9. Restatement of Property, Donative Transfers, Second;
10. Restatement of Property, Mortgages, Third;
11. Restatement of Property, Servitudes, Third;
12. Restatement of Restitution, Quasi Contracts & Constructive Trusts;
13. Restatement of Security;
14. Restatement of Suretyship and Guaranty, Third;
15. Restatement of Torts, Second;
16. Restatement of Torts, Apportionment of Liability, Third;
17. Restatement of Torts, General Principles, Third (discussion draft);
18. Restatement of Torts, Products Liability, Third;
19. Restatement of Trusts, Second;
20. Restatement of Trusts, Prudent Investor Rule, Third;
21. Restatement of Trusts, General Principles, Third (tentative draft);
22. Restatement of Unfair Competition, Third

Exhibit XI-P

TOPIC 3. DEFINITIONS

§ 19. Definition of "Product"

For purposes of this Restatement:

(a) A product is tangible personal property distributed commercially for use or consumption. Other items, such as real property and electricity, are products when the context of their distribution and use is sufficiently analogous to the distribution and use of tangible personal property that it is appropriate to apply the rules stated in this Restatement.

(b) Services, even when provided commercially, are not products.

(c) Human blood and human tissue, even when provided commercially, are not subject to the rules of this Restatement.

Comment:

a. *History.* The question of whether something distributed in commerce is a product for purposes of tort liability is important in this Restatement, but relatively less so than it was in the period from the early 1960s to the early 1980s. Before 1960, American courts had not yet recognized strict liability in tort for harm caused by defective products, particularly if there was no privity of contract between

c. *Tangible personal property: human blood and human tissue.* Although human blood and human tissue meet the formal requisites of Subsection (a), they are specifically excluded from the coverage of this Restatement. Almost all the litigation regarding such products has dealt with contamination of human blood and blood-related products by the hepatitis virus or the HIV virus. Absent a special rule dealing with human blood and tissue, such contamination presumably would be subject to the rules of §§ 1 and 2(a). Those Sections impose strict liability when a product departs from its intended design even though all possible care was exercised in the preparation and marketing of the product. However, legislation in almost all jurisdictions limits the liability of sellers of human blood and human tissue to the failure to

Black letter rule

Comments

Annotations – blurbs from cases interpreting Restatement provisions

Rule B12.1.3 & 12.9.4

Title — Section — Copyright (year published)

Restatement (Third) of Torts: Products Liability § 19 **(A.L.I. 1998).**

Exhibit XII-B

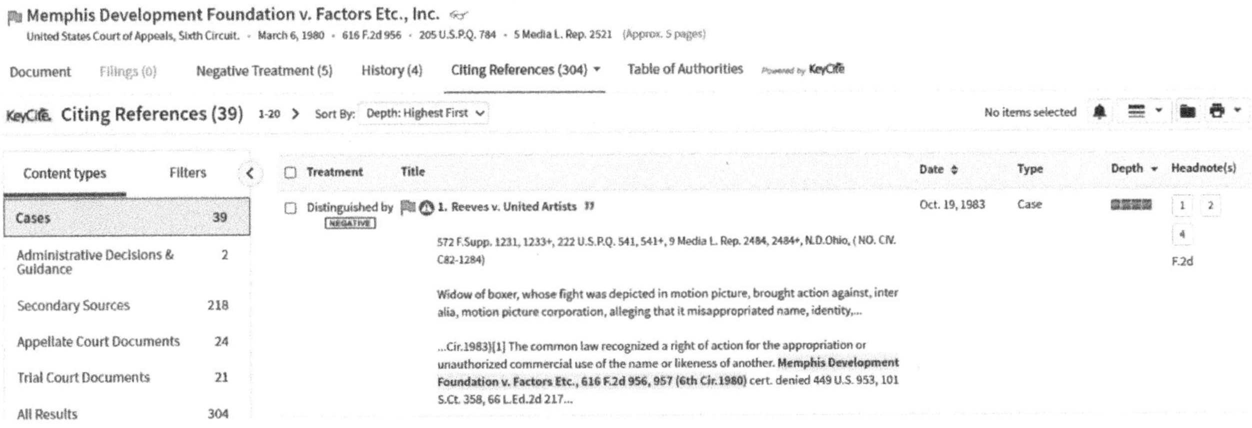

Memphis Development Foundation v. Factors Etc., Inc.

United States Court of Appeals, Sixth Circuit. · March 6, 1980 · 616 F.2d 956 · 205 U.S.P.Q. 784 · 5 Media L. Rep. 2521 (Approx. 5 pages)

Document | Filings (0) | Negative Treatment (5) | History (4) | Citing References (304) | Table of Authorities | Powered by KeyCite

KeyCite. **Citing References (39)** 1-20 > Sort By: Depth: Highest First

No items selected

Content types	Filters
Cases	39
Administrative Decisions & Guidance	2
Secondary Sources	218
Appellate Court Documents	24
Trial Court Documents	21
All Results	304

Treatment	Title	Date	Type	Depth	Headnote(s)
Distinguished by NEGATIVE	**1. Reeves v. United Artists** 572 F.Supp. 1231, 1233+, 222 U.S.P.Q. 541, 541+, 9 Media L. Rep. 2484, 2484+, N.D.Ohio, (NO. CIV. C82-1284) Widow of boxer, whose fight was depicted in motion picture, brought action against, inter alia, motion picture corporation, alleging that it misappropriated name, identity,... ...Cir.1983)[1] The common law recognized a right of action for the appropriation or unauthorized commercial use of the name or likeness of another. **Memphis Development Foundation v. Factors Etc., 616 F.2d 956, 957 (6th Cir.1980)** cert. denied 449 U.S. 953, 101 S.Ct. 358, 66 L.Ed.2d 217...	Oct. 19, 1983	Case		1 2 4 F.2d

Exhibit XII-C

Memphis Dev. Foundation v. Factors Etc., Inc., 616 F.2d 956

6th Cir. Tenn. March 6, 1980

Document | Citing Decisions 39 | Other Citing Sources 156 | History 4 | Table of Authorities 6

exclusive right ...

20 **Reeves v. United Artists** 572 F. Supp. 1231 | Show more

Northern Dist. Ohio | October 19, 1983 | HN2

Distinguished by

572 F. Supp. 1231 p.1234

However, the law in this Circuit is not in accord with the majority of other courts which have considered the issue. In Memphis Development, supra, the Sixth Circuit held that the right of publicity is not descendible under Tennessee

Followed by

572 F. Supp. 1231 p.1235

This Court must determine which view of the right of publicity to apply in this case. In Memphis Development, supra, the Sixth Circuit applied Tennessee law. While Memphis Development provides useful guidance, it must be distinguished from this case because of the difference in state law to be applied; therefore, Memphis is not clearly dispositive. ... In the case at bar, Ohio substantive law must be applied. See, Carson v. Here's Johnny Portable Toilets, Inc., supra at 834 n.1; Memphis Development, supra at 958.

Recently Amended Code Section That Is Not Yet Included in the Database on Westlaw

Exhibit XIII-A

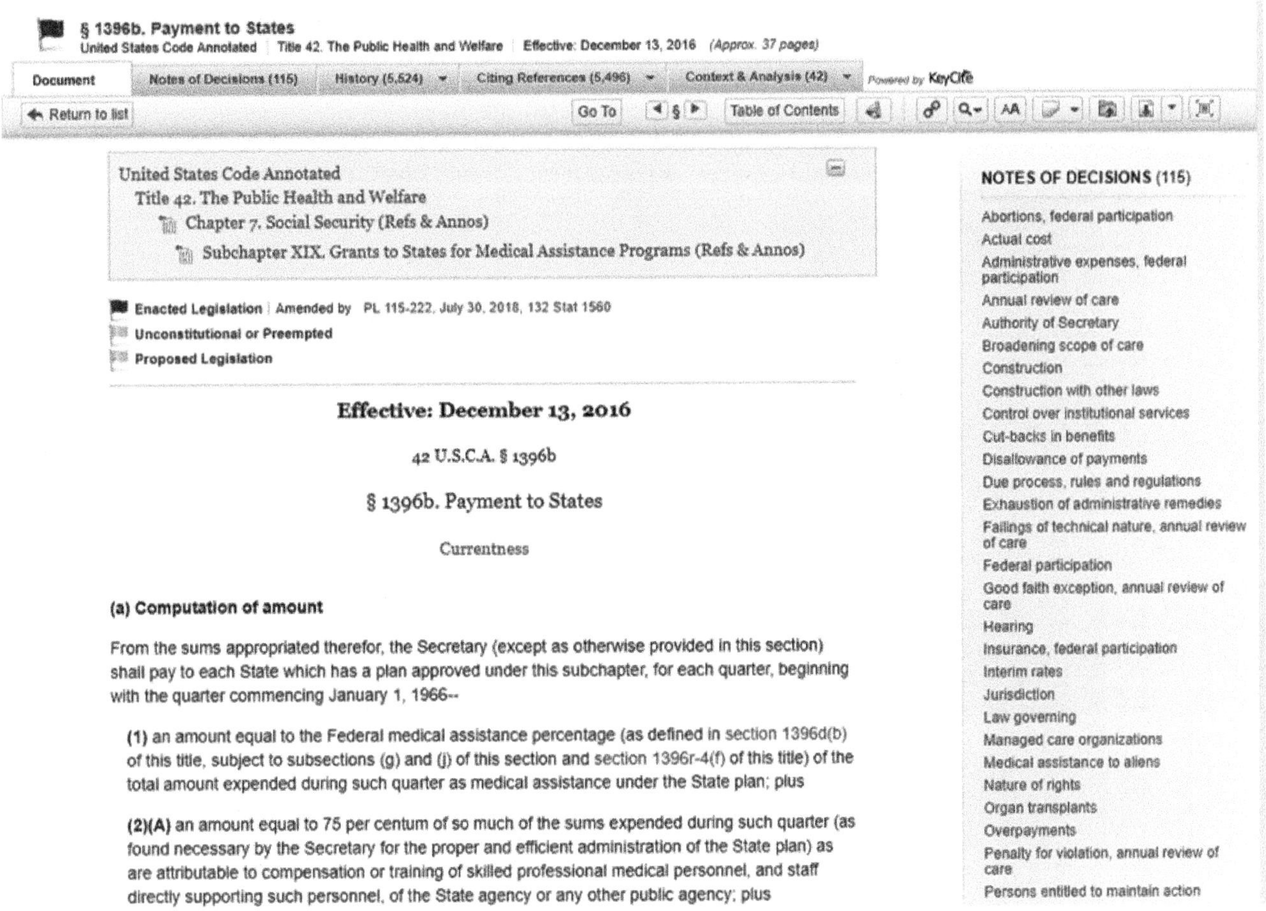

§ 1396b. Payment to States
United States Code Annotated | Title 42. The Public Health and Welfare | Effective: December 13, 2016 (Approx. 37 pages)

Document | Notes of Decisions (115) | History (5,524) | Citing References (5,496) | Context & Analysis (42) | Powered by KeyCite

Return to list | Go To | § | Table of Contents

United States Code Annotated
Title 42. The Public Health and Welfare
Chapter 7. Social Security (Refs & Annos)
Subchapter XIX. Grants to States for Medical Assistance Programs (Refs & Annos)

Enacted Legislation | Amended by PL 115-222, July 30, 2018, 132 Stat 1560
Unconstitutional or Preempted
Proposed Legislation

Effective: December 13, 2016

42 U.S.C.A. § 1396b

§ 1396b. Payment to States

Currentness

(a) Computation of amount

From the sums appropriated therefor, the Secretary (except as otherwise provided in this section) shall pay to each State which has a plan approved under this subchapter, for each quarter, beginning with the quarter commencing January 1, 1966--

(1) an amount equal to the Federal medical assistance percentage (as defined in section 1396d(b) of this title, subject to subsections (g) and (j) of this section and section 1396r-4(f) of this title) of the total amount expended during such quarter as medical assistance under the State plan; plus

(2)(A) an amount equal to 75 per centum of so much of the sums expended during such quarter (as found necessary by the Secretary for the proper and efficient administration of the State plan) as are attributable to compensation or training of skilled professional medical personnel, and staff directly supporting such personnel, of the State agency or any other public agency; plus

NOTES OF DECISIONS (115)

Abortions, federal participation
Actual cost
Administrative expenses, federal participation
Annual review of care
Authority of Secretary
Broadening scope of care
Construction
Construction with other laws
Control over institutional services
Cut-backs in benefits
Disallowance of payments
Due process, rules and regulations
Exhaustion of administrative remedies
Failings of technical nature, annual review of care
Federal participation
Good faith exception, annual review of care
Hearing
Insurance, federal participation
Interim rates
Jurisdiction
Law governing
Managed care organizations
Medical assistance to aliens
Nature of rights
Organ transplants
Overpayments
Penalty for violation, annual review of care
Persons entitled to maintain action

Exhibit XIII-B

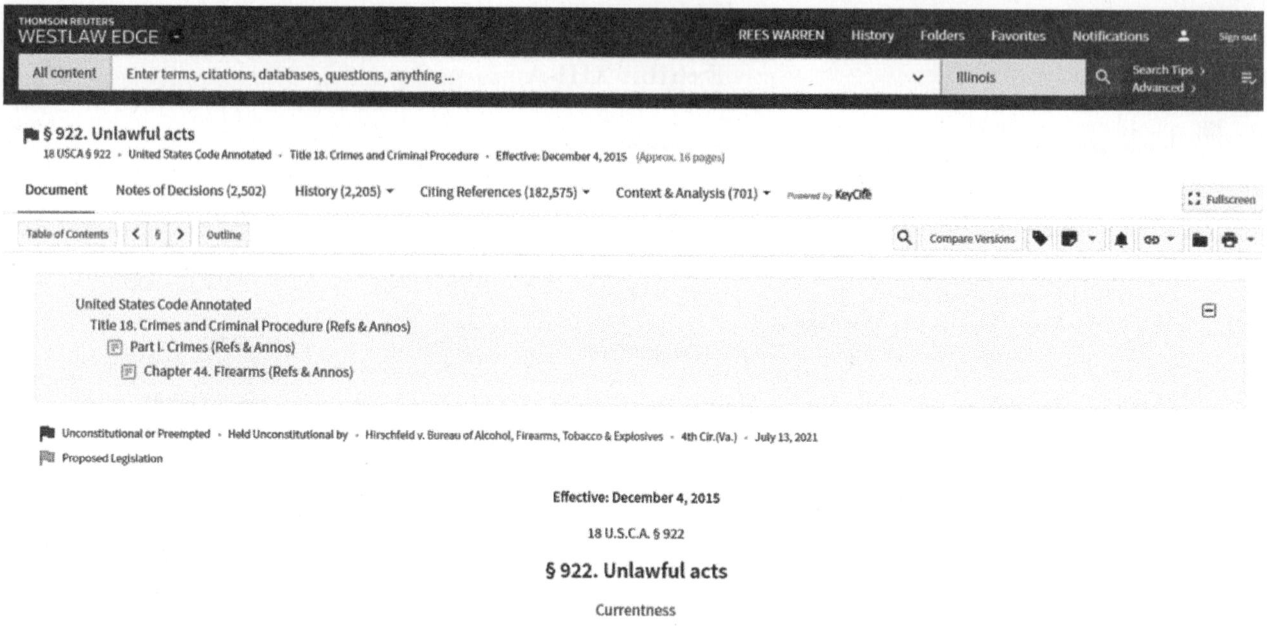

Exhibit XIII-C

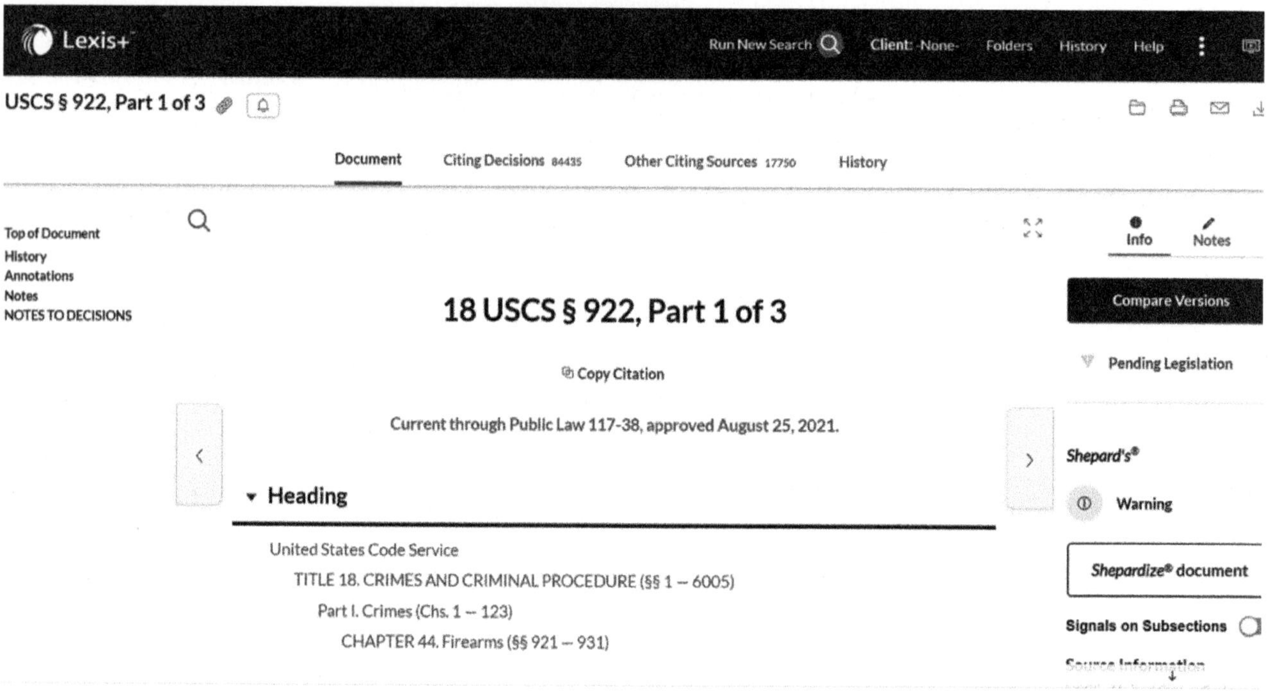